D1281709

Bloom's Modern Critical Views

African-American
  Poets: Volume 1
African-American
  Poets: Volume 2
Aldous Huxley
Alfred, Lord Tennyson
Alice Munro
Alice Walker
American Women
  Poets: 1650–1950
Amy Tan
Anton Chekhov
Arthur Miller
Asian-American
  Writers
August Wilson
The Bible
The Brontës
Carson McCullers
Charles Dickens
Christopher Marlowe
Contemporary Poets
Cormac McCarthy
C.S. Lewis
Dante Alighieri
David Mamet
Derek Walcott
Don DeLillo
Doris Lessing
Edgar Allan Poe
Émile Zola
Emily Dickinson
Ernest Hemingway
Eudora Welty
Eugene O'Neill
F. Scott Fitzgerald
Flannery O'Connor
Franz Kafka
Gabriel García
  Márquez
Geoffrey Chaucer
George Orwell
G.K. Chesterton

Gwendolyn Brooks
Hans Christian
  Andersen
Henry David Thoreau
Herman Melville
Hermann Hesse
H.G. Wells
Hispanic-American
  Writers
Homer
Honoré de Balzac
Jamaica Kincaid
James Joyce
Jane Austen
Jay Wright
J.D. Salinger
Jean-Paul Sartre
John Donne and the
  Metaphysical Poets
John Irving
John Keats
John Milton
John Steinbeck
José Saramago
Joseph Conrad
J.R.R. Tolkien
Julio Cortázar
Kate Chopin
Kurt Vonnegut
Langston Hughes
Leo Tolstoy
Marcel Proust
Margaret Atwood
Mark Twain
Mary Wollstonecraft
  Shelley
Maya Angelou
Miguel de Cervantes
Milan Kundera
Nathaniel Hawthorne
Native American
  Writers
Norman Mailer

Octavio Paz
Oscar Wilde
Paul Auster
Philip Roth
Ralph Ellison
Ralph Waldo Emerson
Ray Bradbury
Richard Wright
Robert Browning
Robert Frost
Robert Hayden
Robert Louis
  Stevenson
The Romantic Poets
Salman Rushdie
Samuel Beckett
Samuel Taylor
  Coleridge
Stephen Crane
Stephen King
Sylvia Plath
Tennessee Williams
Thomas Hardy
Thomas Pynchon
Tom Wolfe
Toni Morrison
Tony Kushner
Truman Capote
Walt Whitman
W.E.B. Du Bois
William Blake
William Faulkner
William Gaddis
William Shakespeare:
  Comedies
William Shakespeare:
  Histories
William Shakespeare:
  Romances
William Shakespeare:
  Tragedies
William Wordsworth
Zora Neale Hurston

Bloom's Modern Critical Views

GEORGE BERNARD SHAW
New Edition

Edited and with an introduction by
Harold Bloom
Sterling Professor of the Humanities
Yale University

BLOOM'S
LITERARY CRITICISM
An imprint of Infobase Publishing

Bloom's Modern Critical Views: George Bernard Shaw—New Edition

Copyright © 2011 by Infobase Publishing
Introduction © 2011 by Harold Bloom

All rights reserved. No part of this publication may be reproduced or utilized in any form or by any means, electronic or mechanical, including photocopying, recording, or by any information storage or retrieval systems, without permission in writing from the publisher. For more information contact:

Bloom's Literary Criticism
An imprint of Infobase Publishing
132 West 31st Street
New York NY 10001

Library of Congress Cataloging-in-Publication Data
George Bernard Shaw / edited and with an introduction by Harold Bloom.
— New ed.
    p. cm. — (Bloom's modern critical views)
  Includes bibliographical references and index.
  ISBN 978-1-60413-882-5 (hardcover)
  1. Shaw, Bernard, 1856–1950—Criticism and interpretation. I. Bloom, Harold.
  PR5367.G43 2011
  822'.912—dc22   2010021839

Bloom's Literary Criticism books are available at special discounts when purchased in bulk quantities for businesses, associations, institutions, or sales promotions. Please call our Special Sales Department in New York at (212) 967-8800 or (800) 322-8755.

You can find Bloom's Literary Criticism on the World Wide Web at
http://www.chelseahouse.com

Contributing editor: Pamela Loos
Cover designed by Alicia Post
Composition by IBT Global, Troy NY
Cover printed by IBT Global, Troy NY
Book printed and bound by IBT Global, Troy NY
Date printed: October 2010
Printed in the United States of America

10 9 8 7 6 5 4 3 2 1

This book is printed on acid-free paper.

All links and Web addresses were checked and verified to be correct at the time of publication. Because of the dynamic nature of the Web, some addresses and links may have changed since publication and may no longer be valid.

Contents

Editor's Note

My introduction, which considers Shaw's copious intellectual debts, offers critical readings of *Man and Superman*, *Major Barbara*, *Pygmalion*, and *Saint Joan*, in the hope of arriving at a freshly balanced estimate both of Shaw's limitations and of his varied achievement as a comic melodramatist.

John A. Bertolini marks *Saint Joan* as a new phase in Shaw's preoccupation with the workings of the imagination, after which Jean Reynolds borrows Eric Bentley's phrase "Shavian inclusiveness" to explore elements of postmodernism in the plays.

Celia Marshik traces *Pygmalion*'s long journey to the page and stage, locating the comedy within the context of turn-of-the-century purity movements. Stuart E. Baker identifies *Major Barbara* as containing the fullest expression of Shavian philosophy and dramatic method.

Lagretta Tallent Lenker considers Shaw's varied and contradictory ideas about war, followed by Jan McDonald's appraisal of Shaw's views of art and artists as expressed in the plays.

Michael Goldman grapples with the relationship between style and ideology in the plays and the influence of Shaw's evolving critical reputation. Emil Roy concludes the volume by comparing the implosive comedy of *Heartbreak House* with Pinter's *The Homecoming*.

HAROLD BLOOM

Introduction

"With the single exception of Homer there is no eminent writer, not even Sir Walter Scott, whom I despise so entirely as I despise Shakespear when I measure my mind against his." Shaw, obsessive polemicist, would write anything, even that unfortunate sentence. No critic would wish to measure Shaw's mind against Shakespeare's, particularly since originality was hardly Shaw's strength. Shavian ideas are quarried from Schopenhauer, Nietzsche, Ibsen, Wagner, Ruskin, Samuel Butler, Shelley, Carlyle, Marx (more or less), William Morris, Lamarck, Bergson—the list could be extended. Though an intellectual dramatist, Shaw essentially popularized the concepts and images of others. He continues to hold the stage and might appear to have earned his reputation of being the principal writer of English comic drama since Shakespeare. Yet his limitations are disconcerting, and the experience of rereading even his most famous plays, after many years away from them, is disappointingly mixed. They are much more than period pieces, but they hardly seem to be for all time. No single comedy by Shaw matches Wilde's *The Importance of Being Earnest* or the tragic farces of Beckett.

Eric Bentley best demonstrated that Shaw viewed himself as a prose prophet in direct succession to Carlyle, Ruskin, and Morris. This is the Shaw of the prefaces, of *Essays in Fabian Socialism*, of *Doctors' Delusions, Crude Criminology, Sham Education*. Only the prefaces to the plays are still read, and of course they are not really prefaces to the plays. They expound Shaw's very odd personal religion, the rather cold worship of creative evolution. Of this religion, one can say that it is no more bizarre than most and less distasteful than many, but it is still quite grotesque. To judge religions by aesthetic

1

criteria may seem perverse, but what others are relevant for poems, plays, stories, novels, personal essays? By any aesthetic standard, Shaw's heretical faith
is considerably less interesting or impressive than D.H. Lawrence's barbaric
vitalism in *The Plumed Serpent* or even Thomas Hardy's negative homage to
the immanent will in *The Dynasts*.

G.K. Chesterton, in his book on Shaw (1909), observed that the heroine
of *Major Barbara*

> ends by suggesting that she will serve God without personal hope,
> so that she may owe nothing to God and He owe everything to
> her. It does not seem to strike her that if God owes everything
> to her He is not God. These things affect me merely as tedious
> perversions of a phrase. It is as if you said, "I will never have a father
> unless I have begotten him."

"He who is willing to do the work gives birth to his own father," Kierkeg-
aard wrote, and Nietzsche mused: "If one hasn't had a good father, then it is
necessary to invent one." Shaw was neither a Darwinian nor a Freudian, and
I think he was a bad Nietzschean, who had misread rather weakly the sage of
Zarathustra. But in his life he had suffered an inadequate father and certainly
he was willing to do the work. Like his own Major Barbara, he wished to have
a God who would owe everything to G.B.S. That requires a writer to possess superb mythopoeic powers, and fortunately for Shaw his greatest literary
strength was as an inventor of new myths. Shaw endures in a high literary
sense and remains eminently readable as well as actable because of his mythmaking faculty, a power he shared with Blake and Shelley, Wagner and Ibsen.
He was not a stylist, not a thinker, not a psychologist, and utterly lacked
even an iota of the uncanny Shakespearean ability to represent character and
personality with overwhelming persuasiveness. His dialogue is marred by his
garrulous tendencies, and the way he embodied his ideas is too often weari-
somely simplistic. And yet his dramas linger in us because his beings transcend their inadequate status as representations of the human, with which
he was hopelessly impatient anyway. They suggest something more obsessive
than daily life, something that moves and has its being in the cosmos we learn
to call Shavian, a comic version of Schopenhauer's terrible world dominated
by the remorseless will to live.

As a critic, Shaw was genial only where he was not menaced, and he
felt deeply menaced by the Aesthetic vision, of which his socialism never
quite got free. Like Oscar Wilde and Wilde's mentor, Walter Pater, Shaw
was the direct descendant of Ruskin, and his animus against Wilde and Pater
reflects the anxiety of an ambitious son toward rival claimants to a heritage.

Pater insisted on style, as did Wilde, and Shaw has no style to speak of, not much more, say, than Eugene O'Neill. Reviewing Wilde's *An Ideal Husband* on January 12, 1895, for Frank Harris's *Saturday Review*, Shaw was both generous and just:

> Mr. Wilde, an arch-artist, is so colossally lazy that he trifles even with the work by which an artist escapes work. He distils the very quintessence, and gets as product plays which are so unapproachably playful that they are the delight of every playgoer with twopenn'orth of brains.

A month later, confronted by *The Importance of Being Earnest: A Trivial Comedy for Serious People*, Shaw lost his composure, his generosity, and his sense of critical justice:

> I cannot say that I greatly cared for The Importance of Being Earnest. It amused me, of course; but unless comedy touches me as well as amuses me, it leaves me with a sense of having wasted my evening. I go to the theatre to be moved to laughter, not to be tickled or bustled into it; and that is why, though I laugh as much as anybody at a farcical comedy, I am out of spirits before the end of the second act, and out of temper before the end of the third, my miserable mechanical laughter intensifying these symptoms at every outburst. If the public ever becomes intelligent enough to know when it is really enjoying itself and when it is not, there will be an end of farcical comedy. Now in The Importance of Being Earnest there is plenty of this rib-tickling: for instance, the lies, the deceptions, the cross purposes, the sham mourning, the christening of the two grown-up men, the muffin eating, and so forth. These could only have been raised from the farcical plane by making them occur to characters who had, like Don Quixote, convinced us of their reality and obtained some hold on our sympathy. But that unfortunate moment of Gilbertism breaks our belief in the humanity of the play.

Would it be possible to have a sillier critical reaction to the most delightful comic drama in English since Shakespeare? Twenty-three years later, Shaw wrote a letter (if it is that) to Frank Harris, published by Harris in his *Life of Wilde* (1918) and then reprinted by Shaw in his *Pen Portraits and Reviews*. Again Wilde was an artist of "stupendous laziness" and again was indicted, this time after his death, for heartlessness:

Our sixth meeting, the only other one I can remember, was the one at the Cafe Royal. On that occasion he was not too preoccupied with his danger to be disgusted with me because I, who had praised his first plays handsomely, had turned traitor over The Importance of Being Earnest. Clever as it was, it was his first really heartless play. In the others the chivalry of the eighteenth-century Irishman and the romance of the disciple of Théophile Gautier (Oscar was old-fashioned in the Irish way, except as a critic of morals) not only gave a certain kindness and gallantry to the serious passages and to the handling of the women, but provided that proximity of emotion without which laughter, however irresistible, is destructive and sinister. In The Importance of Being Earnest this had vanished; and the play, though extremely funny, was essentially hateful. I had no idea that Oscar was going to the dogs, and that this represented a real degeneracy produced by his debaucheries. I thought he was still developing; and I hazarded the unhappy guess that The Importance of Being Earnest was in idea a young work written or projected long before under the influence of Gilbert and furbished up for Alexander as a potboiler. At the Cafe Royal that day I calmly asked him whether I was not right. He indignantly repudiated my guess, and said loftily (the only time he ever tried on me the attitude he took to John Gray and his more abject disciples) that he was disappointed in me. I suppose I said, "Then what on earth has happened to you?" but I recollect nothing more on that subject except that we did not quarrel over it.

Shaw remains unique in finding *The Importance of Being Earnest* (of all plays!) "essentially hateful." A clue to this astonishing reaction can be found in Shaw's outraged response to Max Beerbohm's review of *Man and Super-man*, as expressed in his letter to Beerbohm, on September 15, 1903:

You idiot, do you suppose I don't know my own powers? I tell you in this book as plainly as the thing can be told, that the reason Bunyan reached such a pitch of mastery in literary art (and knew it) whilst poor Pater could never get beyond a nerveless amateur affectation which had not even the common workaday quality of vulgar journalism (and, alas! didn't know it, though he died of his own futility), was that it was life or death with the tinker to make people understand his message and see his vision, whilst Pater had neither message nor vision & only wanted to cultivate style, with the result that of the two attempts I have made to read him the first broke down at the tenth sentence & the second at the first. Pater took a genteel walk up Parnassus: Bunyan fled from the wrath to come: that explains the difference in their pace & in the length they covered.

Poor Pater is dragged in and beaten up because he was the apostle of style, while Bunyan is summoned up supposedly as the model for Shaw, who also has a message and a vision. It is a little difficult to associate *The Pilgrim's Progress* with *Man and Superman*, but one can suspect shrewdly that Pater here is a surrogate for Wilde, who had achieved an absolute comic music of perfect style and stance in *The Importance of Being Earnest*. Shavians become indignant at the comparison, but Shaw does poorly when one reads side by side any of the *Fabian Essays* and Wilde's extraordinary essay "The Soul of Man under Socialism." Something even darker happens when we juxtapose *Man and Superman* with *The Importance of Being Earnest*, but then Shaw is not unique in not being able to survive such a comparison.

Man and Superman

Everything about *Man and Superman*, paradoxical as the play was to begin with, now seems almost absurdly problematical. The very title cannot mean (any more) what Shaw doubtless intended it to mean: the Superman of Nietzsche, Zarathustra, the heroic vitalist who prophesies the next phase of creative evolution, the next resting place of that cold god, the life force. Nietzsche's Zarathustra, as Shaw blandly chose never to see, is a god-man who is free of what Freud came to call the Over-I (superego), the shadow or specter of bad conscience that hovers above each separate self. But Shaw's Superman is simply Bunyan's Pilgrim writ large and brought (supposedly) up to date, Shaw being about as much an immoralist as Bunyan.

Nietzsche transvalued all values (perhaps) or tried to (in some moods), and at the least developed an extraordinary perspectivism that really does call every stance—rhetorical, cosmological, psychological—into question. Shaw was interested neither in rhetoric (which he dismissed as Paterian "style") nor in psychology (associationist or Freudian), and his cosmological speculations, though mythologically powerful, are informed primarily by his post-Ruskinian and only quasi-Marxist political economics. His Fabian socialism marries the British Protestant or evangelical sensibility (Bunyan, Carlyle, Ruskin) to philosophical speculation that might transcend Darwinian-Freudian scientism (Schopenhauer, Lamarck, Nietzsche, Bergson). Such a sensibility is moral and indeed puritanical, so that Shaw always remained in spirit very close to Carlyle rather than to Nietzsche (who despised Carlyle and loved

Emerson for his slyly immoralistic self-reliance). Shaw's Superman, alas, in consequence looks a lot more like Thomas Carlyle crying out "work, for the night cometh in which no man can work" than he does like Zarathustra-Nietzsche urging us: "Try to live as though it were morning."

In Shaw's defense, he took from the Nietzschean metaphor of the Superman what he most needed of it: a political and therefore literal reading, in which the Superman is nothing but what Shaw called "a general raising of human character through the deliberate cultivation and endowment of democratic virtue without consideration of property or class." That is a boring idealization, from an aesthetic or epistemological perspective, but pragmatically it is indeed what we most require and never will attain, which is why doubtless we must perish as a civilization. Such a consideration, fortunately, has nothing to do with *Man and Superman* as a farce and a sexual comedy, or with its glory, the extraordinary inserted drama of dialectic and mythology, "Don Juan in Hell," certainly the outstanding instance of a play-within-a-play from Shakespeare to Pirandello.

The preface to *Man and Superman* is a dedicatory epistle to the drama critic Arthur Bingham Walkley and is a piece of Shavian outrageousness, particularly in promising far more than the play can begin to deliver. Shakespeare, perpetual origin of Shavian aesthetic anxiety, is associated with Dickens as being obsessed with the world's diversities rather than its unities. Consequently, they are irreligious, anarchical, nihilistic, apolitical, and their human figures are lacking in will. Against them, Shaw ranges Bunyan, Nietzsche, and himself—the artist-philosophers! Shakespeare did not understand virtue and courage, which is the province of the artist-philosophers.

The shrewdest reply one could make to Shaw is to contrast Shakespeare's Falstaff (whom Shaw praises) to Nietzsche's Zarathustra. Which is the Superman, embodiment of the drive to live, person free of the superego? Hamlet, to Shaw, is an inadequate Don Juan, since he is famously irresolute. The sadness is that the Don Juan we will see debating the Devil in Hell is only (at best) a wistful impersonation of Hamlet, who remains the West's paradigm of intellectuality even as Falstaff abides forever as its paradigm of wit.

Yet this epistle commencing *Man and Superman* is one of Shaw's grandest performances, reminding us of how soundly he trained as a Hyde Park soapbox orator, a splendid preparation for a polemical playwright of ideas. In the midst of his perpetual advertisements for himself, he utters a poignant credo:

> Now you cannot say this of the works of the artist-philosophers. You cannot say it, for instance, of The Pilgrim's Progress. Put your Shakespearian hero and coward, Henry V and Pistol or Parolles, beside Mr Valiant and Mr Fearing, and you have a sudden

revelation of the abyss that lies between the fashionable author who could see nothing in the world but personal aims and the tragedy of their disappointment or the comedy of their incongruity, and the field preacher who achieved virtue and courage by identifying himself with the purpose of the world as he understood it. The contrast is enormous: Bunyan's coward stirs your blood more than Shakespear's hero, who actually leaves you cold and secretly hostile. You suddenly see that Shakespear, with all his flashes and divinations, never understood virtue and courage, never conceived how any man who was not a fool could, like Bunyan's hero, look back from the brink of the river of death over the strife and labor of his pilgrimage, and say "yet do I not repent me"; or, with the panache of a millionaire, bequeath "my sword to him that shall succeed me in my pilgrimage, and my courage and skill to him that can get it." This is the true joy in life, the being used for a purpose recognized by yourself as a mighty one; the being thoroughly worn out before you are thrown on the scrap heap; the being a force of Nature instead of a feverish selfish little clod of ailments and grievances complaining that the world will not devote itself to making you happy. And also the only real tragedy in life is the being used by personally minded men for purposes which you recognize to be base. All the rest is at worst mere misfortune or mortality: this alone is misery, slavery, hell on earth; and the revolt against it is the only force that offers a man's work to the poor artist, whom our personally minded rich people would so willingly employ as pandar, buffoon, beauty monger, sentimentalizer and the like.

Shakespeare then is not a prophet or at least does not himself suffer personally the burden of his prophecy. Bunyan and Shaw are prophets, and if they suffer, then also they experience the "true joy in life . . . the being a force of Nature." The passage has in it the accent of Carlyle, except that Carlyle rendered it with more gusto in his sublimely outrageous style, and Carlyle (not being in direct competition with Shakespeare) set Shakespeare first among the artist-prophets, higher even than Goethe. We are moved by Shaw, yet he has not the rhetorical power to overwhelm us (however dubiously) as Carlyle sometimes does.

Why has Shaw, of all dramatists, written a play about Don Juan Tenorio, or John Tanner, as he is called in *Man and Superman*? And in what way is the bumbling Tanner, cravenly fleeing the life force that is Ann Whitefield, a Don Juan? A crafty ironist, Shaw knows that all Don Juans, whether literary or experiential, are anything but audacious seducers. Poor Tanner is a relatively deliberate Shavian self-parody and is all too clearly an Edwardian gentleman, a pillar of society, and very much a Puritan. He is all superego, and from the start is Ann's destined victim, her proper and inevitable husband, the father of her children. She will let him go on talking; she acts, and that is the end of it. The true Don Juan does not like women, which is why he needs so many of them. Tanner adores and needs Ann, though perhaps he will never know how early on the adoration and the need commenced in him.

Don Juan, as Shaw revises the myth, is Faust (whom Shaw calls the Don's cousin). He is the enemy of God, in direct descent from Faust's ancestor, Simon Magus, the first Gnostic, who took the cognomen of Faustus ("the favored one") when he moved his campaign of charlatanry to Rome. Shaw's Don Juan is Prometheus as well as Faust and so is an enemy not so much of God as of Jehovah (Shelley's Jupiter in *Prometheus Unbound*) the sky-tyrant, the deity of finance capitalism, repressive sexual morality, and institutional or historical Christianity.

It is manifest that *Man and Superman* does not have a Faustian or Promethean hero in the absurdly inadequate though amiable John Tanner. Tanner is, as Eric Bentley economically observes, a fool and a windbag, all too human rather than Don Juan Tenorio the Superman. But Shaw gives him a great dream: "Don Juan in Hell." Again Bentley is incisive: "Take away the episode in hell, and Shaw has written an anti-intellectual comedy." I would go a touch further and say: "Take away the episode in hell, and Shaw has written a very unfunny comedy." Though it can be directed and acted effectively, most of the play singularly lacks wit; its paradoxes are sadly obvious. But the paradoxes of "Don Juan in Hell" continue to delight and disturb, as in the contrast between the erotic philosophies of Don Juan and the Statue:

DON JUAN: I learnt it by experience: When I was on earth, and made those proposals to ladies which, though universally condemned, have made me so interesting a hero of legend, I was not infrequently met in some such way as this. The lady would say that she would countenance my advances, provided they were honorable. On inquiring what that proviso meant, I found that it meant that I proposed to get possession of her property if she had any, or to undertake her support for life if she had not; that I desired her continual companionship, counsel, and conversation to the end of my days, and would take a most solemn oath to be always enraptured by them: above all, that I would turn my back on all other women for ever for her sake. I did not object to these conditions because they were exorbitant and inhuman: it was their extraordinary irrelevance that prostrated me. I invariably replied with perfect frankness that I had never dreamt of any of these things; that unless the lady's character and intellect were equal or superior to my own, her conversation must degrade and her counsel mislead me; that her constant companionship might, for all I knew, become intolerably tedious to me; that I could not answer for my feelings for a week in advance, much less to the end of my life; that to cut me off from all natural and unconstrained intercourse with half my fellowcreatures would narrow and warp me if I submitted to it, and, if not, would bring me under the curse of clandestinity; that, finally, my proposals to her were wholly unconnected with any of these matters, and were the outcome of a perfectly simple impulse of my manhood towards her womanhood.

ANA: You mean that it was an immoral impulse.

DON JUAN: Nature, my dear lady, is what you call immoral. I blush for it; but I cannot help it. Nature is a pandar, Time a wrecker, and Death a murderer. I have always preferred to stand up to those facts and build institutions on their recognition. You prefer to propitiate the three devils by proclaiming their chastity, their thrift, and their loving kindness; and to base your institutions on these flatteries. Is it any wonder that the institutions do not work smoothly?

THE STATUE: What used the ladies to say, Juan?

DON JUAN: Oh, come! Confidence for confidence. First tell me what you used to say to the ladies.

THE STATUE: I! Oh, I swore that I would be faithful to the death; that I should die if they refused me; that no woman could ever be to me what she was—

ANA: She! Who?

THE STATUE: Whoever it happened to be at the time, my dear. I had certain things I always said. One of them was that even when I was eighty, one white hair of the woman I loved would make me tremble more than the thickest gold tress from the most beautiful young head. Another was that I could not bear the thought of anyone else being the mother of my children.

DON JUAN [revolted]: You old rascal!

THE STATUE [stoutly]: Not a bit; for I really believed it with all my soul at the moment. I had a heart: not like you. And it was this sincerity that made me successful.

DON JUAN: Sincerity! To be fool enough to believe a ramping, stamping, thumping lie: that is what you call sincerity! To be so greedy for a woman that you deceive yourself in your eagerness to deceive her: sincerity, you call it!

THE STATUE: Oh, damn your sophistries! I was a man in love, not a law-
yer. And the women loved me for it, bless them!

Does Shaw take sides? Don Juan, advance guard for the Superman, presumably speaks for the dramatist, but our sympathies are divided or perhaps
not called upon at all. I hear the stance of Shelley's *Epipsychidion* taken up
in Don Juan's rhetoric, probably as a deliberate allusion on Shaw's part. The
Statue though, splendid fellow, speaks the universal rhetoric of all ordinary
men in love, and his rather dialectical "sincerity" has its own persuasiveness. Much trickier, and a larger achievement, is Shaw's management of the
fencing match between the Shavian Don Juan and that Wildean-Paterian
Aesthete, the Devil. Shaw's lifelong animus against Pater, and his repressed
anxiety caused by Wilde's genius as an Anglo-Irish comic dramatist, emerge
with authentic sharpness and turbulence as Don Juan and the Devil face off.
They are as elaborately courteous as Shaw and Wilde always were with each
other, but their mutual distaste is palpable, as pervasive as the deep dislike of
Shaw and Wilde for each other's works, ideas, and personalities:

THE DEVIL: None, my friend. You think, because you have a purpose,
Nature must have one. You might as well expect it to have fingers and
toes because you have them.

DON JUAN: But I should not have them if they served no purpose. And
I, my friend, am as much a part of Nature as my own finger is a part
of me. If my finger is the organ by which I grasp the sword and the
mandoline, my brain is the organ by which Nature strives to understand itself. My dog's brain serves only my dog's purposes; but my own
brain labors at a knowledge which does nothing for me personally
but make my body bitter to me and my decay and death a calamity.
Were I not possessed with a purpose beyond my own I had better be
a ploughman than a philosopher; for the ploughman lives as long as
the philosopher, eats more, sleeps better, and rejoices in the wife of
his bosom with less misgiving. This is because the philosopher is in
the grip of the Life Force. This Life Force says to him "I have done
a thousand wonderful things unconsciously by merely willing to live
and following the line of least resistance: now I want to know myself
and my destination, and choose my path; so I have made a special
brain—a philosopher's brain—to grasp this knowledge for me as the
husbandman's hand grasps the plough for me. And this" says the Life
Force to the philosopher "must thou strive to do for me until thou
diest, when I will make another brain and another philosopher to
carry on the work."

THE DEVIL: What is the use of knowing?

DON JUAN: Why, to be able to choose the line of greatest advantage instead of yielding in the direction of the least resistance. Does a ship sail to its destination no better than a log drifts nowhither? The philosopher is Nature's pilot. And there you have our difference: to be in hell is to drift: to be in heaven is to steer.

THE DEVIL: On the rocks, most likely.

DON JUAN: Pooh! which ship goes oftenest on the rocks or to the bottom? the drifting ship or the ship with a pilot on board?

THE DEVIL: Well, well, go your way, Señor Don Juan. I prefer to be my own master and not the tool of any blundering universal force. I know that beauty is good to look at; that music is good to hear; that love is good to feel; and that they are all good to think about and talk about. I know that to be well exercised in these sensations, emotions, and studies is to be a refined and cultivated being. Whatever they may say of me in churches on earth, I know that it is universally admitted in good society that the Prince of Darkness is a gentleman; and that is enough for me. As to your Life Force, which you think irresistible, it is the most resistable thing in the world for a person of any character. But if you are naturally vulgar and credulous, as all reformers are, it will thrust you first into religion, where you will sprinkle water on babies to save their souls from me; then it will drive you from religion into science, where you will snatch the babies from the water sprinkling and inoculate them with disease to save them from catching it accidentally; then you will take to politics, where you will become the catspaw of corrupt functionaries and the henchman of ambitious humbugs; and the end will be despair and decrepitude, broken nerve and shattered hopes, vain regrets for that worst and silliest of wastes and sacrifices, the waste and sacrifice of the power of enjoyment: in a word, the punishment of the fool who pursues the better before he has secured the good.

DON JUAN: But at least I shall not be bored. The service of the Life Force has that advantage, at all events. So fare you well, Señor Satan.

THE DEVIL [amiably]: Fare you well, Don Juan. I shall often think of our interesting chats about things in general. I wish you every happiness: heaven, as I said before, suits some people. But if you should change your mind, do not forget that the gates are always open here to the repentant prodigal. If you feel at any time that warmth of heart, sincere unforced affection, innocent enjoyment, and warm, breathing, palpitating reality—

This is hardly fair to the Devil, whose Paterian sense of repetition is a powerful answer to the idealism of Schopenhauer's life force, and whose Ecclesiastes-like vision of vanity does not exclude the holiness of the heart's affections. Don Juan regards the Devil as a sentimentalist, but the creative evolution preached by the Shavian Don now seems precisely the sentimentality of a lost world. By a paradox that Shaw would not have enjoyed, the Aesthetic vision of Pater and Wilde now appears to be Ruskin's abiding legacy, while Shaw's Fabian evolutionism would seem to have been a Ruskinian dead end. *Man and Superman* is effective enough farce, and its "Don Juan in Hell" is more than that, being one of the rare efforts to turn intellectual debate into actable and readable drama. Yet *Man and Superman* survives as theater; if you want an artist-philosopher in social comedy, then you are better off returning to the sublime nonsense and Aesthetic vision of *The Importance of Being Earnest*, a play that Shaw so curiously condemned as being "heartless."

Major Barbara

Shaw initially planned to call *Major Barbara* by the rather more imposing title of *Andrew Undershaft's Profession*. The play has been so popular (deservedly so) that we cannot think of it by any other title, but the earlier notion would have emphasized Undershaft's strength and centrality. He dwarfs Cusins and dominates Barbara, as much during her rebellion against him as in her return. And he raises the fascinating question of Shaw's own ambivalence toward the socialist ideal, despite Shaw's lifelong labor in behalf of that ideal. Undershaft may be the archetype of the capitalist as amoral munitions monger, but his arms establishment dangerously resembles a benign state socialism, and the drama moves finally in a direction equally available for interpretation by the extreme left or the extreme right.

Despite his ignorance of Freud, Shaw in *Major Barbara* (1905) wrote a drama wholly consonant with Freud's contemporary works, *The Interpretation of Dreams* and *Three Essays on the Theory of Sexuality*. Consider the first amiable confrontation of Barbara and her father Undershaft, who has not seen her since she was a baby:

UNDERSHAFT: For me there is only one true morality; but it might not fit you, as you do not manufacture aerial battleships. There is only one true morality for every man; but every man has not the same true morality.

LOMAX [*overtaxed*]: Would you mind saying that again? I didnt quite follow it.

CUSINS: It's quite simple. As Euripides says, one man's meat is another man's poison morally as well as physically.

UNDERSHAFT: Precisely.

LOMAX: Oh, that! Yes, yes, yes. True. True.

STEPHEN: In other words, some men are honest and some are scoundrels.

BARBARA: Bosh! There are no scoundrels.

UNDERSHAFT: Indeed? Are there any good men?

BARBARA: No. Not one. There are neither good men nor scoundrels: there are just children of one Father; and the sooner they stop calling one another names the better. You neednt talk to me: I know them. Ive had scores of them through my hands: scoundrels, criminals, infidels, philanthropists, missionaries, county councillors, all sorts. Theyre all just the same sort of sinner; and theres the same salvation ready for them all.

UNDERSHAFT: May I ask have you ever saved a maker of cannons?

BARBARA: No. Will you let me try?

UNDERSHAFT: Well, I will make a bargain with you. If I go to see you tomorrow in your Salvation Shelter, will you come the day after to see me in my cannon works?

BARBARA: Take care. It may end in your giving up the cannons for the sake of the Salvation Army.

UNDERSHAFT: Are you sure it will not end in your giving up the Salvation Army for the sake of the cannons?

BARBARA: I will take my chance of that.

UNDERSHAFT: And I will take my chance of the other. [*They shake hands on it.*] Where is your shelter?

BARBARA: In West Ham. At the sign of the cross. Ask anybody in Canning Town. Where are your works?

UNDERSHAFT: In Perivale St Andrews. At the sign of the sword. Ask anybody in Europe.

LOMAX: Hadnt I better play something?

BARBARA: Yes. Give us Onward, Christian Soldiers.

LOMAX: Well, thats rather a strong order to begin with, dont you know. Suppose I sing Thourt passing hence, my brother. It's much the same tune.

BARBARA: It's too melancholy. You get saved, Cholly; and youll pass hence, my brother, without making such a fuss about it.

LADY BRITOMART: Really, Barbara, you go on as if religion were a pleasant subject. Do have some sense of propriety.

UNDERSHAFT: I do not find it an unpleasant subject, my dear. It is the only one that capable people really care for.

Barbara, having replaced the absent Undershaft by God the Father in his Salvation Army guise, begins by accepting her phallic father as one more sinner to be saved. Their prophetic interchange of signs—daughterly cross and fatherly sword—bonds them against the mother, as each stands for a version of the only subject that the capable Shaw really cares for: religion as the life force, creative evolution. The daughter and the father, in mutual recognition, have commenced on their inevitably narcissistic dance of repressed psychosexual courtship. Cusins shrewdly sums up the enigma in his act 2 dialogue with Undershaft:

UNDERSHAFT: Religion is our business at present, because it is through religion alone that we can win Barbara.

CUSINS: Have you, too, fallen in love with Barbara?

UNDERSHAFT: Yes, with a father's love.

CUSINS: A father's love for a grown-up daughter is the most dangerous of all infatuations. I apologize for mentioning my own pale, coy, mistrustful fancy in the same breath with it.

Undershaft's love for Barbara is conversionary and therefore complex; its aim is to transform family romance into societal romance. After three-quarters of a century, G.K. Chesterton remains much the best of Shaw's early critics, but he insisted on a weak misreading of Undershaft's (and Shaw's) scheme:

The ultimate epigram of *Major Barbara* can be put thus. People say that poverty is no crime; Shaw says that poverty is a crime; that it is a crime to endure it, a crime to be content with it, that it is the mother of all crimes of brutality, corruption, and fear. If a man says to Shaw that he is born of poor but honest parents, Shaw tells him that the very word "but" shows that his parents were probably dishonest. In short, he maintains here what he had maintained elsewhere: that what the people at this moment require is not more patriotism or more art or more religion or more morality or more sociology, but simply more money. The evil is not ignorance or decadence or sin or pessimism; the evil is poverty. The point of this particular drama is that even the noblest enthusiasm of the girl who becomes a Salvation Army officer fails under the brute money power of her father who is a modern capitalist. When I have said this it will be clear why this play, fine and full of bitter sincerity as it is, must in a manner be cleared out of the way before we come to talk of Shaw's final and serious faith. For this serious faith is in the sanctity of human will, in the divine capacity for creation and choice rising higher than environment and doom; and so far as that goes, *Major Barbara* is not only apart from his faith but against his faith. *Major Barbara* is an account of environment victorious over heroic will. There are a thousand answers to the ethic in *Major Barbara* which I should be inclined to offer. I might point out that the rich do not so much buy honesty as curtains to cover dishonesty: that they do not so much buy health as cushions to comfort disease. And I might suggest that the doctrine that poverty degrades the poor is much more likely to be used as an argument for keeping them powerless than as an argument for making them rich. But there is no need to find such answers to the materialistic pessimism of *Major Barbara*. The best answer to it is in Shaw's own best and crowning philosophy.

Is the environment of Undershaft's "spotlessly clean and beautiful hillside town" of well-cared-for munitions workers victorious over Barbara's heroic will? Has the sanctity of human will, its divine capacity for creation and choice, been violated by Undershaft playing the part of Machiavel? Who could be more Shavian than the great life forcer, Undershaft, who cheerfully provides the explosives with which the present can blast itself into the future, in a perhaps involuntary parody of creative evolution? How far is Undershaft from the Caesar of *Caesar and Cleopatra?* The questions are so self-answering as to put Chesterton, splendid as he is, out of court.

But that still gives us the problem of Barbara's conversion: To what precisely has she come? The scene of her instruction is a characteristic Shavian outrage, persuasive and absurd. Cusins asks Undershaft the crucial question as to his munitions enterprise: "What drives the place?"

UNDERSHAFT [*enigmatically*]: A will of which I am a part.

BARBARA [*startled*]: Father! Do you know what you are saying; or are you laying a snare for my soul?

CUSINS: Dont listen to his metaphysics, Barbara. The place is driven by the most rascally part of society, the money hunters, the pleasure hunters, the military promotion hunters; and he is their slave.

UNDERSHAFT: Not necessarily. Remember the Armorer's Faith. I will take an order from a good man as cheerfully as from a bad one. If you good people prefer preaching and shirking to buying my weapons and fighting the rascals, dont blame me. I can make cannons: I cannot make courage and conviction. Bah! you tire me, Euripides, with your morality mongering. Ask Barbara: she understands. [*He suddenly reaches up and takes Barbara's hands, looking powerfully into her eyes.*] Tell him, my love, what power really means.

BARBARA [*hypnotized*]: Before I joined the Salvation Army, I was in my own power; and the consequence was that I never knew what to do with myself. When I joined it, I had not time enough for all the things I had to do.

UNDERSHAFT [*approvingly*]: Just so. And why was that, do you suppose?

BARBARA: Yesterday I should have said, because I was in the power of God. [*She resumes her self-possession, withdrawing her hands from his with a power equal to his own.*] But you came and shewed me that I was in the power of Bodger and Undershaft. Today I feel—oh! how can I put it into words? Sarah: do you remember the earthquake at Cannes, when we were little children?—how little the surprise of the first shock mattered compared to the dread and horror of waiting for the second? That is how I feel in this place today. I stood on the rock I thought eternal; and without a word of warning it reeled and crumbled under me. I was safe with an infinite wisdom watching me, an army marching to Salvation with me; and in a moment, at a stroke of your pen in a cheque book, I stood alone; and the heavens were empty. That was the first shock of the earthquake: I am waiting for the second.

There will not be a second shock, nor need there be. The dialectic of Barbara's conversion is all there in the single moment when Undershaft speaks of "a will of which I am a part" and Barbara is startled into the realization that her two fathers, Undershaft and God, are one. The realization is confirmed in the covenant of power that springs up between father and daughter as Undershaft takes Barbara's hands, while hypnotizing her through the will of which he is a part. Having been driven by one version of the life force, she yields now to another, but it is the same force. We somehow wish to find Shavian irony here, but there is less than we seek to find. What we discover is Shavian cruelty at Barbara's expense. Yielding her will to Undershaft sends Barbara into a massive regression, which calls into question her Christian idealism at the play's opening. A baby clutching at her mother's skirt, poor Barbara ends as the most reduced and humiliated heroine anywhere in Shaw. Why is he so harsh to so vivacious a figure, exuberant in her early idealism?

Eric Bentley observes accurately that "Barbara's final conversion has much less force than her previous disillusionment." This is useful as far as it goes, but Bentley is too fond of Shaw to see and say that her final conversion destroys her as an adult. *Major Barbara* is not a text for feminists, and if it can be construed as one for socialists, then they are very unsocial socialists indeed. Undershaft was a brilliant indication of where Shaw was heading, toward Carlyle's worship of heroes, strong men who would impose socialism because the Superman still waited to be born. Playful, wise, and charming, Undershaft nevertheless is a dangerous vision of the father-god enforcing the will of creative evolution. One remembers that Shaw, though knowing better, always retained a fondness for Stalin.

Nothing is got for nothing, and Shaw makes Barbara pay the price for this extravagant triumph of the religion of power. To be reconciled with the father, she becomes a child again, in a very curious parody of the Christian second birth. Perhaps she is a Shavian self-punishment that masquerades as a Nietzschean will revenging itself against time. Her pathetic dwindling remains a dark tonality at the conclusion of one of Shaw's most enduring farces.

Pygmalion

Part of the lovely afterglow of *Pygmalion* (1913) resides in its positioning both in Shaw's career and in modern history. The First World War (1914–18) changed Shaw's life and work, and nothing like so effective and untroubled a comedy was to be written by him again. If we seek his strong plays after *Pygmalion*, we find *Heartbreak House* (1916), *Back to Methuselah* (1921), *Saint Joan* (1923), and *Too True to be Good* (1932), none of them free of heavy doctrine, tendentious prophecy, and an unpleasant ambivalence toward human beings as they merely are. Fifty-eight and upon the heights of his comedic inventiveness, Shaw reacted to the onset of a catastrophic war with his bitter satiric pamphlet *Common Sense About the War*, which denounced both sides and called for instant peace.

British reaction, justifiably predictable, was hostile to Shaw until late 1916, when the increasing slaughter confirmed the accuracy of his prophetic views. By war's end, Shaw's public reputation was more than restored, but an impressively impersonal bitterness pervades his work from *Heartbreak House* until his death. *Pygmalion*, hardly by design, is Shaw's farewell to the age of Ruskin, to an era when that precursor prophet, Elijah to his Elisha, cried out in the wilderness to the most class-ridden of societies. Since Great Britain now is now more than ever two nations, Shaw's loving fable of class distinctions and of a working girl's apotheosis, her rise into hard-won self-esteem, has a particular poignance that seems in no immediate danger of vanishing.

Pygmalion manifests Shaw's mythopoeic powers at their most adroit, and it is certainly Shaw himself who is still central and triumphant both in the film (which he wrote) and in the musical *My Fair Lady*. Mythmaking most affects us when it simultaneously both confirms and subverts sexual stereotypes, which is clearly Shaw's dramatic advantage over such male vitalists as D.H. Lawrence or the entire coven of literary feminists, from Doris Lessing to Margaret Atwood.

The best judgment of *Pygmalion* as drama that I have encountered is again Eric Bentley's:

> It is Shavian, not in being made up of political or philosophic discussions, but in being based on the standard conflict of vitality and system, in working out this conflict through an inversion of romance, in bringing matters to a head in a battle of wills and words, in having an inner psychological action in counterpoint to the outer romantic action, in existing on two contrasted levels of mentality, both of which are related to the main theme, in delighting and surprising us with a constant flow of verbal music and more than verbal wit.

That is grand, but is *Pygmalion* more "an inversion of romance," more a *Galatea*, as it were, than it is a *Pygmalion*? Shaw subtitled it "A Romance in Five Acts." All romance, literary or experiential, depends on enchantment, and enchantment depends on power or potential rather than on knowledge. In Bentley's reading, Eliza acquires knowledge both of her own vitality and of something lacking in Higgins, since he is incarcerated by "system," by his science of phonetics. This means, as Bentley severely and lucidly phrases it, that Higgins is suspect: "He is not really a life-giver at all." The title of the play, and its subtitle, are thus revealed as Shaw's own interpretive ironies. Higgins is not Pygmalion, and the work is not a romance.

That Eliza is more sympathetic than Higgins is palpably true, but it remains his play (and his film, though not his musical). In making that assertion, I do not dissent wholly from Bentley, since I agree that Higgins is no life giver, no Prometheus. Shaw, after all, has no heroes, only heroines, partly because he is his own hero, as prophet of creative evolution, servant only of God, who is the life force. Higgins is another Shavian self-parody, since Shaw's passion for himself was nobly unbounded. The splendid preface to *Pygmalion*, called "A Professor of Phonetics," makes clear that Shaw considers Higgins a man of genius, a composite of Shaw himself, Henry Sweet who was reader of phonetics at Oxford, and the poet Robert Bridges, "to whom perhaps Higgins may owe his Miltonic sympathies," as Shaw slyly added.

Higgins, like Carlyle and Shaw, is a fierce Miltonist, an elitist who adopts toward women that great Miltonic maxim (so beloved by literary feminists):

"He for God only, she for God in him," where the reference is to Adam and Eve in their relation to Milton's God. The myth of Shaw's *Pygmalion* is that of Pygmalion and Galatea but also that of Adam and Eve, though as a Shavian couple they are never to mate (at least in Shaw's interpretation). Shaw rewrote some aspects of his *Pygmalion* in the first play, *In the Beginning*, of his *Back to Methuselah* cycle. There Adam and Eve repeat, in a sadly less comedic tone, the contrast between Higgins and Eliza:

ADAM: There is a voice in the garden that tells me things.

EVE: The garden is full of voices sometimes. They put all sorts of thoughts into my head.

ADAM: To me there is only one voice. It is very low; but it is so near that it is like a whisper from within myself. There is no mistaking it for any voice of the birds or beasts, or for your voice.

EVE: It is strange that I should hear voices from all sides and you only one from within. But I have some thoughts that come from within me and not from the voices. The thought that we must not cease to be comes from within.

Like Adam, Higgins hears the inner voice only, which is the Miltonic response to reality. Eve, like Eliza, hears the voice of the life force. Yet Adam, like Higgins, is no slave to "system." They serve the same God as Eve and Eliza, but they cannot accommodate themselves to change even when they have brought about change, as Higgins has worked to develop Eliza and wrought better than, at first, he has been able to know or to accept or ever be able to accept fully.

The famous final confrontation of Higgins and Eliza is capable of several antithetical interpretations, which is a tribute to Shaw's dialectical cunning, as he too wrought better (perhaps) than he knew, but then he truly was a Pygmalion:

HIGGINS [*wondering at her*]: You damned impudent slut, you! But it's better than snivelling; better than fetching slippers and finding spectacles, isn't it? [*Rising*] By George, Eliza, I said I'd make a woman of you; and I have. I like you like this.

LIZA: Yes: you turn round and make up to me now that I'm not afraid of you, and can do without you.

HIGGINS: Of course I do, you little fool. Five minutes ago you were like a millstone round my neck. Now youre a tower of strength: a consort battleship. You and I and Pickering will be three old bachelors instead of only two men and a silly girl. *Mrs Higgins returns, dressed for the wedding. Eliza instantly becomes cool and elegant.*

MRS HIGGINS: The carriage is waiting, Eliza. Are you ready?

LIZA: Quite. Is the Professor coming?

MRS HIGGINS: Certainly not. He cant behave himself in church. He makes remarks out loud all the time on the clergyman's pronunciation.

LIZA: Then I shall not see you again, Professor. Goodbye. [*She goes to the door.*]

MRS HIGGINS [*coming to Higgins*]: Goodbye, dear.

HIGGINS: Goodbye, mother. [*He is about to kiss her, when he recollects something.*] Oh, by the way, Eliza, order a ham and a Stilton cheese, will you? And buy me a pair of reindeer gloves, number eights, and a tie to match that new suit of mine. You can choose the color. [*His cheerful, careless, vigorous voice shews that he is incorrigible.*]

LIZA [*disdainfully*]: Number eights are too small for you if you want them lined with lamb's wool. You have three new ties that you have forgotten in the drawer of your washstand. Colonel Pickering prefers double Gloucester to Stilton; and you dont notice the difference. I telephoned Mrs Pearce this morning not to forget the ham. What you are to do without me I cannot imagine. [*She sweeps out.*]

MRS HIGGINS: I'm afraid youve spoilt that girl, Henry. I should be uneasy about you and her if she were less fond of Colonel Pickering.

HIGGINS: Pickering! Nonsense: she's going to marry Freddy. Ha ha! Freddy! Freddy!! Ha ha ha ha ha!!!!! [*He roars with laughter as the play ends.*]

Shaw, in an epilogue to the play, married Eliza off to Freddy and maintained Higgins and Eliza in a perpetual transference, both positive and negative, in which Higgins took the place of her father, Doolittle:

> That is all. That is how it has turned out. It is astonishing how much Eliza still manages to meddle in the housekeeping at Wimpole Street in spite of the shop and her own family. And it is notable that though she never nags her husband, and frankly loves the Colonel as if she were his favorite daughter, she has never got out of the habit of nagging Higgins that was established on the fatal night when she won his bet for him. She snaps his head off on the faintest provocation, or on none. He no longer dares to tease her by assuming an abysmal inferiority of Freddy's mind to his own.

He storms and bullies and derides; but she stands up to him so ruthlessly that the Colonel has to ask her from time to time to be kinder to Higgins; and it is the only request of his that brings a mulish expression into her face. Nothing but some emergency or calamity great enough to break down all likes and dislikes, and throw them both back on their common humanity—and may they be spared any such trial!—will ever alter this. She knows that Higgins does not need her, just as her father did not need her. The very scrupulousness with which he told her that day that he had become used to having her there, and dependent on her for all sorts of little services, and that he should miss her if she went away (it would never have occurred to Freddy or the Colonel to say anything of the sort) deepens her inner certainty that she is "no more to him than them slippers"; yet she has a sense, too, that his indifference is deeper than the infatuation of commoner souls. She is immensely interested in him. She has even secret mischievous moments in which she wishes she could get him alone, on a desert island, away from all ties and with nobody else in the world to consider, and just drag him off his pedestal and see him making love like any common man. We all have private imaginations of that sort. But when it comes to business, to the life that she really leads as distinguished from the life of dreams and fancies, she likes Freddy and she likes the Colonel; and she does not like Higgins and Mr Doolittle. Galatea never does quite like Pygmalion: his relation to her is too godlike to be altogether agreeable.

Shaw is clearly Pygmalion-Higgins here, and Mrs. Patrick Campbell is Galatea-Eliza. Mrs. Campbell, the actress who first played Eliza, had jilted Shaw definitively the year before *Pygmalion* opened in London, thus ending their never-consummated love affair. The price of being the prophet of creative evolution, in art as in experience, is that you never do get to make love to the life force.

Saint Joan

Saint Joan (1923) is a work written against its own literary age, the era of Proust, Joyce, Kafka, and above all others, Freud. It seems astonishing that *Saint Joan* is contemporary with Eliot's *The Waste Land* (1922). Eliot, whose own once-fashionable neo-Christianity now seems a refined superstition, rejected Shaw with his customary generosity of spirit: "The potent ju-ju of the Life Force is a gross superstition." That might be Stagumber crying out as he drags Joan out to be burned in Shaw's play, but then Eliot had become more English than the English. Luigi Pirandello, Shaw's peer as dramatist (as Eliot was not; *Murder in the Cathedral* weirdly concludes with a blatant imitation of the end of *Saint Joan*) made the inevitably accurate comment on the play, which is that it could as well have been called *Saint Bernard Shaw*:

> Joan, at bottom, quite without knowing it, and still declaring herself a faithful daughter of the Church, is a Puritan, like Shaw himself—affirming her own life impulse, her unshakable, her even tyrannical will to live, by accepting death itself.

That "tyrannical will to live" is once again Shaw's revision of Schopenhauer by way of Ruskin and Lamarck—the only wealth is life, as Ruskin taught, and the will creatively modifies the evolution of life in the individual, as Shaw strongly misread Lamarck. Eric Bentley, always the brilliantly sympathetic defender of Shaw, reads *Saint Joan* as a triumphant resolution of Shaw's worn-out agon between system and vitality, between society and the individual, a resolution that is comprised of an exactly equal sympathy for the old antagonists. The sympathy cannot be denied, but the play is overwhelmingly Protestant and its rhetoric wars against its argument, and so takes the side of Joan.

What precisely is Joan's religion, which is to ask: Can we make a coherent doctrine out of the religion of Bernard Shaw—his religion as a dramatist rather than as G.B.S. the polemicist and public personality? Did he indeed believe that what he called the evolutionary appetite was "the only surviving member of the Trinity," the Holy Spirit? Milton, Shaw's greatest precursor as exalter of the Protestant will and its holy right of private judgment, had invoked that spirit as one that descended, in preference to all temples, in order to visit the pure and upright heart—of John Milton in particular. We know how prophetically serious Milton was in this declaration, and his sublime rhetoric persuades us to wrestle with his self-election. But what are we to do with Shaw, whose rhetoric perhaps can beguile us sometimes but never can persuade?

Joan, like Shaw, does very well without either God the Father or Jesus Christ His Son. Though her ghost concludes the epilogue by addressing the "God that madest this beautiful earth," she does not intend her auditor to be the Jehovah of Genesis. Her initial divine reference in the play is to "orders from my Lord," but immediately she tells us that "that is the will of God that you are to do what He has put into my mind," which means that her own will simply is the will of God. Since she is, like Shaw, an Anglo-Irish Protestant, she never once invokes Jesus or His Mother. Instead, she listens to the voices of "the blessed saints Catherine and Margaret, who speak to me every day" and who might as well be girls from her own village. Her battle cry is: "Who is for God and His Maid?" And her last words, before she is pushed offstage to the stake, make dear that she is Shaw's substitute for Jesus of Nazareth:

> His ways are not your ways. He wills that I go through the fire to His bosom; for I am His child, and you are not fit that I should live among you. This is my last word to you.

In the queer but effective *The Adventures of the Black Girl in Her Search for God*, Shaw has his surrogate, whose "face was all intelligence," explain to the black girl his doctrine of work: "For we shall never be able to bear His full presence until we have fulfilled all His purposes and become gods ourselves.... If our work were done we should be of no further use: that would be the end of us." Carlyle would have winced at our becoming gods ourselves, but the gospel of labor remains essentially Carlyle's and Ruskin's. Defending *The Black Girl* in a letter to a friendly but pugnacious abbess, Shaw associated himself with the prophet Micah and refused to take as his idea of God "the anti-vegetarian deity who, after trying to exterminate the human race by drowning it, was coaxed out of finishing the job by a gorgeous smell of roast meat." That is good enough fun, but we return to *Saint Joan* to ask a question that has nothing in common with the Anglo-Catholic Eliot's indictment of a gross superstition. Vocabulary aside, is Joan at all interested in God, any God at all? Is Shaw?

If the term *God* is to retain any crucial aspect of its biblical range of reference, then Joan and Shaw could not care less. The life force has no personality, whereas Jehovah most certainly does, however uncomfortable it makes us. Is Joan anything except an embodiment of the life force? Has Shaw endowed her with a personality? Alas, I think not. The play holds the stage, but that will not always be true. Shaw's rhetoric is not provident or strong enough to give us the representation of a coherent psychology in Joan. The figure of the first few scenes has nothing in common with the heroine who repudiates her own surrender at the trial, or with the shade of a saint who appears to the king of France in his dream that forms the epilogue. No development or unfolding authentically links the country girl with the martyr.

Shaw's bravura as a dramatist saves the play as a performance piece, but cannot make it into enduring literature. Its humor works; its caricatures amuse us; its ironies, though too palpable, provoke analysis and argument. But Joan, though she listens to voices, cannot change by listening to her own voice speaking, which is what even the minor figures in Shakespeare never fail to do. Creative evolution, as a literary religion, could not do for Shaw what he could not do for himself. In *Saint Joan*, he fails at representing persons, since they are more than their ideas.

JOHN A. BERTOLINI

Saint Joan: *The Self as Imagination*

Heartbreak House

All of Shaw's plays act as compendiums of his ideas, motifs, and themes, but none does so more than *Heartbreak House*.[1] Its compendiousness signals Shaw's having reached the end of one phase of his playwrighting course and the beginning of another, as if Shaw, having ended *Heartbreak House* with an anticipation of apocalypse in Ellie Dunn's longing to have the bombers return the next night with their eerily aesthetic appeal of powerful sound and sheer energy, the pleasurable prospect of being finally done with the world, he then has to re-create the world in *Back to Methuselah*, just as Shakespeare in *King Lear* had made time go backward and had uncreated the world, and then had to re-create the world in his romances, especially *The Tempest*. Likewise Shaw had to transform the disillusioned young woman of *Heartbreak House* into the inspired young woman, Saint Joan. The despair that Shaw confronted (not succumbed to) in *Heartbreak House* did not of course simply go away, but it was suppressed, relegated to the status of an overtone, as when it appears in Adam's weariness of the world in *Back to Methuselah* and in Joan's resignation to the world's inhospitability to its saints.

Of all Shaw's plays, *Heartbreak House* remains for me the most elusive, the most ambiguous; pieces of it are graspable, but not the whole. Perhaps that makes it a gravel pit in my understanding of Shaw, but for the present, I can only offer the following brief remarks toward a discussion of the play's

From *The Playwriting Self of Bernard Shaw*, pp. 123-44, 191-95. Copyright © 1991 by the Board of Trustees, Southern Illinois University.

25

relationship to Shaw's playwrighting self.[2] Critics have often interpreted Captain Shotover as a Shavian self-portrait; I see him also as one of a long line of artists and artist figures in Shaw's plays from Eugene Marchbanks to Dr. Ridgeon, to Professor Higgins. As an inventor, sea adventurer, and ship captain, he seems to me to figure both the crafter of original plays and the fabulous voyager; I note also that as the designer of his own house, which is modeled after a ship and which serves as the set for the play in which he is a character, he figures Shaw as the master of stagecraft.

Captain Shotover like Ibsen's Master Builder has designed his own set. Our first encounter with that set suggests the incompleteness of *Heartbreak House*: something is being made at a carpenter's bench, for we see a vice with "*a board in its jaws; and the floor is littered with shavings, overflowing from a waste-paper basket.*" Here we have a condensation of the several ways in which Shotover figures Shaw's playwrighting self: the scene of crafting as a scene of writing ("*waste-paper,*" "*littered*"—Louis Dubedat's studio is also "*littered,*" but with "*sketchbooks, loose sheets of paper,*" etc.); the playwright as creator of stage metaphors, making one world behave like another, the stage like reality, a house on land like a ship on the water ("*overflowing*"); and the Shavian signature ("*shavings*")—which is in fragments, as the result of an unfinished piece of work.

As many critics have noted, Shaw sets up the world of *Heartbreak House* as a fragmentary dreamworld: action and dialogue are constantly interrupted or disrupted, characters appear, disappear, reappear, and doubling is a prominent motif, as in Strindberg's *A Dream Play* (Captain Shotover asks Billy Dunn when he first catches sight of him, "Are there two of you?"). The whole of the play can be read as Ellie's dream since at the beginning of the play she falls asleep while reading—Shakespeare of course—*Othello*, and when she awakes the action proper begins. Thus Shaw presents the play as generated by the dreaming self (as Tanner dreams the Don Juan in Hell sequence), its imagination stimulated by the reading of Shakespeare. Ellie might be Joan attending to her voices, except that Ellie's imagination contemplates the destruction of the world with a certain gleeful anticipation, or, at the least, she seems reckless of the safety of her immediate world.

The dreamlike state in which the action of *Heartbreak House* occurs insures that order will always be threatened, whether by bombs from an aeroplane or one of Captain Shotover's sudden entrances or exits. What order there is, whether aesthetic, moral, or social, is fragile. Whatever is built or arranged may topple over, or be wrecked, or be bombed. Shaw provides the key to this aspect of the play when he begins it with a pantomime that enacts the fragility of all order: Nurse Guinness "*fills her tray with empty bottles. As she returns with these, the young lady* [Ellie] *lets her book drop, awakening herself,*" *and startling the womanservant so that she all but lets the tray fall.*" The tray full of bottles—the attempt to keep order—barely escapes falling into fragments, just as the play will end when the house barely escapes being blown to smithereens (as Andrew Undershaft would have put it). I read Shaw's anxiety for the order of European civilization as extending to the aesthetic realm. Shaw's experiment with dramatic form as rondo discussion in *Heartbreak House* had begun with *Misalliance*; it is a dramatic form that seems always on the verge of formlessness, an aesthetic order always about to collapse under the pressure of impulse or whimsy or lack of will.

Shaw has Captain Shotover, however, meet the prospect of annihilation, as if it were judgment day, and deliver himself of a warning that has frequently been taken to be the lesson of the play, that the business of an Englishman is to learn navigation, "and live; or leave it and be damned." But when the danger passes, he urges "all hands" to "turn in"; and he himself "*goes asleep,*" perhaps to dream another play or to dream of a regenerated world. His sleep ends the play as it began, mysteriously, under the aegis of the dreaming self. In *Back to Methuselah* and in *Saint Joan*, Shaw shows the positive powers of the self that dreams.

Saint Joan: I

In his notice of the first production of Shaw's *Saint Joan*, Pirandello asserted that the play was "a work of poetry from beginning to end."[3] What Pirandello may have meant by that encompassing statement is not clear, but that he thought of the play as something other than either an impudent historical pamphlet masquerading as drama or a flippant treatment of a sacred subject *is* clear. My purpose now is to explore what Pirandello asserted about the play: its deeply poetic nature—a quality of the play that has as often been denied as asserted.[4] The play's poetic nature lives as much in its subject, which I take to be the workings of the imagination more than Joan's particular sainthood, as it does in its artistry. To make my point, I shall begin with the Epilogue, where I see the clearest evidence of Shaw's preoccupation with the nature of imagination. I will then compare the Epilogue with Shaw's explicit discussion of imagination in *Back to Methuselah* and return to *Saint Joan* in order to show how Shaw conceives of Joan as a symbol of imagination.[5]

The famous Epilogue to *Saint Joan* (or notorious Epilogue, if one reads any fair sampling of the reviews and criticism of the play from 1925 on) begins with a description of Charles' reading in bed, or rather, as Shaw puts it, "*looking at the pictures in Fouquet's Boccaccio.*" At first, that stage direction looks like a characteristic good-humored joke at the expense of the foolish Charles, whom Shaw continually portrays as a childishly self-centered individual, shrewd in certain matters, but of nevertheless singularly limited intellectual capacity. The joke is that Charles interests himself only in the dirty pictures found in the book. Neither Fouquet's coloring nor Boccaccio's prose style holds Charles' attention; the dirty pictures do, however. And Charles' insensitivity to art here is meant to tell us how he will respond to Joan's proposal that she return to life. Indeed, it reminds us of how he misunderstood Joan while she was alive. Charles' insensitivity to art and to Joan amount to the same thing.

Fouquet's Boccaccio is only one of the means by which Shaw insinuates into the play notions about art and how people respond to products of the imagination. It is part of a pattern of symbols and metaphors through which Shaw dramatizes his sense of what art can and should be. To continue with the opening stage directions of the Epilogue is to see Shaw's preoccupation with art emerge more and more clearly. From Fouquet's illustrations, Shaw directs our attention to a "*picture of the Virgin lighted by candles of painted wax.*" He then describes the walls of the room as "*hung from ceiling to floor with painted curtains which stir at times in the draughts.*" And lastly, he tells us that Charles' watchman's rattle is "*handsomely designed and gaily painted.*" In short, Shaw takes some pains to point out that Charles is surrounded by painting of one kind or another—a painted manuscript, painted candles, painted curtains, and a painted toy—but painting used to satisfy the human need for a decorous living space, adornment to please the eye.

Against this decorative use of art, Shaw sets Joan as symbol and metaphor. Joan enters when "*A rush of wind through the doors sets the walls swaying agitatedly. The candles go out. He [Charles] calls in the darkness.*" Whatever visual pleasure we took in Charles's colorful surroundings ends as, "*A flash of summer lightning shews up the lancet window*" and "*A figure is seen in silhouette against it.*" The movement of light that Shaw depicts here, from darkness to a figure seen in silhouette, to Joan dimly seen, culminates in the last moments of the Epilogue when "*The last remaining rays of light gather into a white radiance descending on Joan.*" At that moment, Joan stands literally and figuratively illuminated, for Shaw intends the Epilogue to make us see Joan more clearly as a metaphor that has meaning for the world, not merely as a decorative figure in memory and imagination.

Shaw has Joan herself articulate this significance: "I hope men will be the better for remembering me; and they would not remember me so well if you [Peter Cauchon] had not burned me." The rays of white light are also a transfiguration of the light from the fire that burned her, a connection Shaw suggests to us through Cauchon's words, "even as she burned, the flames whitened into the radiance of the Church Triumphant," as well as through the description of the curtains in Charles' bedroom: "*At first glance the prevailing yellow and red in these hanging pictures is somewhat flamelike when the folds breathe in the wind.*" Since the Epilogue follows shortly after Joan is dragged away to be burned, Shaw's stage directions cannot fail to remind us of those flames.

It could be charged that the final vision of the illuminated and solitary Saint Joan is a conventional tableau that has no more meaning that other such melodramatic stage-lighting effects, that it is visual rhetoric merely, a counterpart to her final rhetorical question: "O God that madest this beautiful earth, when will it be ready to receive Thy saints? How long, O Lord, how long?" No doubt the emotion of those last moments derives partly from the rhetorical strategy, but the emotion is also genuinely and complexly poetic. The final "radiance" fulfills the imagistic movement from darkness to light that the figure of Joan follows before our eyes. Poetic, too, is the ritualistic structuring of the immediately preceding episode. With a Te Deum-like sequence of lauds to Joan, each character in the Epilogue kneels in turn to hymn her praises, only to be asked by Joan if she should then return to earth. With their sadly comic volte-faces, each one rises to reject her proposal and leave her on stage alone. This ritual-like stage action points to Joan's isolation as a symbolic figure as well as to her personal isolation. She remains a scapegoat rejected by her comrades and community, and therefore a tragic figure. The kneeling to praise, the rising to reject, and the successive desertions of Joan in the Epilogue reenact the whole drama, which consists of her rise to influence and power in Scenes I to III and her fall in Scenes IV and V.[6]

Shaw liked this patterned action of successive desertions so well he used versions of it for the conclusions of *The Apple Cart* (1928) and *Too True to be Good* (1931), but he did not invent it for *Saint Joan*; he invented it for the conclusion of *Back to Methuselah*, where Lilith corresponds to Joan figuratively and where Adam, Eve, Cain, and the Serpent correspond to Charles, Dunois, and the rest. Shaw there uses a similar ritual-like stage action and plays similarly with light and darkness: "*It is now quite dark. A vague radiance appears near the temple and shapes itself into the ghost of Adam.*" As each ghost appears, it announces itself, hears the voice of the next to appear, and asks whose the voice is. Then the voice introduces itself, and the person appears.

This progress repeats itself for Adam, Eve, Cain, the Serpent, and lastly Lilith, who then starts a new pattern, whereby each ghost defines its contribution to life, notes the condition of the world, and asks the next ghost what he or she makes of it. The new pattern ends with the Serpent, who defines her contribution thus: "I chose wisdom and the knowledge of good and evil; and now there is no evil; and wisdom and good are one. It is enough." With her muted expression of philosophical content, the new ritual enters its final phase as, first the Serpent vanishes, and then Cain, Eve, and Adam express resignation, confidence, and dismay, respectively, and each vanishes in turn, leaving Lilith alone on stage to give her peroration to the whole play cycle that makes up *Back to Methuselah*. The order of the ghosts' exit lines reverses the order of their entrance lines, just as in *Saint Joan*, the order of the Te Deum speakers is reversed for their exit speeches. (The order of exits in *Saint Joan* is not so schematic as in *Back to Methuselah*; but it is close enough so that the audience has the sense of reverse order.)

Shaw's use of similarly structured endings for both plays suggests that Shaw's imagination connects Lilith's ritualistic isolation with Joan's. Both are icons in the scripture of Creative Evolution; both look to the future for fulfillment of their meaning. Here is how Lilith does so (with a strange consciousness of her metaphoric dimension):

> I brought life into the whirlpool of force, and compelled my enemy, Matter, to obey a living soul. . . . and now I shall see . . . the whirlpool become all life and no matter. And because these infants that call themselves ancients are reaching out towards that, I will have patience with them still; though I know well that when they attain it they shall become one with me and supersede me, and Lilith will be only a legend and a lay that has lost its meaning. Of Life only is there no end; and though of its million starry mansions many are empty and many still unbuilt, and though its vast domain is as yet unbearably desert, my seed shall one day fill it and master its matter to its uttermost confines. And for what may be beyond, the eyesight of Lilith is too short. It is enough that there is a beyond. [*She vanishes*].

Lilith looks forward to the time when she will have been so successfully incorporated into the imagination of humankind ("they shall become one with me") that she will become a dead metaphor ("a lay that has lost its meaning"). But in that incorporation and that becoming Lilith is reborn ("my seed shall one day fill it"), for she lives on in her acceptance by the imagination. Joan looks forward to a similar death and rebirth in the imagination of her audience (with, however, less visionary confidence), when her meaning will be so fully understood and accepted that her image is no longer necessary in humankind's memory. Joan's illuminated isolation at the end of the Epilogue is an attempt by Shaw the poet to help us imagine Saint Joan, which means above all to see her clearly.

But seeing Joan clearly requires imagination from the audience and reader. That is why the basic metaphors for lack of imagination in this play are poor eyesight and darkness, images that are associated chiefly with John de Stogumber and Charles. When de Stogumber realizes (in the Epilogue) that he may again be in Joan's presence, he reacts immediately by denying that she is Joan: "My sight is bad; I cannot distinguish your features: but you are not she." Just before he says this, de Stogumber explains how he was saved: "I had not seen it [cruelty] you know. That is the great thing: you must see it. And then you are redeemed and saved." Cauchon asks him if the sufferings of Christ were not enough for him, and de Stogumber replies: "I had seen them in pictures, and read of them in books, and been greatly moved by them, as I thought. But it was no use: it was not our Lord that redeemed me, but a young woman whom I saw actually burned to death. It was dreadful. But it saved me." Cauchon then asks what I take to be a central question of the play, "Must then a Christ perish in torment in every age to save those that have no imagination?" In the play's terms, then, imagination is how the human mind bridges the gap between life and art, between reality and fantasy, distinguishes the real toad in the imaginary garden. For that gap to be bridged the word must be made flesh in our minds. It is not so much a question of action in the real world (though that may be partly its consequence), but rather of what takes place in the human mind: understanding.

To understand Shaw's art and thought here it will be helpful to turn to two other plays that contain both imagistic connections with *Saint Joan* and explicit illustrations of Shaw's idea of the imagination: *Back to Methuselah* (again) and *On the Rocks*. As part of the Preface to *On the Rocks*, Shaw presents a short imaginary dialogue between Jesus and Pontius Pilate in which the following exchange takes place:

PILATE. A Salutary severity—

JESUS. Oh please! . . . I am so made by God that official phrases make me violently sick. . . . I have spoken to you as one man to another in living words. Do not be so ungrateful as to answer me in dead ones. . . . a thought is the substance of a word. I am no mere chance pile of flesh and bone: If I were only that, I should fall into corruption and dust before your eyes. I am the embodiment of a thought of God: I am the Word made flesh: that is what holds me together before you in the image of God. . . . The Word is God. And God is within you. . . .

PILATE. There are many sorts of words; and they are all made flesh sooner or later. . . . Your truth, as you call it, can be nothing but the thoughts for which you have found words which will take effect in deeds if I set you loose to scatter your words broadcast among the people.

What is most striking at first in this dialogue is Shaw's evident concern with language, that words matter, that they are efficacious in the real world. But words are not reality (and here Shaw shows his intellectual inheritance from Coleridge); their substance is thought. When Shaw has Jesus declare Himself to be "the embodiment of a thought of God ... the Word made flesh," and then has Him explain "that is what holds me together ... in the image of God," Shaw means that God created humankind by first imagining it. Things can become real after they have been imagined. Shaw as a dramatist habitually converts words into flesh on stage before an audience, but that conversion is only complete when the audience accepts the imaginative reality of Joan, in short, when the audience also imagines Joan.

Back to Methuselah: A Digression

Shaw most clearly set forth his view of imagination in the first part of *Back to Methuselah* (the play which in composition immediately precedes *Saint Joan*), "In the Beginning."[7] The first clue to the nexus in Shaw's mind between the Jesus–Pilate dialogue, *Saint Joan*, and *Back to Methuselah* comes in the opening stage directions of "In the Beginning" where the Serpent is described as *"sleeping with her head buried in a thick bed of Johnswort."* Johnswort is not a commonly known plant; Shaw has chosen it because in a punning sense it means John's Word: "In the beginning was the Word and the Word was with God." *Back to Methuselah* is Shaw's Word—a fifth gospel, picking up where Saint John's left off, or a third testament in ambition (if not in execution), an attempt to account for man's purpose on earth, a new iconography for man's purpose on earth, a new iconography for the new religion of Creative Evolution. At the center of that new religion is an intimate connection between life and imagination,[8] a connection which Shaw expounds in the wonderful dialogue between the Serpent and Eve.

The idea of imagination first appears when the Serpent explains to Eve how Lilith divided herself in two in order to make Adam and Eve. Eve asks how Lilith worked the miracle and the Serpent replies that Lilith "imagined it." Eve then wants to know what "imagined" is.

THE SERPENT. She [Lilith] told it to me as a marvelous story of something that never happened to a Lilith that never was. She did not know that imagination is the beginning of creation. You imagine what you desire; you will what you imagine; and at last you create what you will. . . . When Lilith told me what she had imagined in our silent language (for there were no words then) I bade her desire it, and then, to our great wonder, the thing she had desired and willed created itself in her under the urging of her will. . . .

EVE. Find me a word for the story Lilith imagined and told you in your silent language: the story that was too wonderful to be true, and yet came true.

THE SERPENT. A poem.

As Shaw conceives it, imagination precedes words, and the act of procreation is analogous to literary creation. Shaw had already drawn this analogy in *Man and Superman* (I argue in chapter two), when he made Tanner's acceptance of fatherhood analogous to his own acceptance of the authorship of *Man and Superman*. Shaw generates writing in the same way that Tanner comes to see himself as a procreator. Shaw needs Don Juan as Tanner's ancestor because Shaw wants to turn Don Juan from a mere seducer into a procreator of new life and a creator of new thought; and that is also what Shaw does with the Serpent and Eve in *Back to Methuselah*. For what the Serpent does here is seduce (but not corrupt) Eve into procreation with a "poem." Shaw quite directly dramatizes Eve's impregnation with imagination. Here, for example, is how he describes the Serpent's first appearance: "*The body of the serpent becomes visible, glowing with wonderful new colors. She rears her head slowly from the bed of Johnswort, and speaks into Eve's ear in a strange, seductively musical whisper.*"[9] The Serpent approaches Eve like a lover, and Eve responds to her unabashedly:

THE SERPENT. I have come to chew you my beautiful new hood. See [*she spreads a magnificent amethystine hood*]! . . . I am the most subtle of all the creatures of the field.

EVE. Your hood is most lovely. [*She strokes it and pets the serpent*]. Pretty thing! Do you love your godmother Eve?

THE SERPENT. I adore her. [*She licks Eve's neck with her double tongue*].

Though the interplay between them clearly resembles a sexual seduction, the Serpent's scope is wider than that: she wants Eve to use her imagination to procreate herself in order to defeat the nothingness of death.

THE SERPENT. Life must not cease. . . .

EVE [*thoughtfully*] There can be no such thing as nothing. The garden is full, not empty.

THE SERPENT. That is true, Darling Eve: this is a great thought. Yes: there is no such thing as nothing, only things we cannot see. The chameleon eats the air.

What seems to have been in the back of Shaw's mind while composing this scene is Hamlet's confrontation of death.[10] The Serpent's line above, for example, echoes Hamlet's reply to Claudius's nervous inquiry after his well-being, "Excellent, i' faith, of the chameleon's dish: I eat the air promise cramm'd" (III, 2). But, more particularly, Shaw seems to be playing variations on the theme of the gravediggers' scene (V, 1). In *Back to Methuselah*, Adam and Eve first become aware of death's having entered the world when Adam sees a playing fawn trip head over heels in the garden and break its neck. Adam realizes that someday he will die too: "Sooner or later I shall fall and trip. . . . We shall fall like the fawn and be broken." (Shaw died at the age of ninety-four, after he had stumbled in his garden and broken a leg. He had been pruning a tree.)

Adam expresses his weariness of the gardener's life of weeding and pruning thus: "If only the care of this terrible garden may pass to some other gardener! . . . If only the rest and sleep that enable me to bear it from day to day could grow into an eternal rest, an eternal sleep, then I could face my days, however long they may last. Only there must be some end, some end. I am not strong enough to bear eternity." The Preface to *Buoyant Billions* begins magnificently this way: "I commit this to print within a few weeks of completing my 92nd year. . . . I can hardly walk through my garden without a tumble or two; and it seems out of all reason to believe that a man who cannot do a simple thing like that can practise the craft of Shakespeare. . . . Should it not warn me that my bolt is shot and my place silent in the chimney corner?" The juxtaposition in Shaw's mind between the recreation of a walk in his garden with the creation of playwrighting indicates that Shaw conceived of his essential self as the playwrighting self, and that when he could no longer write plays his life would be at its end. Is it too fanciful to think that in *Back to Methuselah* Shaw imagined the death he then willed in his ninety-fourth year?[11] One of the things Eve notices especially about the dead fawn is: "It has a queer smell. Pah!"—an exclamation that Hamlet makes when he considers Alexander's dead body:

HAMLET. Dost thou think Alexander look'd o' this fashion i' the earth?
HORATIO. Een so.
HAMLET. And smelt so? Pah!
HORATIO. Een so, my lord.

HAMLET. To what base uses we may return, Horatio! Why may not imagination trace the noble dust of Alexander, till 'a find it stopping a bung-hole?

HORATIO. 'Twere to consider too curiously, to consider so.[12]

Shaw concerns himself in *Back to Methuselah* precisely with Hamlet's question: what may imagination do when it considers death?

In the remaining four parts of the play Shaw fantasizes that certain individuals find the secret of long life. Shaw, of course, intends this fantasy to be a metaphor, as in other such symbolic visions of the future. His basic idea is that man does not live long enough to solve the problems of human society; Shaw therefore posits an Aristophanic fantasy, whereby man imagines himself able to live three hundred years, wills what he imagines, and finally achieves his will. Shaw's metaphor of long life surely means that people should live their seventy-odd years *as if* they were three hundred years or more. With each successive part of *Back to Methuselah*, humankind keeps extending the life-span (in Part V, "As Far as Thought Can Reach," to eight hundred years and more), but accidental death remains. And that is the key point that insures the metaphoric import of Shaw's fantasy: death does not disappear; it diminishes in importance though. Thus, *Back to Methuselah* assumes the generic function of all comedy, to thumb the nose at death.

In Part II, "The Thing Happens," the mockery of death forms itself in the person of Bill Haslam, who has lived to be 245 years old, without anyone knowing about it, by pretending to have drowned several times, each time assuming a new identity upon emergence.[13] His sham drownings are metaphorically a braving of death, a denial of its importance, and hence a freeing of the human imagination from its obsessive fear of death, what Horatio calls considering "too curiously," and what Ophelia's "muddy death" symbolizes.

Shaw dramatizes one such failure of imagination in the confrontation with death at the end of "The Thing Happens." Burge-Lubin, the president of the British Isles in the year 2170 A.D., finds himself attracted sexually to the Minister of Health, a beautiful Negress who invites him to a rendezvous aboard a "*steam yacht in glorious sea weather*":

THE NEGRESS. There is a lightning express on the Irish Air service at half-past sixteen. They will drop you by parachute into the bay. The dip will do you good. I will pick you up and dry you and give you a first-rate time.

BURGE-LUBIN. Delightful. But a little risky, isn't it?

THE NEGRESS. Risky! I thought you were afraid of nothing.

As it turns out Burge-Lubin *is* afraid of *nothing*, that is, the nothingness of death. For, although he at first seems willing to risk death by water when Confucius tells him they will give him an "unsinkable tunic," finally he rejects the chance because, as Confucius tells him, "the water is not safe . . . the sea is very cold," and he "may get rheumatism for life": "BURGE-LUBIN. That settles it: I won't risk it."

Burge-Lubin's refusal to take the physical risk is a metaphor for his refusal to take metaphysical risks. A sexual alliance with the Negress requires the daring of imagination, which he lacks. Earlier in the play, Shaw carefully sets in our minds Burge-Lubin's fear of death by drowning, when we hear him warning Barnabas, the Accountant-General: "You know you never never look where you are going when you are immersed in your calculations. Some day you will walk into the Serpentine." It is precisely being *immersed* in the waters of imagination that Burge-Lubin himself fears—the imagination that reduces the importance of death, that defeats death. The Serpent is an archetypal symbol of eternity, and thus, of the idea that life is cyclical, that death is not final. Burge-Lubin fears the risk involved: he is afraid to walk into the Serpentine because he refuses to dare—exactly what the Serpent in Part I is willing to do and does:

THE SERPENT. You see things; and you say "why?" But I dream things that never were; and I say "Why not?" . . . and I have eaten strange things: stones and apples that you are afraid to eat.

EVE. You dared!

THE SERPENT. I dared everything. And at last I found a way of gathering together a part of the life in my body—

Back to Methuselah announces its main theme when the Serpent tells Eve: "Death is not an unhappy thing when you have learnt how to conquer it . . . by another thing, called birth."

Saint Joan: II

The Serpent's "daring," which is really her imaginative triumph over death and loneliness, is the same "daring" that Joan talks about:

Do not think you can frighten me by telling me that I am alone. France is alone; and God is alone; and what is my loneliness before the loneliness of my country and my God? I see that the loneliness of God is his strength: what would He be if He listened to your jealous little counsels? Well, my loneliness shall be my strength too; it is better to be alone with God: His friendship will not fail me, nor His counsel, nor His love. In His strength I will dare, and dare, and dare, until I die.[14]

The central drama of *Saint Joan* lies in her conquest of the fear of death in the trial scene. Plainly, the locus of powerful emotion in the play is Joan's recantation when she tears up her confession. Learning that she will not go free, but suffer life imprisonment instead, makes her assert the value of freedom over life itself. However, the freedom she desires is not merely freedom of movement (though that is important to her), but also the freedom of the imagination: "if only I could still hear the wind in the trees, the larks in the sunshine, the young lambs crying through the healthy frost, and the blessed blessed church bells that send my angel voices floating to me on the wind. But without these I cannot live." The imaginative freedom Joan asserts here is exclusively aural.[15] In Shaw's mind Joan's voices replicate the voices Adam and Eve hear in the garden in "In the Beginning." Real death for Joan means being cut off from the voice of imagination: her dread of the imprisoning of her imagination crushes her fear of the fire.

Shaw makes Joan not only imaginative herself, but a stimulus to imagination in others (that is one of the reasons why she, like Falstaff, can be seen as an emblem of the imagination). The first Shaw does, humorously, through a pair of stage directions. At her first entrance, Shaw describes Joan as having *"eyes very wide apart and bulging as they often do in very imaginative people."* In contrast, when Shaw introduces the Dauphin, he describes him as having *"little narrow eyes, near together."* Shaw does not need to indicate any more explicitly the Dauphin's lack of imagination. We remember his description of Joan and draw our own conclusion: the Dauphin has no imagination (rather like Herodias in Wilde's *Salome*, for whom "the moon is like the moon, that is all"). The Dauphin's later assertion to Joan, "I have my eyes open," adds ironic counterpoint to Shaw's humorous hinting at Charles' lack of imagination: his eyes may be open, but only to see what lies in front of him; he has no vision of what France should be as Joan does.

Shaw also makes Joan stimulate imagination in others (again humorously). For example, after de Baudricourt is finally convinced to send her to the Dauphin, Joan says, "Oh squire! Your head is all circled with light, like a saint's," and he looks *"up for his halo rather apprehensively."* Joan can make people see more than what is in front of their eyes. In short, Joan enables people to see the metaphoric dimension of reality. That poetic power in her is brought into high relief through the discussion of miracles between the Archbishop and La Tremouille, where the Archbishop explains that the church nourishes the people's "faith by poetry."

THE ARCHBISHOP. Parables are not lies because they describe events that never happened. . . . if they [the people] feel the thrill of the supernatural, and forget their sinful clay in a sudden sense of the glory of God, it will be a miracle.

Shortly thereafter, Shaw underlines his point through a deft bit of characterization, when he has the Archbishop identify Pythagoras as "A sage who held that the earth is round and that it moves round the sun," at which La Tremouille exclaims; "What an utter fool! Couldnt he use his eyes?" La Tremouille, like Charles and like de Stogumber, has limited vision because he cannot see the metaphoric dimension of reality, the poetry in life, its miracles.

More important, however, than these two aspects of Joan is her identity as an emblem of imagination itself, especially in its essence of freedom. Nowhere does Shaw bring this identification out more clearly than in the short scene before Orleans between Dunois and his Page. That scene opens with Dunois invoking the west wind in an attempt at poetic incantation (echoing Shelley's "Ode to the West Wind," of which more later). As Dunois finishes his prayer-poem, the Page bounds to his feet:

THE PAGE. See! There! There she goes!

DUNOIS. Who? the Maid?

THE PAGE. No: the kingfisher. Like blue lightning.

A bit later, they watch another kingfisher fly by the reeds and "*they follow the flight till the bird takes cover.*" That they are waiting for Joan, and that Dunois thinks the Page means Joan when he first cries out, suffices to enforce our identifying Joan with the kingfisher. But if we think of the bird's name and back to how Joan, at the court of the Dauphin in the preceding scene, searches "*along the row of courtiers, and presently makes a dive, and drags out Charles by the arm,*" we can see that Shaw's mind symbolically identifies Joan with the kingfisher bird. (Summer lightning presages Joan's appearance in the Epilogue—a reminder of the "blue lightning" to which the Page compares the kingfisher.) That identification, however, goes beyond the merely picturesque or the punning senses in the bird's name and in Charles' label, Dauphin (Dolphin), for in the next exchange between the Page and Dunois, we see the kingfisher image expand into a mutivalent metaphor for Joan that reaches to the core of the play's meaning:

THE PAGE. Arent they lovely? I wish I could catch them.

DUNOIS. Let me catch you trying to trap them, and I will put you in the iron cage for a month to teach you what a cage feels like.

Dunois' words proleptically point to the trial scene where Joan's imprisonment is in question, and where Shaw maintains Joan's association with the
image of flying: "JOAN. And why must I be chained by the feet to a log of
wood? Are you afraid I will fly away? . . . COURCELLES. If you cannot
fly like a witch, how is it that you are still alive?"[16] The instinctive reaction
of unimaginative people to the "lovely" things in life, the free things, like
the kingfisher, is to capture and cage them. So too it is with Joan: her lovely,
free imagination provokes them to want to destroy her, or failing that, at
least to cage her for life. In their desire to imprison Joan, Shaw shows that
they want to deny metaphor. For Joan embodies imagination, the freedom
to soar beyond things, to metaphorize the world by seeing more. After
Dunois utters a second prayer-poem, this time to the kingfisher bird, asking it to send a west wind, Joan immediately enters, and at the end of the
scene the west wind comes, as if there were a silent consonance between
them. Indeed, there is, but the consonance alludes loudly to Shelley's "Ode
to the West Wind":

> Be thou, Spirit fierce,
> My spirit! Be thou me, impetuous one!
>
> Drive my dead thoughts over the universe
> Like withered leaves to quicken a new birth!
> And, by the incantation of this verse,
>
> Scatter, as from an unextinguished hearth
> Ashes and sparks, my words among mankind!
> Be through my lips to unawakened earth
>
> The trumpet of a prophecy!
> O wind, If Winter comes, can Spring be far behind?[17]

Joan imagines into existence a new France out of the blood and death
of Orleans. That is why Shaw sounds overtones of sexual attraction between
Joan and Dunois as they discuss tactics for laying siege to Orleans. Their
conversation veers off midway onto the topic of love and marriage. With her
enthusiasm and familiarity Joan could be said to seduce Dunois into believing in her, not through feminine wiles or any means so overt, but through
her innocent self-assurance and intimacy of address, even as she seduces de
Baudricourt and Charles. In Joan's meeting with Dunois, feminine sexuality
combines with maternal caring (as is typical in Shaw). Dunois' decorative
masculinity asserts itself playfully even before Joan arrives: he "*has had his*

lance stuck up with a pennon" and *"has his commander's baton in his hand."* And when the wind changes, the seduction ends in union: the surrender of Dunois (he kneels and hands her his baton), and Joan's seizing of him (she flings *"her arms around Dunois, kissing him on both cheeks"*). But Joan's conquest of Dunois is not only a lover's conquest, for she simultaneously mothers him: "I will deliver you from fear." (In Scene V she says to him, "You are the pick of the basket here, Jack.")

The crowning of Charles as king of a new France out of the victory at Orleans adumbrates Shelley's imagery only in a general way, with Joan as a rejuvenating, fertility figure, but what Joan as a martyred saint can do for the rejuvenation of the world echoes Shelley more specifically: "You will all be glad to see me burnt; but if I go through the fire I shall go through it to their hearts [of the common people] for ever and ever."

Shelley's prayer that the west wind "Scatter, as from an unextinguished hearth / Ashes and sparks, my words among mankind!"[18] turns into "the trumpet of a prophecy," like Joan's prediction, and modulates finally into a temperate, yet half-fearful, faith in time's transforming power—"If Winter comes, can Spring be far behind?"—tonally not unlike the ending of *Saint Joan*, "How long, O Lord, how long?" (though there is also anguish in Joan's question).

Shelley's theme of time brings me to my final point about the central drama in *Saint Joan*: the possibility of overcoming the fear of death through imagination. For Joan's final question, "O God that madest this beautiful earth, when will it be ready to receive thy saints? How long, O Lord, how long?," is a real question, not just a rhetorical flourish to conclude the play.

Shaw calls *Saint Joan* a *chronicle* play, and he means it in three senses. *Saint Joan* is a historical play that represents actual persons and events of the past. It is play that rivals Shakespeare's history plays (based as they were on sixteenth-century chronicles), particularly *Henry VI, Part One*, which had so maligned the historical Joan that Shaw could appear to be rewriting Shakespeare for the sake of justice. But it is also a play about time. Much of what characters spend their time doing in *Saint Joan* is waiting: in the first scene, waiting for the hens to lay; in Scene II, the court waits for the Dauphin ("LA TREMOUILLE. What the devil does the Dauphin mean by keeping us waiting like this?"); in Scene III, Dunois waits for the west wind and for Joan; in Scene IV, Warwick waits for Cauchon to arrive; in Scene V, after the coronation, the people wait to see Joan; in Scene VI, the English wait for the outcome of the trial ("WARWICK. Is this trial never going to end?"); and in the Epilogue, Joan remains waiting for the earth to be ready to receive God's saints. The recurring sense of expectancy, of wait-ing upon time, works as a structural force in the play and gives Joan's last line its peculiar power to move. We have been waiting all through the play for historical time to unfold, and at the end of the play we wait for imaginative time to unfold; that is, we ask ourselves what our imaginations can create in time.

Shaw places the Epilogue in historical time: *"night in June 1456."* But more than that, he tells us the exact time for the beginning, the middle, and the end of the scene, midnight. Before the dialogue begins, he tells us, *"A distant clock strikes the half-hour softly,"* which we know means 11:30 P.M. Approximately halfway through the scene, just before the Soldier enters, *"The clock strikes the third quarter."* In other words, the time Shaw indicates as passing during the action of the Epilogue equals half an hour. Although Shaw locates the action chronologically and represents it as transpiring in real time, yet the action is not realistic, for characters who are dead appear in it (Joan herself, Cauchon, et al.), as well as characters who are alive but who could not actually be present in Charles' chamber.

Moreover, Shaw creates unrealistic entrances for his characters. For example, Dunois enters *"through the tapestry on Joan's left, the candles relighting themselves at the same moment, and illuminating his armor and surcoat cheerfully,"* and Shaw thereby metaphorically underlines his sense of the Epilogue as a pure product of art and the imagination, while at the same time rehearsing the larger illumination provided by the end of the play. Thus, Shaw collapses time and space in the Epilogue[19]—a normal procedure for a dramatist who wishes to represent the action of a dream on stage. It is clear, however, that Shaw does not intend the Epilogue to be Charles' dream merely, and certainly not his wish fulfillment.[20] Indeed, it cannot be the dream of any character on stage, for toward the end of the scene, *"a clerical looking gentleman,"* dressed *"in the fashion of 1920, suddenly appears."* It can only be the audience's dream projected on stage as a fantastical, Lucianic adventure: a "what if Joan were free to talk with her friends and foes after her death and learn of her canonization?" proposition.

The author helps the audience to imagine the situation, to ask itself when it will be ready to receive God's saints. And the moment when it contemplates this question is midnight, in stage time and in real time (Shaw surely must have planned that the last half-hour of the play from 11:30 to midnight would also correspond to the time the audience would be hearing the play—assuming an evening performance beginning at 8:00), so that imagination and reality come together artfully on the borderline between the death of the midnight bell's last chime and the day's rebirth into the white radiance descending on Joan. In the ritualized ending to the play, the pallid green light of the false images and dim sight yields to the visionary white light around the lonely figure of Joan, praying her quietly urgent question,

"How long, O Lord, how long?" Shaw wrote *Saint Joan* to help us imagine Saint Joan, that is to help us sense what imagination is.

But Shaw knows he can only go so far in the direction of representing imagination. In doing so he appeals to three kinds of imagination in the audience: the hallucinatory imagination through the dream setting; the auditory through the chimes; and the visual through the white radiance. Yet there remains something ineffable about the imagination that the dramatist can only hint at—JOAN: "I cannot tell you the whole truth: God does not allow the whole truth to be told." Shaw has Joan express this idea during the cathedral scene (V), midway through the play, where he creates a moment that rehearses the use of the chimes in the Epilogue. In speaking to Dunois after Charles' coronation, Joan tries to explain her sense of imagination resonating within her:

> It is in the bells I hear my voices. Not to-day, when they all rang: that was nothing but jangling. But here in this corner, where the bells come from a distance through the quiet of the country-side, my voices are in them. [*The cathedral clock chimes the quarter*] Hark! [*She becomes rapt*] Do you hear? "Dear-child-of-God": just what you said. At the half-hour they will say "Be-brave-go-on." At the three-quarters they will say "I-am-thy-Help." But it is at the hour, when the great bell goes after "God-will-save-France": it is then that St. Margaret and St. Catherine and sometimes even the blessed Michael will say things that I cannot tell beforehand. Then, oh then—

Dunois interrupts her at this point, for to him, when Joan talks this way, she seems "a bit cracked," but surely his interruption is timely. The filling in of that dash that halts her speech is the Epilogue, especially its final moments when we hear those chimes Joan only describes here, and we see the white radiance descending on her head. The poetry of the play concentrates itself in the theatrical gestures of light, sound, and language combining together to make us feel what we might otherwise be incapable of feeling. Shaw's use of theatrical metaphor creates a heightened and therefore new sense of reality in his audience, as well as in those of his readers who have imagination themselves.

The delicacy and feeling with which Shaw accomplishes his meaning elude demonstration somewhat, in part because aural and visual stage rhythm account for much of the proper effect. The ritual isolation of Joan proceeds regularly as each character in turn demurs from her proposal that she return to life, and then rises and exits. When we reach the last two characters, Charles and the Soldier, Shaw applies a *ritardando* to the rhythm of the exit speeches: first, as Charles "[*mumbling in his pillows*] Goo ni," falls asleep, finally weary of Joan and irredeemably unconscious of her sadness, while Joan bids him "Goodnight, Charlie," showing her affection for him in her use of his nickname, notwithstanding his indifference to her; and second, as the Soldier with an instinctive, if not fully conscious, sense of the pain caused by the others' rejection of her, counsels her not to pay any heed to such lofty personages as kings and archbishops. He even starts to explain why she "has as good a right to [her] notions as they have to theirs," but before he can get on with his "lecture," the chimes of midnight begin to sound and Joan never hears his lecture: "Excuse me: a pressing appointment—[*He goes on tiptoe*]." All during his half-attempted consolation of her, his friendly chattiness focuses the audience's attention, not on himself, but on the chimes and on Joan's silence as she attends to them.[21]

"A work of poetry from beginning to end," wrote Pirandello. What Joan hears in those chimes—the Word made flesh, poetic imagination overcoming the fear of death—Shaw makes her embody as a character and a symbol, thus helping us to imagine imagination herself, Saint Joan.

NOTES

1. These have been well catalogued and analyzed by several critics (see for example J. L. Wisenthal's chapter on *Heartbreak House* in *The Marriage of Contraries* (Cambridge: Harvard Univ. Press, 1974) for the play's relationship to *Man and Superman*, *Major Barbara*, and *John Bull's Other Island*), and I will not repeat their findings here.

2. Shaw himself strongly identified with the inexplicability of the play; for example, he said about it (in the *Sunday Herald*, London, Oct. 23, 1921): "I am not an explicable phenomenon: neither is 'Heartbreak House'" (see *Collected Plays*, Vol. 5, 185).

3. "Bernard Shaw's *Saint Joan*" in *Bernard Shaw's Plays*, ed. Warren S. Smith (New York: W. W. Norton, 1970), 450.

4. Denied in *The Harvest of Tragedy* (New York: Barnes and Noble, 1966), 194–95, by T. R. Henn, for example (whose objections to Joan's diction seem to me way off the mark insofar as they do not take into account Joan's mystical bent); asserted by J. I. M. Stewart, *Eight Modern Writers*, Vol. 12 of the *Oxford History of English Literature* (Oxford: Oxford Univ. Press, 1963), 179: " . . . certainly Shaw's outstanding play, conceivably the finest and most moving English drama since *The Winter's Tale* or *The Tempest*."

5. A shorter version of this chapter was published in 1983 in *Shaw: The Annual of Bernard Shaw Studies*, Vol. 3, *Shaw's Plays in Performance*, ed. Daniel Leary (University Park: The Pennsylvania State Univ. Press, 1983), as "Imagining *Saint Joan*"; almost at the same time, Bryan Tyson published his fine book, *The Story of Saint Joan* (Kingston and Montreal: McGill-Queen's Univ. Press, 1982). It is a pleasure to note here that Tyson and I had reached independently similar readings of

how Shaw used the theme of imagination in *Saint Joan*. I refer the reader to Tyson's book for insights parallel and additional to those I try to articulate here regarding the role of imagination in the play.

6. I should like to note here that I believe Robert Bolt borrowed this structure (whether consciously or unconsciously) for the screenplay of *Lawrence of Arabia*, where the "miraculous" taking of Aquaba corresponds to Joan's victory at Orleans, and where Lawrence's becoming persona non grata to the British and the Arabs corresponds to Joan's becoming a thorn to both church and state. There are many further parallels.

7. Actually, *Jitta's Atonement* intervenes between the two plays, but can be considered a parenthesis in Shaw's imaginative course as a dramatist, since it was a translation-adaptation of a Siegfried Trebitsch play, *Frau Gittas Suhne*, which Shaw made as a gesture of gratitude to his German translator.

8. In this, as in so many other intellectual and visionary matters, Shaw follows Blake, for whom imagination was not merely another faculty but the substance of life. For a convenient index to Blake's statements on imagination, see S. Foster Damon, *A Blake Dictionary* (New York: E.P. Dutton, 1971). See also, Northrop Frye, *Fearful Symmetry: A Study of William Blake* (Princeton: Princeton Univ. Press, 1947), 114: "A thing's name is its numen, its imaginative reality in the eternal world of the human mind. That is another reason why Jesus is called the Word of God. Reality is intelligibility, and a poet who has put things into words has lifted 'things' from the barren chaos of nature into the created order of thought."

9. Shaw seems to have based the Serpent's courtship of Eve on his own of Mrs. Patrick Campbell—or hers of him. In a letter to Shaw, postmarked Sept. 2, 1912, she refers to his "beloved Irish accent! which I believe the serpent had or Eve would never have noticed the apple far less eaten it." See *Bernard Shaw and Mrs. Patrick Campbell: Their Correspondence*, ed. Alan Dent (New York: Alfred A. Knopf, 1952). Several years later, after Shaw had written *Back to Methuselah*, he twice professed to have imagined *her* as the Serpent: "God intended you to play the serpent in Methuselah: I wrote it for your voice" (letter of Mar. 27, 1924): and in a letter of July 28, 1929, he refers to "the Serpentin *Methuselah*, whom l always hear speaking with your voice."

10. In the Postscript (1944) to *Back to Methuselah*, Shaw identifies *Hamlet* as the play Shakespeare would most likely have selected for inclusion ("if he could be consulted"), in the Oxford series of World's Classics.

11. Shaw seems particularly to have identified himself with Adam's perplexity in the face of longevity. Almost twenty years after writing *Back to Methuselah*, he echoes the following (one of Adam's more desperate utterances): "It is the horror of having to be with myself for ever. I like you [Eve]; but I do not like myself. I want to be different; to be better; to begin again and again; to shed my skin as a snake sheds its skin. I am tired of myself. And yet I must endure myself, not for a day, but for ever. That is a dreadful thought." At the age of eighty-one Shaw said about what he thought was his imminent death: "I find I cannot like myself without so many reservations that I look forward to my death, which cannot now be far off, as a good riddance." (See *The Religious Speeches of Bernard Shaw*, ed. Warren S. Smith [New York: McGraw-Hill, 1965], 96.) Anyone who has heard the tape of this broadcast speech can miss neither the sincerity nor the detachment in Shaw's tone. His and Adam's attitude is neither a romantic longing for dissolution, nor a desire to embrace darkness, but rather the poise of one who feels his life's work is done and who accepts death as a necessary condition for the continuation of life as a whole.

12. Another indication that Shaw had the gravediggers' scene in mind is Cain's line, "When Adam delved and Eve span, who was then the gentleman?" from Act II of *In the Beginning*, which begins and ends with a tableau of Adam's digging and Eve's spinning. Behind this, it seems to me, lies the clown's identification of "gard'ners, ditchers, and gravemakers. They hold up Adam's profession . . . the Scripture says Adam digged."

13. In Sir Arthur Sullivan's operetta, *Cox and Box*, based on the farce *Box and Cox* by J. Maddison Morton (a well-known 1847 play alluded to by Shaw), Box pretends to have drowned in order to avoid marrying a widow. Martin Meisel notes that in *Back to Methuselah* Shaw imitated the farcical device of the feigned drowning from *Box and Cox*. See *Shaw and the Nineteenth-Century Theater* (Princeton: Princeton Univ. Press, 1963), 246.

14. The idea that God can feel lonely is not, I believe, an invention of theologians, but rather of poets. For example, Milton, in Bk. VIII of *Paradise Lost*, has God say to Adam, "Seem I to thee sufficiently possessed / Of happiness, or not? who am alone / From all eternity, for none I know / Second to me or like, equal much less" (404–7). Shaw refers to the idea of the loneliness of God in a letter to Mrs. Patrick Campbell, New Year's Eve, 1913: "On the last New Years eve . . . there was eternity and Beauty . . . and if your part in it was an illusion, then I am as lonely as God. Therefore you must still be the Mother of the angels to me. . . . And now let us again hear the bells ring: you on your throne in your blue hood, and I watching and praying." See *Collected Letters: 1911–1925*, ed. Dan H. Laurence (New York: Viking, 1985), 212. It was for her that Shaw first conceived the idea of writing a play about St. Joan (see his letter of Sept. 8, 1913, in Laurence, 201). Shaw transforms his vision of Mrs. Patrick Campbell into Dunois' prayer before Orleans, "Mary in the blue snood, kingfisher color: will you grudge me a west wind?" Below in the text I discuss the kingfisher as a symbol of Joan, and the sexual chemistry between Joan and Dunois.

15. That is partly because her speech derives from Milton's invocation to Light at the beginning of Bk. III of *Paradise Lost*: "Thus with the year / Seasons return, but not to me returns / Day, or the sweet approach of ev'n or morn, / Or sight of vernal bloom, or summer's rose, / Or flocks, or herds, or human face divine" (40–44). Both set pieces express the feeling of loss, but Shaw disguises his inspiration by shifting the terms of loss from the visual in Milton to the aural in Joan. Moreover, Shaw characteristically shifts the emphasis away from the experience of the loss to the affirmation of Joan's feeling for nature.

16. When Shaw prepared a screenplay of *Saint Joan*, he added a scene set in the marketplace of Rouen in which the Executioner is seen preparing the stake for Joan's burning; Shaw suggests that "if a bird or two could be induced to light on the stake, the effect would be deadly" (see *Saint Joan: A Screenplay by Bernard Shaw*, ed. Bernard F. Dukore [Seattle: Univ. of Washington Press, 1968], 158)—a Hitchcockian touch, that, and simultaneously additional and ironic enforcement of the connection between Joan and flight.

17. Cf. Milton: "Meanwhile / The world shall burn, and from her ashes spring / New heav'n and earth, wherein the just shall dwell, / And after all their tribulation long / See golden days, fruitful of golden deeds, / With joy and love triumphing and fair truth." *Paradise Lost*, Bk. III, 333–38.

18. Cf. Pilate's speech from *On the Rocks*, particularly, " . . . if I set you loose to scatter your words broadcast among the people."

19. In the Preface, Shaw hints at his self-conscious treatment of time in the play: " . . . as it [the play] is for stage use I have had to condense into three and a half hours a series of events which in their historical happening were spread over four times as many months; for the theatre imposes unities of time and place from which Nature in her boundless wastefulness is free. Therefore the reader must not suppose that Joan really put Robert de Baudricourt in her pocket in fifteen minutes, nor that her excommunication, recantation, relapse, and death were a matter of half an hour or so." The point, as I see it, of Shaw's playful patronizing of his reader here, his exhortation to a willing suspension of disbelief (as if some readers might be unfamiliar with the conventions of stage time), is to make the reader aware in an indirect way that Shaw is playing with time in the play for a reason.

20. "The Epilogue is obviously not a representation of an actual scene, or even of a recorded dream; but it is none the less historical," says Shaw in his "Note by the Author" in *Collected Plays*, Vol. 6, 213. Shaw *does* use the technique of dramatic action as wish-fulfillment dream in *Too True to be Good*, where, as Northrop Frye points out, for the anonymous heroine, "the action . . . is really her own wish-fulfill-ment dream." See *The Secular Scripture: A Study of Romance* (Cambridge: Harvard Univ. Press, 1976), 79.

21. The interplay between Joan and the Soldier repeats that between Major Barbara and Peter Shirley, when the latter tries to console Barbara for her loss of purpose in life at the end of Act II: "Ah, if you would only read Tom Paine in the proper spirit, miss!" Peter's limited awareness (like the Soldier's) intensifies our sense of Barbara's (and Joan's) pain.

JEAN REYNOLDS

The Shavian Inclusiveness

HIGGINS. This is an age of upstarts. Men begin in Kentish Town with 80 £ a year, and end in Park Lane with a hundred thousand. They want to drop Kentish Town; but they give themselves away every time they open their mouths. Now I can teach them—

Eric Bentley's phrase "the Shavian inclusiveness" offers a useful starting point for a study of Shavian postmodernism. Jacques Derrida—like Shaw, powerfully influenced by Karl Marx—consistently rejects traditional dualistic "either/or" thinking. Deconstruction, focusing on the marginal and repressed elements in a text, offers many insights into Shavian "new speech," which encompasses an astonishing range of styles, roles, and rhetorical devices.

Pygmalion can be called an "inclusive" play: A more conventional dramatist than Shaw might not have included an "upstart" like Eliza Doolittle in a drama about gentlemen like Higgins and Pickering. Eliza is a marginal person, startlingly out of place beside the pillars of St. Paul's Church in Covent Garden, where Higgins first sees her. But Shaw, marginal himself because of his Irish origins and radical thinking, was just as unconventional. Regarding himself as "a sojourner on this planet rather than a native of it," he pondered life from the vantage point of an alien (*CP* 3:3 5). In *Mainly about Myself* (1898) he vividly described his outsider status:

From *Pygmalion's Wordplay: The Postmodern Shaw*, pp. 20–42, 138. Copyright © 1999 by the Board of Regents of the State of Florida.

I had no taste for what is called popular art . . . no admiration for popular heroics. As an Irishman I could pretend to patriotism neither for the country I had abandoned nor the country that had ruined it. As a humane person I detested violence and slaughter, whether in war, sport, or the butcher's yard. I was a Socialist, detesting our anarchical scramble for money, and believing in equality as the only possible permanent basis of social organization, discipline, subordination, good manners, and selection of fit persons for high functions. Fashionable life, open on indulgent terms to unencumbered "brilliant" persons, I could not endure, even if I had not feared its demoralizing effect on a character which required looking after as much as my own. (*CP* 1:24)

Shaw used his outsider status to advantage, writing both dramatic and nondramatic works that—like *Pygmalion*—critique contemporary ideologies by exposing what Michael Ryan calls their "gestures of exclusion" (3). Shaw's prose often explores political, social, economic, and religious ideas overlooked by other writers of his day: the necessity of women's rights, the failure of Britain's criminal justice system, the sins of science, and the absurdity of religious orthodoxy. In his Preface to *Misalliance*, Shaw explained that alien and rejected ideas are essential to "progressive enlightenment [which] depends on a fair hearing for doctrines which at first appear seditious, blasphemous, and immoral, and which deeply shock people who never think originally, thought being for them merely a habit and an echo" (*CP* 2:38). This "Shavian inclusiveness" is a hallmark of Shaw's thought.

Shaw's interest in margins and their problems—things excluded and included—links him to Jacques Derrida, who is preoccupied with the seemingly extraneous features in a text or ideology that subtly undermine its primary message. According to Derrida, "Every culture and society requires an internal critique or deconstruction as an essential part of its development. . . . Every culture is haunted by its other" (Kearney 116). This "otherness," so pervasive in Shavian prose, is a vital component of deconstruction, as Derrida explains: "Deconstruction is not an enclosure in nothingness, but an openness towards the other" (Kearney 124). In a 1994 interview, Derrida noted that "otherness" is a prerequisite rather than a detriment to dialogue, community, and national unity: "Once you take into account this inner and other difference, then you pay attention to the other and you understand that fighting for your own identity is not exclusive of another identity, is open to another identity. And this prevents totalitarianism, nationalism, egocentrism, and so on" (*Deconstruction in a Nutshell* 13–14).

Like psychoanalysts, deconstructionists attach great significance to the unspoken, unnoticed "others" that are often repressed and denied. They make a sharp break with the traditional Western metaphysics, which, heavily influenced by Plato, seeks to differentiate and banish everything that does not fit its system. In *The Realm of Rhetoric*, Chaim Perelman explains that Plato "recognized a cleansing role in dialectic—the technique Socrates used to refute his opponent's opinions insofar as he was able to bring out their internal inconsistencies. As soon as they contradict themselves, opinions cannot be simultaneously admitted, and at least one of them has to be abandoned for the sake of truth" (Bizzell and Herzberg 1072).

Shaw, with his "both/and" habit of mind, often exposes such metaphysical "cleansing." In the *Quintessence of Ibsenism*, for example, he tells the story of a contemporary woman, Marie Bashkirtseff, who has shocked Britain with her "unfeminine" intellect and independence. Her critics, Shaw points out, simply deny that she is a woman at all: He quotes one who wrote, "She was the very antithesis of a true woman" (*Selected* 224).

Shaw's prose challenges Platonist metaphysics in still another way, by showing how it smoothly absorbs differences and conflicts into a false appearance of harmony. Christopher Norris points out "that power of logocentric thinking to absorb all differences into itself by viewing them as mere stages or signposts on the way to some grand conceptual synthesis" (*Derrida* 231). A prime example appears in the Preface to *Saint Joan*, in which Shaw shows that contemporary thinkers dismiss religion as an early, inadequate source of knowledge that has been superseded by science, rather than considering the possibility that religion may still have something to offer the modern world.

Shaw's penchant for both/and thinking is clearly visible in *Pygmalion*. Despite her outsider status, Eliza, along with her Angel Court neighbors, is a vital part of English social structure. Like Eliza's dustman father, members of Eliza's class perform distasteful but essential services for the rich. Higgins and his fellows use both strategies mentioned earlier to "cleanse" themselves from the less desirable elements of society. First, the lower classes are banished from view: out of sight, out of mind. Although a small army of workers is required to maintain the standard of living depicted in *Pygmalion*, only a housekeeper, a dustman and a parlormaid are seen onstage. Second, the poor are denied the status of human beings, as in this exchange from Act II of *Pygmalion*:

PICKERING [*in good-humored remonstrance*] Does it occur to you, Higgins, that the girl has some feelings?

HIGGINS [*looking critically at her*] Oh no, I dont think so. Not any feelings that we need bother about. (694–95)

Most important, the poor are stereotyped as morally weak. Moments after *Pygmalion* begins, Mrs. Eynsford-Hill suspects that Eliza is a prostitute and buys a bunch of flowers in hopes of confirming her suspicions:

THE MOTHER [*to the girl*] You can keep the change.

THE FLOWER GIRL Oh, thank you, lady.

THE MOTHER Now tell me how you know that young gentleman's name.

THE FLOWER GIRL I didn't.

THE MOTHER I heard you call him by it. Dont try to deceive me.

THE FLOWER GIRL [*protesting*] Who's trying to deceive you? I called him Freddy or Charlie same as you might yourself if you was talking to a stranger and wished to be pleasant. (672)

Freddy's sister Clara protests her mother's injustice to him: "Really, mamma, you might have spared Freddy that" (672). But Clara does not take offense at the insult directed at another member of her own sex: Eliza is beneath her notice.

Despite the scorn repeatedly heaped on Eliza and others of her class, they perform another vital function that goes beyond their menial services to the rich: They help classify British social structure. Eliza's "Lisson Grove lingo" so clearly defines her social position that when she masters upper-class speech, guests at the embassy reception have no clue to her origin. And it is here, with Eliza's "new speech," that British class ideology breaks down, or "deconstructs." Genteel speech, supposedly a natural acquisition of the well bred, isn't "natural" at all—nor is it a reliable social indicator. Although the embassy guests seem homogeneous, they are a jumbled lot: Their ranks include both "upstarts" who have mastered refined speech and aristocrats who never learned to speak it. Of the latter Higgins complains, "theyre such fools that they think style comes by nature to people in their position; and so they never learn" (746–47).

And Higgins himself is seriously flawed. Despite his social standing and "Miltonic mind," he is boorish and manipulative, with as little respect for his peers as for members of Eliza's class. He airily suggests an arranged marriage for Eliza, who retorts, "We were above that at the corner of Tottenham Court Road.... I sold flowers. I didn't sell myself" (750). At the end of the play she tells Higgins, "I had only to lift up my finger to be as good as you" (781). Eliza has discovered the fallacy of British social-class ideology.

Marxist critic Kenneth Burke defines an ideology as an "inverted gene-alogy of culture, that makes for 'illusion' and 'mystification' by treating ideas as *primary* where they should have been treated as *derivative*" (*Rhetoric* 104). Ideologies naturalize events and relationships, creating the impression of inevitability by concealing their causes and origins in order to deter questions, doubts, and critical thinking. Critic Patricia Waugh says this process is accomplished through the medium of "everyday language" by "power structures through a continuous process of naturalization whereby forms of oppression are constructed in apparently 'innocent' representations" (11).

The insults that Higgins directs at Eliza are linguistic evidence of the "naturalization" process that British class structure has undergone: He can throw epithets at her with no fear of reprisal or contradiction. Eliza's low status seems "primary"—the unchangeable result of heredity—even though it is actually "derivative," resulting from economics, education, demographics, and other social phenomena. Higgins's phonetics game of guessing people's origins in Act I drives the point home: Speech patterns are the product not of genes or inborn character, but geography.

In "Karl Marx and 'Das Kapital'" (1887), Shaw recounts a similar process—the establishment of gold as a "natural" medium of exchange: "The soap-maker . . . finds it troublesome to estimate the value of his ware not only in nails, but in candles, gloves, bread, and every separate ware used by him. So does the nail-maker; and so do all the other exchangers. So they agree upon a suitable ware, such as gold, in which each can estimate the value of his ware. Gold can then be bought for wares; and all wares can be bought for it. Gold becomes money; and values become prices. Money then becomes the customary expression of the "natural price of all things." In the Robinson Crusoe age, before division of labor and exchange, labor seemed the natural price; when wares were exchanged and bartered, wares seemed the natural price" (*Karl Marx* 130).

Such naturalizations reinforce ideologies by concealing the discords simmering within them. Burke's description of an ideology, focusing on the conflicts beneath its surface harmony, sounds much like Derridean deconstruction: "An ideology is not a harmonious structure of beliefs or assumptions; some of its beliefs militate against others, and some of its standards militate against our nature. An ideology is an aggregate of beliefs sufficiently at odds with one another to justify opposite kinds of conduct" (*Counter-Statement* 163).

This commonality between Burke, Shaw, and Derrida should not be surprising, since all three have a Marxist background, and the critiquing of ideologies is a Marxist activity. Shavian critics have tended to underestimate Shaw's debt to Marx because they focus only on the failed socialist economics of *Das Kapital*.[1] Bernard Dukore, describing the myopic views of several of these critics, explains, "To Marxist critics like [Alick] West, Christopher

Caudwell, and E. Strauss, Shaw is a bourgeois playwright who is not as radical as he thinks. Before and after 1917, they denounced his Fabian-inspired plays as unsocialistic, for they fail to dramatize the class struggle, vilify capitalists, applaud the moral preeminence of the working class, and present exemplary socialists with whom audiences of workers might identify" (xviii). Actually, Marx's ideas helped form many features of Shavian "new speech": Shaw's passion for social change, his attraction to people and problems outside mainstream thinking, his hatred of idealism, and his ability to break through surface harmony to expose the discord underneath.

Reading *Das Kapital* in 1882 changed Shaw's whole life. Biographer and friend Hesketh Pearson said that Marx "directed [Shaw's] energy, influenced his art, gave him a religion, and, as he claimed, made a man of him" (52). Shaw himself told Pearson that discovering Marx "was the turning-point in my career. Marx was a revelation. His abstract economics, I discovered later, were wrong, but he rent the veil. He opened my eyes to the facts of history and civilisation, gave me an entirely fresh conception of the universe, provided me with a purpose and a mission in life" (51).

Difficulties multiplied. Only the first two volumes of *Das Kapital* had been published, and Shaw had to go to the British Museum to study Deville's French edition because no English translation was available. Shaw attended meetings of the Democratic Federation, a Marxist organization, but no one there except the leader, J. M. Hyndman, had actually read *Das Kapital*. Nor were there any critical analyses to clarify Marx's difficult ideas—his formidable definition of an ideology, for example: "[It] transforms the predicates, the objects, into independent entities, but divorced from their actual independence their subject. Subsequently the actual subject appears as a result, whereas one must start from the actual subject and look at its objectification. The mystical substance, therefore, becomes the actual subject, and the real subject appears as something else, as an element of the mystical subject" (Marx and Engels 18).

Shaw did have an unusual advantage, however: Several of his friends, including Hyndman, an actress named Mrs. Theodore Wright, and Marx's youngest daughter Eleanor, had actually talked with Marx at length about his ideas. One of Shaw's 1887 essays about Marx refers to these friends without naming them: "The charm of [Marx's] conversation, admitted by those who knew him personally, would not alone account for his reputation, although it is true that his reputation must be measured by its intensity as much as by its width" (*Karl Marx* 106).

Hyndman had discovered *Das Kapital* in 1880 and, learning that Marx lived in London, met with him for long talks at the end of 1880 and early in 1881. Shaw described Mrs. Wright, who was a Fabian, as "a revolutionary beauty" and "the friend of Karl Marx" (*Letters* 2:474). And Shaw was in love with Eleanor, an aspiring actress who was a political activist and had done research for her father in the British Museum and translated *Das Kapital*; she was also a close friend of Friedrich Engels, Marx's collaborator. Eleanor and Shaw, drawn together by their interest in socialism and the theater, often met at Eleanor's home, which she shared with Dr. Edward Aveling, her common-law husband, whom Shaw described as "saturated with Marx" (*Letters* 1:379). She and Shaw also spent time together at the British Museum and at political and literary meetings. From Eleanor, Shaw learned that Marx was intensely interested in British literature, having taught himself English by studying the works of Shakespeare. At one meeting of the Shelley Society, whose members included Shaw, Eleanor presented a lecture about her father's interest in Shelley—a writer who had profoundly influenced Shaw. Although Shaw loved Eleanor, she preferred Aveling and finally killed herself when Aveling betrayed her.

Shaw quickly developed an exceptionally broad understanding of Marx's ideas. Anticipating such twentieth-century thinkers as Erich Fromm, Kenneth Burke, Mikhail Bakhtin, Jacques Derrida, and Terry Eagleton, Shaw recognized that Marx was a psychologist, philosopher, and rhetorician as well as a political economist. Shaw's 1887 essays often mention Marx's rhetorical power: In the first, published on August 7, Shaw wrote, "[Marx] wrote of the nineteenth century as if it were a cloud passing down the wind, changing its shape and fading as it goes" (*Karl Marx* 109). Besides mentioning Marx's "spirit" twice (113 and 121), Shaw discussed "the novelty and fascination of his treatment" (109) and Marx's "remarkable historical sense" (113). According to Shaw, Marx's style had a powerful effect on his readers, demonstrating that "the old order is one of fraud and murder ... [and] it is changing and giving place to the new by an inexorable law of development. It is easy to shew that Mill ... knew this and said this; but the fact is that the average pupil of Marx never forgets it, whilst the average pupil of Mill and the rest never learns it" (117).

Shaw was especially impressed by Marx's humanist assertion that passion is central to a meaningful life. Marx's detractors have often overlooked his humanism because they misunderstand the "materialism" that shapes much of his philosophy and working methods. In the Foreword to Karl Marx, *Selected Writings in Sociology & Social Philosophy*, Erich Fromm explains that Marx's "materialism" has nothing to do with the physical world: It referred instead to "the real man and the real conditions of his life" (xv).

Unlike Freud, whose emphasis on biological instincts was popular with progressive Victorians, Marx declared that humans are motivated by higher drives: "Passion is man's faculties striving to attain their objects" (Fromm,

Marx's Concept 65). Marx was interested in the "spontaneous activity of human fantasy, of the human brain and heart" (69). Similarly, Erich Fromm notes that Marx "speaks in very concrete terms of human passions, particularly that of love," which Marx defined as the human connection to life: "it is love which teaches man to truly believe in the world of objects outside of him" (69).

In the same way, Shaw believed in human drives such as an "appetite for knowledge" that transcend biological longings. In the Preface to *Saint Joan* he explained, "But that there are forces at work which use individuals for purposes far transcending the purpose of keeping these individuals alive and prosperous and respectable and safe and happy in the middle station in life, which is all any good bourgeois can reasonably require, is established by the fact that men will, in the pursuit of knowledge and of social readjustments for which they will not be a penny the better, and are indeed often many pence the worse, face poverty, infamy, exile, imprisonment, dreadful hardship, and death" (*CP* 2:509).

Shaw often used "passion" to describe the inner forces that shaped his character and mission. As a "boy atheist," he discovered that he had "evolved a natural sense of honor" that served as a moral guide: "I ranked it, and still do, as a passion" (*EPWW* 65). Telling Hesketh Pearson about a formative spiritual experience that came to him when he was twelve, he said, "The change that came to me was the birth in me of moral passion; and I declare that according to my experience moral passion is the only real passion" (29). In 1895 Shaw encouraged readers to find their own inner basis of upright behavior: "[Y]ou will find that your passions, if you really and honestly let them all loose impartially, will discipline you with a severity which your conventional friends, abandoning themselves to the mechanical routine of fashion, could not stand for a day" (*Selected* 356). In Act I of *Man and Superman*, Tanner declares, "according to my experience moral passion is the only real passion" (74).

With his emphasis on passionate living, Shaw did not extol science and logic as his Victorian contemporaries did. "In process of time the age of reason had to go its way after the age of faith," Shaw declared in *The Quintessence of Ibsenism* (*Selected* 213). As often happens in Shaw's writings, the "Shavian inclusiveness" prompted him to put human reason into a larger context, rather than discarding it. Shavian "new speech," integrating reason and passion, is consistent with Marx's assertion, in the *Economic and Philosophic Manuscripts*, that "man is affirmed in the objective world not only in the act of thinking, but with *all* his senses" (Marx and Engels 88).[2] In the Preface to *Back to Methuselah* Shaw wrote,

My own Irish XVIII centuryism made it impossible for me to believe anything until I could conceive it as a scientific hypothesis, even though the abominations, quackeries, impostures, venalities, credulities, and delusions of the camp followers of science, and the brazen lies and priestly pretensions of the pseudoscientific cure-mongers, all sedulously inculcated by modern "secondary education," were so monstrous that I was sometimes forced to make a verbal distinction between science and knowledge lest I should mislead my readers. But I never forgot that without knowledge even wisdom is more dangerous than mere opportunist ignorance, and that somebody must take the Garden of Eden in hand and weed it properly. (*CP* 2:429)

As a result, Shaw's "new speech" often "includes the excluded" by appealing to readers' emotions as well as their reasoning powers. He told Henderson, "Emotion evolved and fixed in intellectual conviction—will save the world" (894).[3] In "The New Theology," Shaw declared, "I do not address myself to your logical faculties, but as one human mind trying to put himself in contact with other human minds" (*Religious Speeches* 10). "The Religion of the Pianoforte" (1894) declares, "It is feeling that sets a man thinking, and not thought that sets him feeling" (*Music* 3:127). In 1918 Shaw wrote, "The appalling fact that nobody in this country seems to know that intellect is a passion for solving problems, and that its exercise produces happiness, satisfaction, and a desirable quality of life, shews that we do not yet know even our crude bodily appetites in their higher aspect as passions: a passion being, I take it, an overwhelming impulse towards a more abundant life" (*CP* 2:297). In "Literature and Art," a 1908 lecture, Shaw explained how the power of art is created through the "both/and" of reason and feeling: "Leaving out all that is irrelevant, [the artist] has to connect the significant facts by chains of reasoning, and also to make, as it were, bridges of feeling between them by a sort of ladder, get the whole thing in a connected form into your head, and give you a spiritual, political, social, or religious consciousness. Literally, then, the work of the artist is to create mind" (*Platform* 43–44).

After reading Marx, Shaw committed himself to a lifetime of advocacy for social change. In a self-drafted 1901 interview, "Who I Am, and What I Think," Shaw explained how Marx helped shape his goals: "Now the real secret of Marx's fascination was his appeal to an unnamed, unrecognized passion—a new passion—the passion of hatred in the more generous souls among the respectable and educated sections for the accursed middle-class institutions that had starved, thwarted, misled, and corrupted them from their cradles. Marx's Capital is not a treatise on Socialism; it is a jeremiad against the bourgeoisie" (*Sketches* 83).

Shaw perpetuated Marx's "jeremiad against the bourgeoisie" by using his "new speech" to expose the fallacies and frauds of contemporary life. One might even conjecture that Shaw surpassed Marx since, as J. L. Wisenthal has noted, "in Shaw's view economic considerations have some importance in history, but ideas are much more important" (51). But Marx too gave primary importance to ideas rather than "economic considerations," as this letter of his, written in September 1843, attests: "[O]ur motto must be then: reform of consciousness not through dogmas but by analysing the mystical self-confused consciousness, whether it has a political or a religious content" (Fromm, *Crisis* 74). Marx, declaring that "language is practical consciousness" (*Portable Karl Marx* 173), clearly understood the relationship between words and worldview. That same understanding later engendered Shaw's "new speech" and reformer's mission.

One ideology that Shaw attacked—following Marx's lead—was the popular belief that every human possesses a stable and unchanging essence, or Self. In *Pygmalion*, this ideology causes Higgins to reject Eliza, despite her accomplishments: She will always be a "draggletailed guttersnipe" (691) to him. Shaw held a much broader view of the human potential for change—a view influenced by Marx, who had declared, "As individuals express their life, so they are" (Marx and Engels 150). In the Preface to *The Irrational Knot* (1905) Shaw emphasized his own capacity for endless change: "Physiologists inform us that the substance of our bodies (and consequently of our souls) is shed and renewed at such a rate that no part of us lasts longer than eight years: I am therefore not now in any atom of me the person who wrote *The Irrational Knot* in 1880. The last of that author perished in 1888; and two of his successors have since joined the majority. Fourth of his line, I cannot be expected to take any very lively interest in the novels of my literary great-grandfather" (*CP* 1:171).

Still another ideology challenged by Shaw is the Western belief in transcendent, unchanging artistic principles. Following Marx, Shaw challenged the notion that artists must obey eternal aesthetic laws. In *A Degenerate's View of Nordau* (reissued in 1908 as *The Sanity of Art*), Shaw explained, "The severity of artistic discipline is produced by the fact that in creative art no ready-made rules can help you. There is nothing to guide you to the right expression for your thought except your own sense of beauty and fitness, and as you advance upon those who went before you, that sense of beauty and fitness is necessarily often in conflict, not with fixed rules, because there are no rules, but with precedents" (*Selected* 368).

Excluded from conventional histories of art, Shaw complained, are the clashes and discord that must occur when rising genius breaks with tradition. Critics Richard Poirier, in *The Renewal of Literature*, and Harold Bloom, in *The Anxiety of Influence*, have explored the pressures our Western literary inheritance places upon each new generation of writers, who suffer acutely from the need to create something totally original that surpasses what previous geniuses have done. Bloom describes "the exhaustions of being a late-comer" that he hears in contemporary poetry (12); Poirier cites the "danger of being trapped in language, in the conformities which make language possible" (12).

Shaw's solution was, as usual, paradoxical: He both embraced and rejected the past. In the Preface to *Major Barbara*, repudiating "the hypothesis of complete originality," he insisted that "a man can no more be completely original in that sense than a tree can grow out of air" (*CP* 1:247). He described himself as "standing . . . on [the] shoulders" of "Voltaire, Rousseau, Bentham, Marx, Mill, Dickens, Carlyle, Ruskin, Butler, and Morris all rolled into one, with Euripides, More, Montaigne, Molière, Beaumarchais, Swift, Goethe, Ibsen, Tolstoy, Jesus and the prophets all thrown in" (161). In the Preface to *Three Plays for Puritans* Shaw confessed, "my stories are the old stories; my characters are the familiar harlequin and columbine, clown and pantaloon (note the harlequin's leap in the third act of Caesar and Cleopatra); my stage tricks and suspenses and thrills and jests are the ones in vogue when I was a boy, by which time my grandfather was tired of them. . . . I am a crow who has followed many ploughs" (*CP* 1:83–84).

But Shaw refused to deify the great writers and thinkers whose "ploughs" he was following. Even Mozart, whose brilliance Shaw acclaims in the Epistle Dedicatory to *Man and Superman*, is portrayed as a genius whose time has come and gone. Shaw dealt with the past by freely borrowing from its "magnificent debris of fossils" (*CP* 1:164), and throwing away the rest. Each new era, he declared, had to be dealt with on its own terms. Shavian "new speech" was an attempt to bring an old language into a new age—using words not to sustain established power structures, but to destabilize the world his readers took for granted and show them the possibilities of a new order.

Above all, Shaw rejected the idealist aesthetics that imprison new artists in the values and principles of earlier times. The essence of Shavian philosophy is, in effect, that there is no essence: His metaphysics, like Marx's, strove to escape metaphysics altogether. Shavian Creative Evolution—the closest he ever came to an abstract and systematic explanation of the workings of our world—is intrinsically fluid and mutable. Like Marx and, later, Derrida, Shaw rejected the notion that our world is only an imperfect reflection of a perfect realm that transcends our understanding. These idealistic philosophies, Marx complained, convert language into a medium for social and economic manipulation.

Shaw, following Marx's idea, saw that "new speech" could renew society by teaching men and women how to recognize and resist the misuses of language. In *The German Ideology* Marx had explained how "General interests ... decline into mere idealizing phrases, conscious illusions and deliberate deceits. But the more they are condemned as falsehoods, and the less they satisfy the understanding, the more dogmatically they are asserted and the more deceitful, moralizing and spiritual becomes the language of established society" (Marx, *Selected Writings* 81). This idealism, according to Marx, discounts the realities of human existence:

> The production of ideas, conceptions and consciousness is at first directly interwoven with the material activity and the material intercourse of men, the language of real life. Representation and thought, the mental intercourse of men, still appear at this stage as the direct efflux of their material behaviour. The same applies to mental production as it is expressed in the language of politics, laws, morality, religion, metaphysics, etc., of a people. Men are the producers of their conceptions, ideas, etc.—real, active men, as they are conditioned by a definite development of their productive forces, and of the intercourse which corresponds to these, up to its furthest forms. (Marx and Engels 154)

Both Marx and Shaw saw that such idealism inhibits social change in two ways. First, it devalues human efforts, emphasizing instead the authority and power of transcendent forces. Marx explains that it "presupposes an abstract or absolute spirit which develops in such a way that humanity is nothing but a mass which more or less consciously bears it along" (*Selected Writings* 57). Marx was particularly critical of Christianity, which glorified God at the expense of humanity: "The more of himself man attributes to God, the less he has left in himself" (170).

Shaw's Preface to *Major Barbara* argues the same point: Too often religion fosters complacency by making God, rather than human beings, responsible for the condition of society. In "The New Theology," Shaw encouraged readers to say, "I am working for the purpose of the universe, working for the good of the whole of society and the whole world, instead of merely looking after my personal ends" (*Religious Speeches* 19). Shaw hoped that a human race educated out of its dependence on Jehovah would eventually accept its own responsibility for the condition of the world: "In a sense there is no God as yet achieved, but there is that force at work making God, struggling through us to become an actual organized existence, enjoying what to many of us is the greatest conceivable ecstasy, the ecstasy of a brain, an intelligence, actually conscious of the whole, and with executive force capable of guiding it to a perfectly benevolent and harmonious end" (19).

More seriously, both Marx and Shaw realized that idealism smoothes over the inevitable conflicts that arise with every human endeavor. Class struggles, identity crises, artistic feuds—all are glossed over by the relentless power of idealism. Perceptions of reality become distorted by the struggle to make them fit an idealist system. As an antidote Marx advocated "naturalism"—avoiding idealisms to stay close to human experience. In *The German Ideology* he declared, "In direct contrast to German [idealistic] philosophy, which descends from heaven to earth, here we ascend from earth to heaven. That is to say, we do not set out from what men say, imagine, conceive, nor from men as narrated thought of, imagined, conceived, in order to arrive at men in the flesh. We set out from real, active men, and on the basis of their real life-process we demonstrate the development of the ideological reflexes and echoes of this life-process" (Marx and Engels 154).

Shaw echoes Marx's complaint about the substitution of abstractions for "real, active men" in "Who I Am, and What I Think":

> Men are not real men to us; they are heroes and villains, respectable persons and criminals. Their qualities are virtues and vices; the natural laws that govern them are gods and devils; their destinies are rewards and expiations; their reasoning a formula of cause and effect with the horse mostly behind the cart. They come to me with their heads full of these figments, which they call, if you please, "the world," and ask me what is the meaning of them, as if I or anyone else were God omniscient and could tell them. Pretty funny this: eh? But when they ostracize, punish, murder, and make war to impose by force their grotesque religions and hideous criminal codes, then the comedy becomes a tragedy. The Army, the Navy, the Church, the Bar, the theatres, the picture-galleries, the libraries, and the trade unions are forced to bolster up their pet hallucinations. (*Sketches* 90–91)

Although Shaw was in many ways a Platonist—citing Plato as an example of a true realist, for example (*Selected* 222)—he followed Marx in opposing the optimistic abstractions of Platonic idealism. In the Preface to *Misalliance*, Shaw chastised Britons who prefer abstractions to reality: "in discussing family life we never speak of actual adults or actual children, or of realities of any sort, but always of ideals such as The Home, a Mother's Influence, a Father's Care, Filial Piety, Duty, Affection, Family Life, etc., etc., which are no doubt very comforting phrases, but which beg the question of what a home and a mother's influence and a father's care and so forth really come to in practice" (*CP* 2:14).

Shaw's insistence on dealing with the realities of human experience shaped everything he wrote. Always conscious of the complexity of the human race, Shaw never underestimated his audience. In a 1939 interview about *Pygmalion*'s huge success, he explained that he never tried to appeal to the "low intelligence of the average filmgoer." There was, he insisted, "no such person" (*Collected Plays* 4:821).

Politically, too, Shaw was firmly grounded in reality. In a 1900 letter to H. M. Hyndman, Shaw explained his mission in the Marxist terminology not of economics, but of social reform: "I am a moral revolutionary, interested, not in the class war, but in the struggle between human vitality and the artificial system of morality, and distinguishing, not between capitalist & proletarian, but between moralist and natural historian" (*Letters* 2:163). As a "natural historian," Shaw included himself and his own writings in the category of transient entities. Hence this surprisingly humble self-assessment in the Preface to *Three Plays for Puritans*: "I shall perhaps enjoy a few years of immortality. But the whirligig of time will soon bring my audiences to my own point of view; and then the next Shakespear that comes along will turn these petty tentatives of mine into masterpieces final for their epoch" (*CP* 1:83–84).

Shaw's refusal to canonize himself and his writings clashes with the New Criticism and its insistence on the timelessness of great literature. It is, however, consistent with two twentieth-century outgrowths of Marxism: Russian formalism and Derridean deconstruction. The Russian formalists were a literary group that included such notables as Roman Jakobsen and Viktor Shklovsky; they flourished for about a decade after the Russian Revolution of 1917. They rejected idealist notions of literature, insisting that all writing is temporal, and that its value varies according to the ways in which it is used.

Jacques Derrida—who has acknowledged the importance of Russian formalism to his own thought (*Positions* 70)—similarly argues against metaphysical definitions of literature. In a 1971 interview with Jean-Louis Houdebine and Guy Scarpetta, he explained, "I have tried to describe and to explain how writing structurally carries within itself (counts-discounts) the process of its own erasure and annulation, all the while marking what *remains* of this erasure" (*Positions* 68).

The Quintessence of Ibsenism is a compelling example of Shaw's attacks on ideologies, often along Marxist and deconstructionist lines. It began in 1890 as a paper for a Fabian Society lecture series called "Socialism in Contemporary Literature." In 1891 it was published as a small book; later it was revised and republished several times, and Shaw added a new Preface in 1922.

Although Ibsen was neither a Marxist nor a member of any political movement, his sympathy for socialism made his plays attractive to the Fabians. Ibsen described his own affinity for socialism in an 1890 letter that refers, without naming them, to *The Quintessence of Ibsenism* and its author:

> I should be very much obliged if some of the expressions attributed to me could be corrected. . . . I did not, for instance, say that I have never studied the question of socialism. The fact is that I am much interested in the question and have endeavored to the best of my ability to acquaint myself with its different aspects . . .
>
> What the correspondent writes about my surprise at seeing my name put forward by socialistic agitators as a supporter of their dogmas is particularly liable to be misunderstood.
>
> What I really said was that I was surprised that I, who had made it my chief business in life to depict human character and human destinies, should, without consciously aiming at it, have arrived at some of the same conclusions as the social-democratic moral philosophers had arrived at by scientific processes.
>
> What led me to express my surprise (and, I may add, my satisfaction) was a statement . . . to the effect that one or more lectures had lately been given in London, dealing, according to him, chiefly with *A Doll's House*. (291–92)

Here I will focus on the first three chapters of *The Quintessence of Ibsenism*, which features two aspects of "Shavian inclusiveness." First, Shaw exposes unpopular truths about family life—its prosaic origins, banalities, and injustices. In addition, he foregrounds the marginal members of society—those dissatisfied with traditional marriage—and places them at the center of the quest for human progress. Both arguments serve Shaw's larger purpose: "deconstructing" conventional morality by calling attention to the people and problems at the margins of respectability. Through Shaw's deft handling, margins and mainstream exchange places.

Shaw's primary target is idealistic attitudes that deny the realities of family life. Like Marx, Shaw complains that conventional thought obscures complex relationships by simplifying them into lofty ideals. "In consciousness . . . relations become concepts," wrote Marx (Ryan 54). In *The Quintessence of Ibsenism*, Shaw explains, "The family as a beautiful and holy natural institution is only a fancy picture of what every family would have to be if everybody was to be suited, invented by the minority as a mask for the reality, which in its nakedness is intolerable to them" (*Selected* 219). Almost no one, Shaw declares, acknowledges the truth about family life. Exalted talk about love, sacrifice, and duty prevents people from seeing that marriage "really is a conventional arrangement, legally enforced," says Shaw (219).

This is the pragmatic attitude of the characters in *Pygmalion*. Alfred Doolittle, who has had at least six mistresses, finally gets married only because Eliza's "stepmother" insists on it: "Middle class morality claims its victim," he says sadly (771). Both Higgins and Eliza view marriage as an economic institution whose primary benefit is security for a woman. After the embassy reception, when a desperate Eliza asks what is to happen to her, Higgins replies, "I daresay my mother could find some chap or other who would do very well" (750). Although Eliza indignantly rejects the suggestion, she too takes a practical view of marriage: Better to be married to Freddy than subservient to Higgins. She never says that she loves Freddy, and she acknowledges that he cannot offer her economic security, but she needs the respectability he can provide for her.

In the *Quintessence* Shaw argues that most people are contented "Philistines" who marry for similarly practical reasons. A smaller number are disillusioned "idealists" who, however, vehemently deny their marital failures. Only one in a thousand, suggests Shaw, is a "realist" capable of facing the truth: "The alleged natural attractions and repulsions upon which the family ideal is based do not exist; and it is historically false that the family was founded for the purpose of satisfying them" (220).

Marriage is not a sacrament at all, argues Shaw: It is a pragmatic economic institution, dedicated to perpetuating the status quo:

> When the social organism becomes bent on civilization, it has to force marriage and family life on the individual, because it can perpetuate itself in no other way whilst love is still known only by fitful glimpses, the basis of sexual relationship being in the main mere physical appetite. Under these circumstances men try to graft pleasure on necessity by desperately pretending that the institution forced upon them is a congenial one, making it a point of public decency to assume always that men spontaneously love their kindred better than their chance acquaintances, and that the woman once desired is always desired: also that the family is woman's proper sphere, and that no really womanly woman ever forms an attachment, or even knows what it means, until she is requested to do so by a man. (218–19)

Like Marx, who complained that capitalism glosses over the conflicts between property owners and labor, Shaw explains that marriage only pretends to serve the best interests of men and women. "An overwhelming majority of such marriages as are not purely *de convenance*, are entered into for the gratification of that appetite either in its crudest form or veiled only by those idealistic illusions which the youthful imagination weaves so wonderfully under the stimulus of desire. . . . The man himself keeps her confirmed in her illusion; for the truth is unbearable to him too: he wants to form an affectionate tie, and not to drive a degrading bargain. . . . Then comes the breakdown of the plan" (227–28).

Shaw explains how repression and denial reinforce these deceptions. I have already cited the example of Marie Bashkirtseff, whose enemies repudiated her independent lifestyle by denying that she was a woman at all. Discontented husbands and wives also practice denial, denouncing anyone who speaks honestly about marriage. "[T]he idealists will be terrified beyond measure at the proclamation of their hidden thought—at the presence of the traitor among the conspirators of silence—at the rending of the beautiful veil they and their poets have woven to hide the unbearable face of the truth" (220).

These falsehoods will not prevail indefinitely: Revolution is inevitable. But Shaw reminds his readers that "every step of progress is a duty repudiated, and a scripture torn up" (212). There are echoes of Marx, with his refusal to idealize human progress, in Shaw's insistence that the evolution of more humane attitudes toward marriage will be appear to be the opposite—a regression into immorality: "The point to seize is that social progress takes effect through the replacement of old institutions by new ones; and since every institution involves the recognition of the duty of conforming to it, progress must involve the repudiation of an established duty at every step. . . . This crablike progress of social evolution, in which the individual advances by seeming to go backward, continues to illude us in spite of all the lessons of history" (212).

Shaw, again rejecting the strictures of Enlightenment thought, proposes a revolutionary system based not on reason, but on a new understanding of "the soul or spirit of man" and "justification by faith": "no action, taken apart from the will behind it, has any moral character: for example, the acts which make the murderer and incendiary infamous are exactly similar to those which make the patriotic hero famous. 'Original sin' is the will doing mischief. 'Divine grace' is the will doing good" (214).

Despite such Christian terminology, *The Quintessence of Ibsenism* disavows the Christian ideology of a stable and infallible system of ethics in which "good" and "evil" are opposing polarities. Shaw argued that good and evil, inextricably connected, define each other on a continuum that is constantly changing; no appeal to absolutes is possible. Shaw's shifting moral system of endless displacements anticipates Derrida's rejection of the either/

or thinking that reduces complexities to "the simple exteriority of death to life, evil to good, representation to presence, signifier to signified, representer to represented, mask to face, writing to speech" (*Grammatology* 315). Shaw, declaring he did not "deal in definitions" (*Selected* 222) had a working understanding of *différance* before Derrida was born.

The strongest link between Shaw and Derrida is a deconstructionist twist—margins becoming a mainstream text—in Shaw's classification system. At first it seems that marital malcontents are only a small minority. Shaw speculates that out of a thousand Britons, seven hundred are content enough with traditional marriage; another 299 find it a failure, but only one "is strong enough to face the truth. . . . He says flatly of marriage, 'This thing is a failure for many of us'" (220).

But Shaw then shows that alienated members of society, forced by their frustrations to break with conventional morality, are so numerous that they are not marginal at all: "Now if anyone's childhood has been embittered by the dislike of his mother and the ill-temper of his father; if his wife has ceased to care for him and he is heartily tired of his wife; if his brother is going to law with him over the division of the family property, and his son acting in studied defiance of his plans and wishes, it is hard for him to persuade himself that passion is eternal and that blood is thicker than water. Yet if he tells himself the truth, all his life seems a waste and a failure by the light of it" (219).

Happy families undoubtedly exist, Shaw admits, but they do not prove that men and women have an innate predilection for marriage. The occasional success "depends altogether upon the accident of the woman having some natural vocation for domestic management and the care of children, as well as on the husband being fairly good-natured and livable with" (228). The contented husbands and wives are the real minority. "Shavian inclusiveness" finally draws in all of Shaw's readers, who find that Shaw's "radical" stance against traditional marriage actually encompasses a large percentage of the British population.

"Shavian inclusiveness" takes a different form in Shaw's 1924 Preface to *Saint Joan*, which defends rather than attacks traditional religion. Here Shaw exposes the "gestured of exclusion" practiced by progressive Victorians who dismiss religious beliefs as superstition. Earning Shaw's praise for its inclusiveness is the Roman Catholic Church, which in 1920 reversed its 1431 condemnation of Joan for her "unwomanly and insufferable presumption" (*CP* 2:500). The Church, admitting that "the highest wisdom may come as a divine revelation to the individual" (526), elevated to sainthood this radiant young woman who had, ironically, defied its authority.

But Shaw, a lifelong critic of orthodox Christianity, was far from trying to convert Britain to Catholicism. Instead, again employing his "new speech," he used the Church to remind readers that change, often looking like regression rather than progress, is essential to the forward movement of the human race: "And as the law of God in any sense of the word which can now command a faith proof against science is a law of evolution, it follows that the law of God is a law of change, and that when the Churches set themselves against change as such, they are setting themselves against the law of God" (532).

Throughout the Preface Shaw argues the superiority of the Church to the scientific community, defamiliarizing both and provoking readers to create a new perspective. Many of his arguments are similar to those in the *Quintessence*: Science fosters repression and denial, masks conflict to create the appearance of harmony, and reduces complex relationships to abstract, simplistic concepts.

First, Shaw complains, science represses its similarity to religion. Scientists make extravagant truth claims while indulging in practices and thought processes that resemble sorcery. We have succumbed to them, Shaw charges, not because of their superior explanations, but because "modern science has convinced us that nothing that is obvious is true, and that everything that is magical, improbable, extraordinary, gigantic, microscopic, heartless, or outrageous is scientific" (540). (In *Counter-Statement* Kenneth Burke would later point out the similarity between scientific and religious rhetoric, noting that scientists enjoy the privileges of "circumlocution, implication, and the mystical protection of a technical vocabulary"—66.)

Furthermore, scientists, like sorcerers and seers, deny their humanity, refuse to be held morally accountable for their behavior, and claim infallibility for their discoveries. The Church courageously admitted its error in condemning and burning Joan; its Dogma of Papal Infallibility, Shaw notes approvingly, "is by far the most modest pretension of the kind in existence" (526). But science allows itself to indulge in "hypochondria, melancholia, cowardice, stupidity, cruelty, muckraking curiosity, knowledge without wisdom, and everything that the eternal soul in Nature loathes, instead of the virtues of which St Catherine was the figure head" (511). Ironically, says Shaw, our age is more rather than less susceptible to figments of the imagination than the Middle Ages: "I affirm that the XIX century, and still more the XX, can knock the XV into a cocked hat in point of susceptibility to marvels and saints and prophets and magicians and monsters and fairy tales of all kinds" (540).

The result of this scientific gullibility, Shaw argues, is suppression of the open conflict and debate needed to moderate the truth claims of science. "The proportion of marvel to immediately credible statement in the latest edition of the Encyclopaedia Britannica is enormously greater than in the Bible," he says (540). In one oratorical passage, Shaw warns that the awe of scientists deafens us to other voices trying to convict us of "our credulities that have not the excuse of being superstitious, our cruelties that have not the excuse of barbarism, our persecutions that have not the excuse of religious faith, our shameless substitution of successful swindlers and scoundrels and quacks for saints as objects of worship, and our deafness and blindness to the calls and visions of the inexorable power that made us, and will destroy us if we disregard it" (512).

Finally, science reduces complex relationships to abstract concepts. And which is the healthier mind?" Shaw asks. "[T]he saintly mind or the monkey gland mind?" (512). Science can offer no explanation for the luminous Joan, with her voices, visions, and pretensions. Its only recourse is to argue that she was insane. But "an explanation which amounts to Joan being mentally defective instead of, as she obviously was, mentally excessive, will not wash" (509).

Yet "Shavian inclusiveness" does not really demand a choice between religion and science. Shaw himself is "both/and"—a would-be saint (he once wrote, "there is no reason why I too should not be canonized someday"— *EPWW* 327) and—despite his scientific skepticism—a student of the science of phonetics. One of Shaw's goals in *Pygmalion* and many of his prose writings is to relativize science, rather than destroy it, by undercutting its truth claims. In *Everybody's Political What's What?* he described his vision of an integrated religious science: "Both our science and our religion are gravely wrong; but they are not all wrong; and it is our urgent business to purge them of their errors and get them both as right as possible. If we could get them entirely right the contradictions between them would disappear: we should have a religious science and a scientific religion in a single synthesis. Meanwhile we just do the best we can instead of running away from the conflict as we are cowardly enough to do at present" (362–63).

Shaw's arguments—exposing scientific denial, suppression of conflict, and reductionism—are the same strategies used by Marx. There are also anticipations of Derrida in this Preface, as in *The Quintessence of Ibsenism*, when margins and mainstream exchange places. Again and again Shaw confronts readers with choices that push them beyond the edge of conventional thinking.

First, Shaw's lucid portrait of Joan challenges readers to find a means of reconciling spirituality and science: "Socrates, Luther, Swedenborg, Blake saw visions and heard voices just as Saint Francis and Saint Joan did. If Newton's imagination had been of the same vividly dramatic kind he might have seen the ghost of Pythagoras walk into the orchard and explain why the apples were falling" (507–8). Shaw repeatedly raises provocative questions about the relative merits of spirituality and science: "As to the new rites, which would be the saner Joan? the one who carried little children to be baptized of water and the spirit, or the one who sent the police to force their parents to have the most villainous racial poison we know thrust into their veins? the one who told them the story of the angel and Mary, or the one who questioned them as to their experiences of the Edipus complex?" (511–12).

Second, the Preface challenges readers to take unconventional positions about contemporary scientific, religious, and political issues. For example, Shaw questions the popular concept of tolerance: Should the Church have condemned the ecstatic but insufferable Joan? "At eighteen Joan's pretensions were beyond those of the proudest Pope or the haughtiest emperor. She claimed to be the ambassador and plenipotentiary of God, and to be, in effect, a member of the Church Triumphant whilst still in the flesh on earth. . . . As her actual condition was pure upstart, there were only two opinions about her. One was that she was miraculous: the other that she was unbearable" (500–501).

Faced with this either/or choice, the reader is forced to leave the comfortable mainstream sentiment that Joan was a brave but confused girl whose hidebound Church victimized her: "If Joan was mad, all Christendom was mad too; for people who believe devoutly in the existence of celestial personages are every whit as mad as the people who think they see them" (510). Joan knew full well what she was doing—as did the Church when it burned her. We are left with an uncomfortable choice: taking Joan's side by declaring our allegiance with the "law of change," or positioning ourselves with the medieval Church that condemned her.

Throughout the Preface, Shaw challenges his readers with unpalatable choices and undeniable truths, beginning with "society is founded on intolerance" (534). "The degree of tolerance attainable at any moment depends on the strain under which society is maintaining its cohesion. In war, for instance, we suppress the gospels and put Quakers in prison, muzzle the newspapers, and make it a serious offence to shew a light at night" (534). "Edith [Cavell], like Joan, was an arch heretic. . . . She nursed enemies back to health, and assisted their prisoners to escape, making it abundantly clear that she would help any fugitive or distressed person without asking whose side he was on" (523). "It is, I repeat, what normally innocent people do that concerns us; and if Joan had not been burnt by normally innocent people in the energy of their righteousness, her death at their hands would have no more significance than the Tokyo earthquake, which burnt a great many maidens" (543).

This juxtaposition of tolerance and intolerance, science and spirituality, truth as preached in the Middle Ages and truth taught by science today, again constitutes *différance*—Shaw's rejection of the logocentrism that replaces unstable reality with abstract, unchangeable concepts. Shaw is never satisfied with refuting erroneous ideas: His "new speech" seeks out the ambiguity in commonplace words that form the foundation of conventional thought.

Saint, lunatic, vision, murder, tolerance, justice, science, religion, truth—these words take on broader, unexpected meanings in the "Shavian inclusiveness" of the Preface to *Saint Joan*.

Before this chapter ends, I must point out my own "gestures of exclusion." So far I have not acknowledged the general absence of Shaw's public *persona* from *The Quintessence of Ibsenism* and the Preface to *Saint Joan*. The *Quintessence*, replete with footnotes, seems to come from the pen of a faceless writer who calls attention to his ideas rather than his personality. And while the outrageous G.B.S. shows himself several times in the Preface to *Saint Joan*, those appearances are brief. There is one hyperbolic self-comparison to Shakespeare: "I can only invent appropriate characters for them in Shakespear's manner" (541). Near the end of the Preface, Shaw taunts his critics in the familiar Shavian voice: "I have to thank several critics on both sides of the Atlantic, including some whose admiration for my play is most generously enthusiastic, for their heartfelt instructions as to how it can be improved" (544). Otherwise there is little of G.B.S., Shaw's outspoken literary alter ego, in either work.

Closer scrutiny of the Shavian *persona* will be delayed until chapter 3. For now I want to point out that Shaw, whether openly performing as G.B.S. or not, is always making himself present through his "new speech": His bold wordplay and oratory and daring opinions are present in abundance in both the *Quintessence* and the Preface to *Saint Joan*. (Similarly, Higgins is present in every word that Eliza says, even when he is offstage at the embassy reception.) Paradoxically, the outrageousness of Shavian "new speech" is more honest than the impersonal omniscience affected by more conventional essayists. The outcome is an empowered readership, liberated from their unthinking dependence on a human author disguised as a god. That empowerment is the subject of the next chapter.

Notes

1. Shaw's socialism is discussed in Paul A. Hummert, *Bernard Shaw's Marxian Romance*, Harry Morrison, *The Socialism of Bernard Shaw*; and Eric Bentley, *Bernard Shaw*.

2. Western philosophy has a long tradition of affirming human affective functions. Plato, Aristotle, Descartes, Spinoza, Hume, Kant, and Toulmin, among others, considered emotion an important adjunct to logic.

3. For an analysis of Shaw's synthesis of reason and passion, see R. F. Dietrich, "Shaw and the Passionate Mind."

CELIA MARSHIK

Parodying the £5 Virgin: Bernard Shaw and the Playing of Pygmalion

Although fifteen years would pass before he realized his intentions, Bernard Shaw conceived of the plot of—and cast for—*Pygmalion* in 1897. In September of that year, he informed Ellen Terry that he wanted to write a play for Mrs. Patrick Campbell in which the popular actress would star as "an east end dona in an apron and three orange and red ostrich feathers."[1] *Pygmalion*—starring Mrs. Campbell—did not debut in England until 1914, when it quickly became Shaw's most popular work to date. In the decades that followed, Shaw's tale of a young flower girl turned "duchess" through the exertions of a phonetic expert achieved widespread circulation through revivals, publication, musical adaptation (*My Fair Lady*), and film. It became a popular version of the Cinderella story, with a message about personal transformation that seems to transcend the historical distance between Shaw's era and our own.

If *Pygmalion*'s ongoing popularity demonstrates the comedy's appeal to contemporary tastes and concerns, the play and its initial performance are closely tied to the 1880s and 1890s, decades when Shaw was mainly known as a political speaker and critic of late-Victorian drama. The seeds of *Pygmalion*'s central joke were planted as Shaw saw the political power of social purity movements, which he initially championed, turned against the theater. When Shaw finally wrote and helped to produce *Pygmalion*, he used

From *The Yale Journal of Criticism*, 13, no. 2 (2000): 321–41. Copyright © 2000 by Yale University and the Johns Hopkins University Press.

the play to parody the social movements that had, he felt, assumed hysterical proportions and hampered his early career. The comedy engages in a critique of the "Maiden Tribute of Modern Babylon," a founding document of the purity movement, as it mocks Shaw's old opponents. This parody has, however, escaped the attention of audiences and critics, partly because of the passage of time and partly because Mrs. Patrick Campbell hyper-eroticized the role of Eliza Doolittle in the play's English and American debuts. Shaw may have hoped that his leading lady would sharpen his critique of social purity; instead, Campbell compromised Shaw's spoof as she brought her previous roles with her onto the stage.

Pygmalion has received considerable scholarly attention because it demonstrates Shaw's interest in the role of language in the English class system. It has also drawn the attention of psychoanalytic critics, who see Higgins as a figure for Shaw. The comedy has not, however, been considered in dialogue with the efforts of nineteenth- and twentieth-century purity movements.[2] By contextualizing the play within the Victorian climate that inspired it, I demonstrate that Shaw's early battles with stage censorship and social purity linger in works that seem preoccupied with other concerns. Moreover, I argue that Shaw's casting choice powerfully influenced how *Pygmalion* would be understood by audiences of the 1910s and 1920s, audiences that might otherwise have recognized Shaw's play with moralists' myths.

*   *   *

In July of 1885, the editor and journalist William T. Stead shocked the British public with his "Maiden Tribute," a series of articles in the *Pall Mall Gazette*. After declaring that "the most imperious sense of duty" impelled his pen, Stead documented how working-class girls were

> snared, trapped, and outraged, either when under the influence of drugs or after a prolonged struggle in a locked room, in which the weaker succumbs to sheer downright force. Others are regularly procured; bought at so much per head in some cases, or enticed under various promises into the fatal chamber.[3]

Stead interviewed prostitutes, madams, johns, policemen, and others to unveil systemic efforts in the nation's capital to deprive young, vulnerable females of their virginity, which he asserted a "woman ought to value more than life" (3).

The highlight of Stead's work, "A Child of Thirteen Bought for £5," chronicled the purchase of young "Lily" from her parents. According to

Stead, Lily's drunken mother knew that her daughter was purchased for a brothel, while the child's father, "who was also a drunken man, was told that his daughter was going to a situation. He received the news with indifference, without even inquiring where she was going to" (6). The article went on to describe the ease with which the child was certified a virgin, brought to a brothel, and placed in a bed. The tale ended as a man entered the girl's room, causing Lily to emit "not a loud shriek, but a helpless, startled scream like the bleat of a frightened lamb" (6). The reader was left to conclude that poor Lily had joined the ranks of the "fallen" and to feel outrage at such wanton sexual predation.

Stead's exposé marked a high point in the British public's attention to the sexual exploitation of working-class women. His series led to mass rallies and calls for government intervention; eventually, the outcry led to the passage of the Criminal Law Amendment Act of 1885, which raised the age of consent from thirteen to sixteen and facilitated prosecutions of brothel-keepers and prostitutes. But Stead was not satisfied with mere legislation. He later organized a conference on the subjects covered by the "Maiden Tribute," a conference with a "practical program" of organizing "the Vigilance Association of London."[4] This Association—later known as the National Vigilance Association (NVA)—insured that authorities enforced the provisions of the new Act. Stead argued that the government could not be trusted to protect the nation's purity on its own; the new tools of the state would only be employed if a vigilant public demanded action.

A broad range of individuals joined Stead's initial campaign for social purity. Shaw, who had begun reviewing books for the *Pall Mall Gazette* in May of that year, was among Stead's early supporters.[5] When W.H. Smith and Son, a prominent bookseller, refused to carry the "Maiden Tribute" issues of the *PMG*, Shaw wrote to Stead with an offer to support "the first newspaper which ever inspired respectable men with enthusiasm." He went on to state that he was "quite willing to take as many quires of the paper as I can carry and sell them (for a penny) in any thoroughfare in London." He was sure that he could find "both ladies and gentlemen willing to do the same."[6]

Stead never took advantage of Shaw's offer, but for a brief moment, Shaw was prepared to take the reformer's message to the streets. Subsequent events undermined Shaw's dedication to Stead. In October of 1885, the editor was brought to trial for abduction and technical assault under the Criminal Law Amendment Act—the very law that "The Maiden Tribute" had carried through Parliament. After the series' publication, the mother of thirteen-year-old Eliza Armstrong reported the disappearance of her child to local authorities. Eliza was quickly identified as "Lily," the virgin that Stead had purchased for five pounds and whose tale he had fictionalized in order to arouse his audience's fury. Although the child was not in fact seduced and had been sent to the Salvation Army in France, Stead was indicted for kidnapping because Eliza's father had not given permission for his daughter to leave his house. As the trial unfolded, some observers concluded that the editor's enthusiasm had led him to make "serious errors of judgment."[7] Although Stead's intentions were seemingly pure, his pose as Eliza's purchaser and seducer (the account was written in third person, but it was Stead himself who had startled Eliza in the brothel) complicated his moral position. His actions were illegal, and the journalist was convicted under the law he had helped to pass.

Shaw, disgusted with the revelations about Stead's journalism, dismissed the entire "Maiden Tribute" as a "put-up job" that betrayed "our confidence in him." Stead was "so stupendously ignorant that he never played the game" of professional reporting.[8] While Shaw's reaction was not uncommon among journalists, his subsequent contact with the editor reveals that their point of disagreement ran deeper than professional ethics. Although Shaw appreciated Stead's commitment to reform, the two men disagreed on the means to achieve social change.

While Shaw felt that art—and specifically, theater—was a useful tool for reformers, Stead and the NVA were suspicious of theater's moral impact on its practitioners and audience members. "The Maiden Tribute" contained several examples of Stead's puritan attitude toward the theater; in one column, he alluded to a "notorious" theater where "no girl ever kept her virtue more than three months," and he also mentioned the rumor that "some theatrical managers . . . [insist] upon a claim to ruin actresses whom they allow to appear on their boards."[9] Stead depicted theaters as dens of vice and sexual predation and provided vigilance movements with a mandate to "clean up" public entertainments. This mandate had a direct impact upon Shaw's early career as a playwright.

The English theater of Shaw's era was policed through a combination of government regulation and private initiative. The Theatres Act of 1843 required that all plays performed in England be submitted to the Lord Chamberlain for licensing "at least seven days before the first performance." His office could refuse a license without providing a reason and could fine or close theaters that presented unlicensed plays. The Act did not make any provision for appeal.[10] Although the stage was thus regulated through official, state censorship, individual moral reformers and organizations supported the government's actions and pressured the Lord Chamberlain to apply ever more stringent guidelines to plays. They hoped that the office might eventually prohibit any works that would violate "the conscience of the Bishop or any other decent citizen."[11] Such arguments found a sympathetic ear in public officials; as Jeffrey Weeks notes, "there was a continuing close, and often symbiotic relationship between morality pressure groups, church and state."[12] Shaw was aware of this close relationship and expressed dismay that organizations such as the NVA were "strong enough to . . . bring [their] convictions to bear effectively on our licensing authorities."[13]

A number of Shaw's early works were denied a license for public performance because they might offend bishops and other decent citizens. Between 1895 and 1909, ten percent of the plays banned by the Lord Chamberlain were by Shaw.[14] *Mrs. Warren's Profession* (rejected in 1898), *The Shewing-up of Blanco Posnet* (1909), and *Press Cuttings* (1909) were all banned from the British stage, events that did not surprise Shaw but that drove him into an increasing frenzy over official censorship and the moral reformers who supported it. As a result of these encounters with stage censorship, Shaw issued a number of articles, prefaces, public letters, and statements that protested the government's licensing requirements and berated social purity groups' pretensions to intervene in the theater.[15] He called the Secretary of the NVA "in artistic matters a most intensely stupid man" who was "on sexual questions something of a monomaniac"; he asserted that "the paid officials of [purity and vigilance] societies . . . combine a narrow but terribly sincere sectarian bigotry with a complete ignorance of art and history"; and he called Stead "an abyss of ignorance" who made "a round of theatres as if they were brothels."[16] *Blanco Posnet* contained a clear jibe of its own; in the play, a drunken and dissolute "Vigilance Committee" metes out "justice" to those unfortunate enough to fall in its path.

Such actions did not endear Shaw to the Lord Chamberlain's office or to social purity leaders (one wryly noted that his group had "not often found themselves running in parallel lines of thought to Mr. Bernard Shaw"),[17] but they did earn him public stature as an opponent of stage censorship. Newspaper and journal cartoons depicted Shaw as both victim and critic of censorship. Indeed, one might argue that Shaw's experience of censorship contributed to his status as a public intellectual. It certainly contributed toward a new direction, one that would prove quite popular with audiences, in his playwriting.

In 1895, at the beginning of his career as a playwright, Shaw expressed his belief that "it is quite impossible to legislate and administer with a view to the comfort of . . . abnormal people."[18] In the course of the next two decades, prosecutions of performance halls and publishers—prosecutions instigated and supported by social purity groups—had proved him wrong. So Shaw would write no more of what he called his "unpleasant" plays. Instead of dramatizing a social problem and making undisguised appeals to his audience's reason, later works such as *Pygmalion* seem on the surface deliberately apolitical. But *Pygmalion* was Shaw's parting shot at social purists, and at the increasingly repressive state that they supported, through a parody of the tales circulated by Stead and other moral crusaders. If Shaw couldn't undo their social policing and censorship, he would at least have a good laugh at their expense.

While Shaw was writing *Pygmalion*, Stead's reputation underwent another reversal. The journalist died when the Titanic sank in April of 1912, and his behavior on this occasion led the press to lionize him. According to various survivors, Stead never attempted to board the Titanic's lifeboats, and he was last seen in "a prayerful attitude of profound meditation."[19] After this event, Stead was not a figure Shaw could openly mock or critique; as the playwright finished *Pygmalion* in May and June of that year, a subtle parody was the most he might tactfully direct at the sainted Stead.

The laughing, lighthearted *Pygmalion* has a dark side. From the play's beginning, there are "repeated threats to Eliza [Doolittle's] sexual and physical safety."[20] When the flower girl realizes that her casual remarks about selling flowers and making money have been recorded by an unknown man, she immediately fears that she will be accused of soliciting: "I aint done nothing wrong by speaking to the gentleman. . . . I'm a respectable girl: so help me, I never spoke to him except to ask him to buy a flower off me."[21] Concerned that her "character" will be indicted for "speaking to gentlemen" (20), Eliza panics and works to assure those around her of her respectability. She repeatedly states that she was attempting to sell flowers—not, the audience is to understand, herself.

Other characters initially mock the young woman's attempts to defend her virtue. The crowd, the stage directions state, deprecates "her excessive sensibility" (20). The phoneticist Henry Higgins indicates that he was only noting down her accent; far from being a "copper's nark," he can't wait to get away from Eliza (27). Higgins thus implies that Eliza is making something of nothing—that she need not insist that she's a "good girl" because no one is accusing her of anything (24). And yet, the crowd that surrounds Eliza and Higgins is ready to defend the flower girl, assuring her that "nobody's going to touch you" and telling Higgins to "mind your own affairs" (20, 22). The bystanders think that Eliza is overreacting to Higgins's actions, but they acknowledge that she might be mistreated. Shaw's play thus mocks the working-class woman's anxiety over her "character," but it also implies that such concern is sometimes warranted.

Pygmalion continues to question Higgins's role and his threat to Eliza after she arrives at his house with the intention of paying for lessons that will rid her of her Cockney accent. When Higgins and his friend Colonel Pickering begin to plan their grand educational experiment with and on Eliza, the play returns to the question of Higgins's intentions toward the working-class woman. Just as Stead's actions in the Eliza Armstrong affair were variously interpreted by those surrounding the case, Higgins is implicated as reformer and seducer of Eliza Doolittle as *Pygmalion* reveals the fine line between philanthropy and predation. When he talks about burning Eliza's clothes and buying her new ones, Higgins is ostensibly initiating the flower girl's transformation. Eliza, however, reads his actions as those of a sexual predator: "Youre no gentleman, youre not . . . I know what the like of you are, I do" (41). Eliza sounds like someone who has read "The Maiden Tribute" and committed its lessons to heart: as a "daughter of the people," she is the natural prey of the idle rich and must constantly guard against the temptations they offer.

Eliza's response is framed as a comic misrecognition. Higgins claims to have no sexual interest in the girl and dismisses her words as "Lisson Grove prudery" (41). But the young woman's attempts to protect herself and to assess the safety of her surroundings are not misguided because she is essentially "safe" in Higgins's flat; rather, Eliza's reactions are foolish because she perceives her situation through hysterical tales of lost virtue. Her interpretive structures, what scholars have called her "melodramatic state of mind," cause her to misunderstand the evidence before her.[22] Eliza's reading of the world thus mirrors the text that Shaw parodies in *Pygmalion*; as historian Judith Walkowitz has argued, "The Maiden Tribute" needs to be understood in relation to stage melodrama in its focus on individual actions at the expense of economic and social issues. Eliza, unlike Shaw and *Pygmalion*, reduces the world to "innocent female victims" and "individual evil men," and she is therefore a bad interpreter.[23] Sexual predation certainly exists—that is not "fiction"—but it does not follow the scripts that Eliza anticipates.

If Higgins dismisses Eliza's fears, *Pygmalion* continues to play with the unstable opposition between reformers and sexual predators. Higgins's proposal to "take [Eliza] out of the gutter and dress [her] beautifully and make a lady of [her]" mimics the kind of offer a rake would make to a potential mistress (43). Other characters express reservations about Higgins's intentions: Mrs. Pearce, Higgins's housekeeper, tells him that his offer to remake Eliza is "wicked" and worries about the terms under which "the girl is to be here" (43, 44). She doesn't even know if she can "consent to the arrangement at all" (46). Although Mrs. Pearce insists that Higgins "dont mean . . . any harm" (46), the older woman reminds the audience that any interaction between a male reformer and a working-class woman is fraught with danger—albeit of different kinds—for both parties.

Pygmalion repeatedly exposes the dual nature of relationships between social reformers and young, unmarried women. In a society where sex is a working-class woman's most valuable commodity, a middle-class man's philanthropic interest in an Eliza Doolittle is vexed by her sexual availability and vulnerability. Higgins repeatedly mocks Eliza's attempts to protect herself as unwarranted and melodramatic, but minor characters at the periphery of the action imply that Higgins acts and talks like a seducer. Indeed, Higgins becomes an uncanny double for reformers and sexual predators; he is represented as upright and trustworthy, but as an upper-class man he looks like the johns Stead attacked and follows their script. Eliza may have an overactive imagination, but Higgins—like Stead—becomes implicated in the sexual misdeeds of the very system he appears to reject.

As Shaw's play exposes the unsettling proximity of male philanthropy to sexual predation, it also mocks the fictions of late-Victorian social reform.[24] One widespread belief about sexual predators, or "Minotaurs" as Stead liked to call them, was that they sedated their victims to make abduction and assault easier. Tales of drugged drinks and candies circulated widely as young women were told to regard any stranger's offer of refreshments with caution. For example, at one point in 1913 (just one year before the debut of *Pygmalion*), the 5,000 young women who operated London's telephone exchanges were provided with an official warning to watch out for drugged candy.[25] In *Pygmalion*, Shaw ridicules such stories by having Higgins offer Eliza chocolates. She hesitates, questioning, "How do I know what might be in them? Ive heard of girls being drugged by the like of you" (44). Higgins assuages her concern by cutting the candy in half and eating part himself, and Shaw's play thus asserts that sometimes a chocolate is just a chocolate. This scene once again demonstrates that Eliza makes sense of her world through stories of sexual danger; to a young woman familiar with tales of public injections and unwholesome sweets, Higgins has an uncanny resemblance to a "Minotaur." But since Eliza is proved to have overreacted, Shaw's play indicts the individuals who circulated stories about druggings for making mischief. *Pygmalion* thus deflates calls for increased government intervention into public arenas in the name of protecting young women.[26]

As the comedy unfolds, Shaw continues to spoof reformers' tales of sexual danger. Eliza's father, Alfred Doolittle, appears at Higgins's home bearing his daughter's belongings but not, significantly, her clothes (56). He implies that he's coming "to rescue her from [a fate] worse than death" (56), but he eventually makes the teacher-reformer a seemingly unusual offer:

> Regarded in the light of a young woman, she's a fine handsome girl. As a daughter she's not worth her keep; and so I tell you straight. All I ask is my rights as a father; and youre the last man alive to expect me to let her go for nothing; for I can see youre one of the straight sort, Governor. Well, whats a five-pound note to you? and whats Eliza to me? (57)

Doolittle makes this offer although he is ignorant of Higgins's plan to educate and reform Eliza. He professes to believe that Higgins's intentions are "entirely honorable," but Doolittle states that they are "men of the world" and asks no probing questions about Eliza's future (57). Higgins is tickled by Doolittle's arguments and, after some further discussion, the five pounds change hands.

As Eliza is traded from her father to Higgins, this scene demonstrates how women circulate in a masculine economy.[27] But this exchange is also a parody of such bargains, pointing back toward Stead's "Maiden Tribute" and mocking it in the process. Five pounds is not an arbitrary figure: it is the exact amount that Stead's contact paid Eliza Armstrong's mother in order to demonstrate how easily young girls could be purchased by vicious men. This figure gained widespread "currency" as the proper value for female virgins. Walkowitz reports that in the fall of 1885,

> the *PMG* actually reported two cases of sexual assault of "virgins" where monetary reparations were offered at the valuation set by the "Maiden Tribute": in Manchester, a father whose daughter had been assaulted, "having read the *Pall Mall Gazette* and the *War Cry*" (Salvation Army paper) demanded "no less than £5" as consolation for "wounded honour"; while a farmer, charged with assaulting a domestic servant in his employ, offered £5 to "square the matter."[28]

Five pounds was what "good girls" like Eliza were worth, according to Stead's reports; while his conclusions were later questioned, the amount had entered public consciousness as an appropriate price for female virtue. Although Doolittle has personal reasons for requesting five pounds (more money would force him to be "prudent"), the dustman's demand puts this scene in dialogue with the "Maiden Tribute." Like other (nonfictional) fathers before him, Doolittle seizes on this figure as the amount that another man ought to pay for the services of his child.

Pygmalion is full of similar links to the "The Maiden Tribute." Most obviously, Shaw's heroine shares the first name of Stead's "Lily," Eliza Armstrong.[29] In addition to sharing a first name, the two women share a neighborhood: both Elizas are from Lisson Grove. And, like Eliza Doolittle's, Eliza Armstrong's "grammar was very shaky" and "although her spelling was extraordinary, she was able to express herself with much force and decision."[30] *Pygmalion* thus encourages readers and audiences to connect its comedy with "The Maiden Tribute." At the level of plot, both texts explore the treatment of a working-class "Eliza" at the hands of an acquisitive male reformer. Through particular details about Eliza Doolittle's character and the exchange between her father and Higgins, the play develops more than a passing resemblance to the articles of 1885.

Shaw's comedy thus gestures toward Stead and toward the vigilance groups that the editor had set in motion. *Pygmalion* plays with this connection: Higgins does not sexually assault his new property, and the scene between the phoneticist and Eliza's father is passed off as a joke about the latter's greed. Since Eliza's sexual integrity is not ultimately violated, Shaw's play merely laughs at the idea that a parent would "sell" his child. Instead of confronting Stead's (discredited) claim that "daughters of the people" could be molested for a petty fee, *Pygmalion* displaces Shaw's old editor by making him and his followers the butt of the play's joke. The question of Eliza's relative safety—at the hands of Higgins and of her father—is deflected, and the young woman's sexual vulnerability is laughed off the stage.

Shaw's joke at the expense of Stead may help to explain his frustration with actors, directors, and producers who tinkered with *Pygmalion*'s ending. Although Shaw's play implies that Eliza will eventually marry young Freddy Eynsford-Hill, various productions have found ways to insinuate that Eliza and Higgins have a romantic future. In the 1914 London debut, the actor who played Higgins threw flowers at Eliza as the curtain fell; during the play's first American tour, the actress cast as Eliza returned to Higgins at the comedy's conclusion.[31] Shaw was so troubled by such interpretations that he added a postscript to the play that insists upon the incompatibility of his main characters. While Shaw may have had several reasons for writing his postscript,[32] he needed to combat a romantic reading to preserve his parody of Stead. If Higgins marries Eliza, if he takes her as a sexual partner, he has effectively purchased a £5 virgin and confirmed—rather than undermined—Stead's arguments.[33]

By parodying Stead's tale of £5 virgins, Shaw directed his audience's attention to the absurdities of the social purity movement. This caricature of moral reform is developed by the fate of Alfred Doolittle as the play draws to a close. The drinking, cohabiting dustman becomes a lecturer for the Wannafeller Moral Reform World League (116). This transformation is somewhat less dramatic than it first appears; as a member of the "undeserving poor," Doolittle states that he is "a thinking man and game for politics or religion or social reform same as all the other amusements" (58–59). Through Higgins's intervention, Doolittle is compelled to adopt this "amusement" as a way of life as he is paid handsomely to adopt "middle class morality" and to lecture audiences (115). Doolittle's own morals, skin deep and adopted under economic persuasion, serve to parody the authority of "real" social reformers. If Doolittle can "amuse" himself with social reform, so might anyone, and *Pygmalion* suggests that one requires neither a pure character nor sincerity to take a leading role in contemporary vigilance societies and moral movements.

In a drama of social amelioration that becomes a burlesque of the vigilance craze, Shaw exposed the unstable authority of the social forces born in 1885. Stead had opened the floodgates of censorship and moral policing by writing and publishing a melodrama. Shaw struck back at these repressions by drawing attention to the proximity of philanthropy to sexual predation and by parodying the melodramatic reactions of individuals who had been taught by reformers' tales. Eliza Doolittle could have become a prostitute and madam like Kitty Warren, the protagonist of *Mrs. Warren's Profession*, quite easily. The two characters share a class background and employment options, but Shaw had been pushed away from such "unpleasant" thoughts by a social movement intent on repressing dissent along with indecency. In *Pygmalion*, Shaw worked to undo the damage that social reformers and the paternal state they supported had done to personal relations, the theater, and public life. Through a subversive mime of their work, moral crusaders and purity groups were indicted for circulating hysterical tales, fictions that led to ever more oppressive laws and enforcement. If working-class women were still sexually vulnerable in the 1910s, Shaw insinuated that social purity was not an adequate response to their condition.

When Shaw's play was first performed in London and the United States, his casting decisions complicated *Pygmalion*'s engagement with the late-Victorian reform impulse and its confused sexual mores. As I have noted, he wrote the role of Eliza for, and brought the play to, one of the most famous actresses of the turn-of-the-century stage: Mrs. Patrick Campbell. After a couple years of wrangling over financial backing, the remaining cast, and other production details, Campbell, Shaw, and Sir Herbert Beerbohm Tree finally brought *Pygmalion* to His Majesty's Theatre in April of 1914. Shaw and Tree made sure that the play received a great deal of advance publicity, and much of it focused on Campbell in her role as flower-girl-turned-duchess. When audiences attended *Pygmalion* in 1914 (and during its revival in 1920), they knew three things about the play: the title indicated that it was based on a myth of female transformation, reviewers noted that it featured the then-scandalous profanity "bloody," and advertisements emphasized that Mrs. Campbell was cast in the starring female role.

By tying his play so tightly to the reputation of Stella Campbell, Shaw stood to lose as much as he gained by associating his work with a popular performer. Campbell was nearly fifty in 1914 and was somewhat mature to be playing the eighteen-year-old Eliza Doolittle, a fact that was noted in some reviews. More important, she had made her professional reputation in quite different plays and was ostensibly cross-cast in *Pygmalion*.[34] In her twenty-five years as an actress, Campbell had played a number of roles, but she was strongly associated with ethereal sex objects. In 1901, Shaw wrote that her presence imbued dramas with an "overpowering *odor di femmina*,"[35] an *odor* that was most apparent when she acted in the "woman with a past" play.

In its various manifestations, the late-Victorian "woman with a past" play addressed the question of whether a woman could leave sexual license behind and reenter respectable society as a wife, mother, or friend. Most dramas concluded that she could not. Like Stead's "Maiden Tribute," such plays linked lost virginity with dire consequences, and like Stead, playwrights depicted women as victims destined to suffer for the sexual liberties of upper-class men. Although they challenged the "double standard" by encouraging audiences to sympathize with the "fallen" character[36] (much as Stead drummed up pity for young prostitutes), the majority of such plays ended by ostracizing or killing off the troublesome, erotically charged female protagonist.

If "an entire stage history accompanies an actress onto the stage" when she assumes a new role,[37] Mrs. Patrick Campbell's history was longer—and racier—than most. Her first major role was in Arthur Wing Pinero's *The Second Mrs. Tanqueray*, which debuted in 1893. In this play, Campbell portrayed the title character, a former mistress and perhaps prostitute who attempts to reform but is finally unable to escape her past. *Tanqueray* was enormously popular—Campbell called the work "the most successful modern English play of the century"[38]—and her acting was widely acclaimed. Or rather, her ability to "be" Mrs. Tanqueray was much remarked; Campbell's naturalistic acting style encouraged association between the actress and her part, and audience members and critics alike claimed that she "was" Paula Tanqueray.[39] Campbell was startled to discover that she was identified with her role. A few people called her "Mrs. Tanqueray" by accident, and one woman even investigated her background to see whether she was a *demi-mondaine*.[40] According to Elaine Aston and George Savona, "the image of fallen woman was henceforth encoded in Mrs Pat's on- and offstage identity."[41]

Campbell's subsequent career encouraged further confusion between actress and role. Her next major part was in Pinero's 1895 drama *The Notorious Mrs. Ebbsmith*. In this play, Campbell was cast as a young intellectual (a "New Woman") who lives openly with a married man. In the middle of the play, Agnes Ebbsmith gives up her political ambitions, dons a sensual gown, and resigns herself to becoming a traditional mistress. Although Ebbsmith feels shame when she goes from "workday drudge" to "faerie gown[ed]" enchantress, Campbell's audiences didn't always grasp this point and cheered the actress's costume change.[42] This response indicates that some spectators valued Campbell's physical charms more highly than her ability to create a character. But critics praised the actress's performance while Campbell's audience conflated her with Agnes Ebbsmith; in the words of Edmund Gosse, "the play was [Mrs. Campbell]."[43]

Although Campbell went on to play other characters (including additional women with sexual pasts), Paula Tanqueray and Agnes Ebbsmith remained her most popular roles. Whenever her management, touring company, or Campbell herself needed a guaranteed success, one of Pinero's plays was revived and the actress received new acclaim. Indeed, Campbell played these parts again in 1898, 1901, 1902, 1907, 1913, 1914 (while on the American tour of *Pygmalion*), 1922, and 1924, firmly cementing her reputation as an actress who could bring "fallen women" to the stage in unparalleled ways. Shaw was aware of her reputation and indeed had hoped to exploit it in one of his earlier works. Before the Lord Chamberlain refused to license *Mrs. Warren's Profession*, Shaw had suggested that Campbell be cast in the role of his impenitent former prostitute and madam.[44]

Because of her performance history, Campbell as Eliza Doolittle was—in the words of one critic—a "crosscasting joke."[45] And yet, her presence in *Pygmalion* was generally a hit with critics. As Eliza, Campbell sniveled "I'm a respectable girl" and reminded audiences of all the specific ways in which such a woman might not be respectable, while her presentation of Eliza after her transformation highlighted the character's newfound refinement and beauty.

In retrospect, Campbell's Eliza seems to underline *Pygmalion*'s allusions to the late-Victorian obsession with sexual danger. But her presence compromised that subtext for the play's 1914 and 1920 audiences. Indeed, Campbell brought the "*odor di femmina*" to Shaw's comedy; the frustrated playwright discovered that he could not control the actress and complained that she insisted on wearing costumes that "displayed Mrs. Patrick Campbell while eclipsing Eliza."[46] Pictures of the 1914 production indicate that some of these costumes, and certainly Campbell's appearance in them, were decidedly vampish. Advertisers exploited Campbell's sexual appeal in cartoons based on *Pygmalion* but reminiscent of the actress's famous—and fallen—roles. Like *The Notorious Mrs. Ebbsmith, Pygmalion* threatened to become a play known for Mrs. Campbell's sexual appeal and dramatic costumes.

As Campbell's Eliza paraded around Higgins's bachelor apartments, she alternately raised and undermined the expectation that such a woman would inevitably fall prey to the machinations of male sexuality. While Stead had worried about the fate of "daughters of the people" who became the sexual objects of upper-class men, Shaw's play used Campbell's character to mock such fears. And yet, the playwright had not reckoned with the force of Campbell's status as a sexual icon. Campbell's sexual appeal made her—and

Eliza—popular with audiences, who could gaze upon the actress; her sexual magnetism compromised their ability to laugh at the assumptions that had made Stead—and the woman-with-a-past play—so well known.

Some viewers noted the vexed connection between *Pygmalion* and Campbell's earlier work. The reviewer for *Vanity Fair* observed that "toward the end of the play ... Mrs. Campbell got into her 'Pinero stride,' and the Eliza of the streets faded before one's memories of Paula Tanqueray and Mrs. Ebbsmith."[47] While some might read this comment as a sign of Campbell's failure as an actress, this review indicates that members of the 1914 audience came close to recognizing Shaw's subtext. For Shaw's play is about £5 virgins and phonetics, and Campbell was a physical link between *Pygmalion*'s dialogue and the preoccupations of late-Victorian drama and reform movements.

Implying that the repressive enforcement of British laws was fueled by colossal misreadings, Shaw's "pleasant play" concealed some polemical thoughts underneath its comedic surface. Eliza, he would tell Stella Campbell, "was only a joke," albeit a very successful one.[48] But it is time that readers and audiences remember who Shaw was laughing at and why he had stopped writing his "unpleasant" plays.

Henry Higgins and Alfred Doolittle mime the complicated sexual identities and melodramatic myths that Shaw had first observed in the 1880s. By exposing the proximity of social reform and sexual desire, Shaw put a "modern" spin on the Pygmalion myth while undermining the moral authority of Stead and his followers. His jokes repeatedly worked to challenge the publications and actions of social purity movements, an effort that had become increasingly important as such groups gained political power and government support.

If we do not recognize the butt of Shaw's jokes, it is undoubtedly because William T. Stead, "The Maiden Tribute," and the NVA have largely disappeared from our cultural memory. If Shaw's contemporaries did not fully recognize these jokes, it is perhaps because the playwright overestimated his ability to use Mrs. Campbell's public persona for his own ends. Her Eliza Doolittle was too much of a Galatea to rewrite the Pygmalion myth; Campbell was too desirable and too strongly associated with narratives of sexual consummation.[49] Shaw's casting choice did more than draw audiences to his play; his insistence that Campbell play his "east end dona in an apron and three orange and red ostrich feathers" jeopardized his ability to recast Stead and the purity movement. If we remember Shaw more than the actors who brought his works to the stage, *Pygmalion* demonstrates that certain performers—such as the seductive Mrs. Campbell—shape what we can see at work (and at play) in Shaw's drama.

Notes

1. *Collected Letters*, ed. Dan H. Laurence, 4 vols. (London: Max Reinhardt, 1965–88), 1:803.

2. Jean Reynolds, one of the most recent critics to analyze Shaw's view of language, brings together *Pygmalion* and Derridean deconstruction to argue that the dramatist collapsed "opposing terms into each other in a synthesis that anticipates Derrida's critique of logocentrism" (*Pygmalion's Wordplay: The Postmodern Shaw* [Gainesville: University Press of Florida, 1999], 134). Arnold Silver's *Bernard Shaw: The Darker Side* (Stanford: Stanford University Press, 1982), in contrast, provides a psychoanalytic reading of Shaw's work and presents *Pygmalion* as one of many plays in which the author's "destructive urges" circulate (282). My argument leaves aside the play's concerns with language to reconstruct Shaw's conscious—and quite public—battles with middlebrow moral movements. With the exception of Charles Berst, who notes in passing that "Doolittle's attempt to 'sell' Eliza to Higgins" is "perhaps" linked to "the genteel slave market of Victorian times," critics have not linked Shaw's comedy with late-Victorian sexual myths and scandals (*Pygmalion: Shaw's Spin on Myth and Cinderella* [London: Twayne, 1995], 104).

3. "The Maiden Tribute of Modern Babylon," *Pall Mall Gazette*, 6 Jul. 1885, 3. Subsequent references will be cited parenthetically in the text.

4. Raymond L. Shults, *Crusader in Babylon: W.T. Stead and the Pall Mall Gazette* (Lincoln: University of Nebraska Press, 1972), 171.

5. Michael Holroyd, *Bernard Shaw*, 4 vols. (New York: Random House, 1988–92), 1:138. Shaw was perhaps enthusiastic about the series because Stead opined that the future "belongs to the combined forces of Democracy and Socialism" ("We Bid You Be of Hope," *Pall Mall Gazette*, 6 Jul. 1885, 1).

6. Frederic Whyte, *The Life of W.T. Stead*, 2 vols. (London: Jonathan Cape, 1925), 1:175.

7. Trevor Fisher, *Scandal: The Sexual Politics of Late Victorian England* (Phoenix Mill: Alan Sutton, 1995), 89.

8. Whyte, *The Life of W.T. Stead*, 1:304.

9. "The Maiden Tribute of Modern Babylon," 10 Jul. 1885, 4. Stead later modified his attitude toward the theater; in 1910, he asserted that "theatre can be made a great instrument of public education and inspiration." He acknowledged, however, that many of his readers—supporters of a movement he had initiated—would not agree with this view ("The Relations of the Theatre to Public Morals—Part I," in *The Nation's Morals*, ed. James Marchant [London: Cassell, 1910], 193–94).

10. John Johnston, *The Lord Chamberlain's Blue Pencil* (London: Hodder and Stoughton, 1990), 29–30.

11. Rev. Thos. Philips, "The Relations of the Theatre to Public Morals—Part II," in *The Nation's Morals*, 195.

12. Jeffrey Weeks, *Sex, Politics, and Society: The Regulation of Sexuality since 1800* (London: Longman, 1989), 214.

13. George Bernard Shaw, "The Living Pictures," in *Our Theatres in the Nineties* (London: Constable and Co., 1932), 84.

14. Sally Peters, *Bernard Shaw: The Ascent of the Superman* (New Haven: Yale University Press, 1996), 220.

15. Shaw's battle with stage censorship has received considerable attention from scholars, so I do not recount his specific campaigns here. See Leon Hugo,

Edwardian Shaw: The Writer and his Age (New York: St. Martin's, 1999), 197–230; Lucy McDiarmid, "Augusta Gregory, Bernard Shaw, and the Shewing-Up of Dublin Castle," *PMLA* 109 (1994): 26–44; and Holroyd, *Bernard Shaw*, 2:224–38. For a general discussion of Edwardian stage censorship, see Samuel Hynes, *The Edwardian Turn of Mind* (Princeton: Princeton University Press, 1968), 212–53.

16. Shaw, "Living Pictures," 84; *The Shewing-up of Blanco Posnet*, in *Bernard Shaw: Collected Plays with Their Prefaces* (London: The Bodley Head, 1971), 3:733; "Theatres and Reviews Then and Now," in *Shaw on Theatre* (New York: Hill and Wang, 1958), 173; *Collected Letters*, 1:448.

17. James Marchant, *The Master Problem* (New York: Moffat, Yard, and Co., 1917), 281.

18. Shaw, "Living Pictures," 89.

19. Whyte, *The Life of W.T. Stead*, 2:314.

20. J. Ellen Gainor, *Shaw's Daughters: Dramatic and Narrative Constructions of Gender* (Ann Arbor: University of Michigan Press, 1991), 229. Gainor argues that these threats are finally realized in a "lesbian 'rape' scene" that displaces Higgins's actions onto those of Mrs. Pearce, his housekeeper (235–36). Nigel Alexander, Louis Crompton, Errol Durbach, and Charles Berst also note that *Pygmalion* raises questions about Eliza's fate at the hand of Higgins. Unlike Gainor, they assume that the play eventually "clears up" these concerns. See Alexander, *A Critical Commentary on Bernard Shaw's* Arms and the Man *and* Pygmalion (London: Macmillan, 1968), 62–65; Crompton, "Improving *Pygmalion*," *Prairie Schooner* 41 (1967): 74; Durbach, "*Pygmalion*: Myth and Anti-Myth in the Plays of Ibsen and Shaw," *English Studies in Africa* 21 (1978): 29; and Berst, *Pygmalion*, 63.

21. Bernard Shaw, *Pygmalion* (1916; reprint, London: Penguin, 1944), 19–20. Subsequent references are to this edition and will be cited parenthetically in the text.

22. Berst, *Bernard Shaw*, 204.

23. Judith Walkowitz, *City of Dreadful Delight: Narratives of Sexual Danger in Late-Victorian England* (Chicago: University of Chicago Press, 1992), 94.

24. Walkowitz notes that reformers concerned with young girls as "sexual objects" often pursued their reform work in "perverse" or "prurient" ways, revealing the fine line between predation and philanthropy (*Prostitution and Victorian Society: Women, Class, and the State* [Cambridge: Cambridge University Press, 1980], 249).

25. Edward Bristow, *Vice and Vigilance: Purity Movements in Britain since 1700* (Totowa: Rowman and Littlefield, 1977), 193.

26. Shaw's dismissal of the drugging myth might seem callous, but it appears that there were few facts to substantiate such tales. The *Vigilance Record* noted that "in spite of careful investigation, [the NVA] had never been able to establish the truth of such statements" ("An Incredible Story—But True," *The Vigilance Record* 9 [1915]: 75). The case of Mrs. Allen, investigated in November of 1927, reveals that the meaning of "drugging" was unstable. The widow claimed that a male friend had drugged her coffee and impregnated her; after several interviews, the NVA investigator concluded that a small amount of beer had been added to the coffee in front of Mrs. Allen. A female friend of the widow, present at the time, insisted that Allen did not seem "drugged" by the concoction (NVA Archives, Fawcett Library, Box 116, file 14).

27. Gainor, *Shaw's Daughters*, 230.

28. Walkowitz, *City*, 124.

29. Shaw remembered Eliza Armstrong's name years after the "Maiden Tribute" scandal; in 1922, he joked that "Armstrong (not Eliza)" smuggled him onto the *PMG* staff (Whyte, *The Life of W.T. Stead*, 1:305).

30. "The Maiden Tribute of Modern Babylon," 6 Jul. 1885, 6.

31. For additional variations on Shaw's ending, see Robert G. Everding, "Shaw and the popular context," in *The Cambridge Companion to George Bernard Shaw*, ed. Christopher Innes (Cambridge: Cambridge University Press, 1998), 315–16.

32. See, for example, Arnold Silver's contention that the postscript enabled Shaw to indirectly attack Stella Campbell, who brought their year-long flirtation to an end in the fall of 1913 (Silver, *Bernard*, 255). While the "affair" with Campbell may have influenced Shaw's revisions of *Pygmalion*, this interpretation requires a biographical reading of the play. I am arguing that *Pygmalion* needs to be placed within larger socio-political contexts and that the postscript works to preserve the "Maiden Tribute" parody.

33. Tracy C. Davis notes that Higgins has "in effect enslaved" Eliza "by taking away [her] independence as a kerbstone flower seller" ("Shaw's interstices of empire: decolonizing at home and abroad," in *The Cambridge Companion to George Bernard Shaw*, 225). By depriving Eliza of economic self-sufficiency, and thus leaving her no option but to marry, Higgins brutalizes Eliza in a way that Stead never imagined.

34. On the day that the play opened, the *Daily Sketch* covered its front page with pictures of Mrs. Patrick Campbell in her most famous parts (Richard Huggett, *The Truth about* Pygmalion [New York: Random House, 1969], 127). Such publications insured that audiences would associate Mrs. Campbell's Eliza with the actress's previous roles.

35. Shaw, *Collected Letters*, 2:219.

36. Elliott Simon, "Arthur Wing Pinero's *The Second Mrs Tanqueray*: A Reappraisal," *Ball State University Forum* 28 (1987): 47.

37. Sos Ann Eltis, "'Did Good Woman Ever Play Bad Woman So Well?': Typecasting and Cross-Casting the Victorian Actress," Women on the British Stage Panel, MLA Convention, San Francisco Hilton, 29 Dec. 1998.

38. Mrs. Patrick Campbell, *My Life and Some Letters* (London: Hutchinson, 1922), 62. Pinero's biographer states that the play achieved "a total . . . of 228 performances and a profit of over £10,000" during its first run. It also made a successful tour of provincial centers. See John Dawick, *Pinero: A Theatrical Life* (Niwot: University Press of Colorado, 1993), 200.

39. Eltis, "Did Good Woman,'" 29 Dec. 1998.

40. Campbell, *My Life*, 83.

41. Elaine Aston and George Savona, *Theatre as Sign-System: A semiotics of text and performance* (London: Routledge, 1991), 103.

42. Joel Kaplan, "Pineroticism and the problem play: Mrs Tanqueray, Mrs Ebbsmith and 'Mrs Pat,'" in *British Theatre in the 1890s*, ed. Richard Foulkes (Cambridge: Cambridge University Press, 1992), 55. In a review of a different production that same year, the theater critic William Archer observed that such applause was mainly due to Campbell's "extraordinary beauty and elegance" ("Fedora," in *The Theatrical 'World' of 1895* [London: Walter Scott, 1896], 179).

43. Margot Peters, *Mrs. Pat: The Life of Mrs. Patrick Campbell* (New York: Alfred A. Knopf, 1984), 106.

44. Peters, *Mrs. Pat*, 106–107.

45. Eltis, "Did Good Woman,'" 29 Dec. 1998.

46. Peters, *Mrs. Pat*, 365.

47. *Vanity Fair*, 30 Apr. 1914, 26.

48. Shaw, *Collected Letters*, 4:157.

49. Gail Marshall argues that nineteenth-century actresses had to negotiate a "sculpture metaphor" that was authorized by the Pygmalion-Galatea myth (*Actresses on the Victorian Stage: Feminine Performance and the Galatea Myth* [Cambridge: Cambridge University Press, 1998], 4). Marshall largely ignores Mrs. Campbell in her study; in a brief endnote, she simply observes that the actress was criticized for her adherence to the sculptural (Galatean) model when other actresses, such as Eleanora Duse, were becoming known for their interpretive engagement (214 n. 67). I describe Campbell as "Galatean" because of her profound sexual appeal; while I find Marshall's study suggestive, I do not here consider Campbell's intellectual engagement with the roles she performed.

STUART E. BAKER

Major Barbara

The Organic and the Didactic

*M*ajor *Barbara* provides the first step of Shaw's journey out of hell into heaven, out of the despair of impotency to the triumph of Godhead. We should not expect it to supply a map, for the region is uncharted. It does show us how we must start, which is task enough, for the first step is as difficult and terrifying as the exit from the womb. *Major Barbara* is the single most complete statement of Shaw's philosophy and the epitome of the dramatic method he developed to express that philosophy. It is the most Shavian of Shaw's plays. By now he had mastered the technique, first successfully used in *Candida*, of presenting a reality both difficult to contemplate and worthy of respect. His chosen role as "interpreter of life" is no longer disguised in popular theatrical confectionery but is brought into the foreground, while the action moves simply where his dramatic imagination takes him. And for the first time we see evidence of internal conflict in his dramatic method: a clash between the free narrative of real people struggling with their circumstances and the need to provide an "interpretation" of something far below the surface of life as it is consciously lived. To serve the parable, Shaw put constraints on his characters that we do not see in any previous play. There are awkward moments when one character is clearly feeding a line to another, such as the following exchange in the second act:

From *Bernard Shaw's Remarkable Religion: A Faith That Fits the Facts*, pp. 123–46, 247–49. Copyright © 2002 by Stuart E. Baker.

CUSINS. . . . Barbara is quite original in her religion.

UNDERSHAFT [*triumphantly*] Aha! Barbara Undershaft would be. Her
inspiration comes from within herself.

CUSINS. How do you suppose it got there?

UNDERSHAFT [*in towering excitement*] It is the Undershaft inheritance.
(3:120)

"How do you suppose it got there?" is not a question worthy of Cusins, but
it allows Undershaft to makes his paradoxical point.

This conflict of purpose may be the reason Shaw found it necessary to
do the must extensive revision he had yet undertaken of any play since *The
Philanderer.* The changes were of a different nature from those applied to the
early play. The revisions of *The Philanderer* tended to cut out Shaw's penchant
for letting the characters dictate to their author where to take the play and to
bring it more into the familiar, structured pattern of farcical comedy, that is,
to make it less "organic" and more conventional; the changes made to *Major
Barbara* help resolve potential conflicts between Shaw's "organic" and didactic
tendencies and so help make it even more Shavian, rather than more conventional. The most sweeping changes were to the second scene of the third
act, which was entirely rewritten. Shaw was right in his dissatisfaction with
the original, for the first draft was dramatically inferior to the final product,
but missteps can be illuminating.[1] One of the most interesting changes is an
alteration in the moral and intellectual debate between Cusins and Undershaft. In the original draft (called the "Derry" manuscript), Undershaft is
unambiguously the winner and Cusins is clearly brought around to Undershaft's point of view. In the final version, Cusins is changed but remains his
own man at the end. The resulting intellectual ambiguity is interesting, and
the exact nature of its significance is an important question in determining
the play's meaning.

Anomalies in the Action

The dramatic structure of the play is especially unusual. In all of the preceding plays the action is a clear development of the desires of the characters
in conflict with each other and their circumstances: classic examples for a
teacher of play analysis. *Caesar and Cleopatra* may appear an exception, but
its episodic nature is merely a shell for the true action: the partly successful education of Cleopatra. When Shaw uses a conventional "complication"
to change the course of the action, it helps complete the picture, showing
us more fully how the characters behave by altering their circumstances.
The change in the status of the slums proposed by Lickcheese in *Widowers' Houses* and the arrival of the American navy in *Captain Brassbound's*

Conversion both change the action in order to illuminate it. The fundamental conflict remains clear and consistent. Despite the intense philosophical concerns of both *Man and Superman* and *John Bull's Other Island*, Shaw lets the unfolding of the story take precedence over any attempt to contrive the morality of the piece. The result is a pair of organic if unconventional works that are more successful as art than as complete statements of Shaw's beliefs. *Major Barbara* is a different case.

An overview of the play's action will make its oddness clear. The first scene ends with a reversal that sets the tone for numerous shifts the action will take as the play progresses. We are led to believe that Lady Britomart is (apparently for the first time) asking her eldest child to make an important decision regarding the family finances, then we suddenly learn that the decision has been made and that Stephen was being asked only to take responsibility for it. This might be just an amusing way to provide exposition, but it is characteristic of the entire play, which is a mosaic of altered and overturned expectations. Indeed, the scene between Lady Britomart and Stephen introduces an action that is dropped toward the end of the first act, ignored entirely in the second, and picked up again in the third only to be resolved in a casual anticlimax. The problem presented by the first act, like that of *Widowers' Houses*, is the need for money and the moral difficulty of obtaining it from a "tainted" source—in this case the profits from the death and destruction factory of Stephen's father, Andrew Undershaft. We are made to suspect that Stephen's sister Barbara, a recent convert to the Salvation Army, will have moral objections to both the money and her father's character. As soon as the father makes his entrance, this expected conflict melts away and is forgotten. The money is not mentioned, the daughter shows herself to be surprisingly free of moralizing priggishness, and the father becomes unaccountably fascinated with both the daughter he has just met and her religion of poverty. A new question arises from the meeting of father and daughter. It is a kind of battle of missionaries; each will try to convert the other and both agree to submit to the attempt. Undershaft will visit the Salvation Army shelter, and Barbara will come to the munitions works. This action, which involves two distinct steps, is also interrupted by the resumption of the question raised in the first act. The question of obtaining additional income for the two sisters, which is treated with awkwardly indelicate delicacy in the first act, is settled with casual abruptness in the first scene of the third act. When Andrew, obviously ignorant of the purpose of his invitation, asks after his first entrance, "What can I do for you all?," Lady Brit tells him that he need not do anything but sit and enjoy himself, a remark that puts everyone out of countenance and successfully evades the issue. Andrew's entrance in the third act is very different; he barely has time to draw a breath before Lady Brit peremptorily and emphatically demands more money for the girls. Undershaft agrees without a murmur. Strife occurs when she demands the inheritance of the factory for Stephen, but as Undershaft is resolute that it will go to a foundling as the tradition demands, and Stephen immediately renounces his claim, that conflict, too, disappears. Then the only difficulty—obviously not the central conflict of the play—is for Undershaft to find a suitable profession for Stephen, whose priggishly aristocratic upbringing has made him unfit for almost all gainful employment. But just as Stephen's inheritance of the factory is put entirely out of question, we casually learn that Undershaft has yet to find a foundling to inherit the munitions works. In the middle of the last act a new "action" is introduced. Then that is forgotten for the moment, as they gather together to accompany Barbara on her promised visit to the factory of death. It turns out to be a model of cleanliness and respectability rather than the pit of Hell, and Cusins, the neurasthenic and bespectacled professor of Greek, claims by a quibble to be an eligible foundling, offering himself as a candidate for the inheritance. His proposal is accepted virtually without hesitation. The conflict is not Cusins's trying to persuade Undershaft to accept a weak, inexperienced academic as his apprentice; it is not about his struggle to become the master of an arms empire that dominates Europe. No, it is Cusins's inner struggle with his conscience over the moral propriety of acceptance. The battle between Undershaft and Cusins at the end of the play is about the arms manufacturer's attempt to persuade the professor to abandon his moral standards. So many strange things have happened by now that we are not surprised when he accepts, or even when Barbara tells him that if he turned it down she would jilt him for the man who accepted. The "big" question at the end of the play is whether the young idealists will take on the factory; Cusins is the only one who asks the eminently sensible question: Why would Undershaft take on Cusins?

There is a sense in which we are being overly scrupulous here; it is a little like looking at the complexion of a beautiful woman with a powerful magnifying glass so as to "prove" how grotesque she really looks. The play is not incoherent, for the overall action is limpid: the mutual challenge of father and daughter and its conclusion in the father's favor. But there are many digressions and extraneous details whose purpose is not immediately apparent. We might expect that in a historical epic like *Caesar and Cleopatra*, where the busy pattern of historic fact is apt to clutter up the picture, but *Major Barbara* is presented frankly as a parable.[2] One expects a parable to be simple and—at least relatively—uncluttered. Part of the problem is that Shaw is using "real people I have met and talked to" as a means of telling his tale (*Collected Screenplays* 485). That makes the play much more interesting, but it complicates the task. Even more important is that the moral of this parable is not simple, Shaw crams a great deal into an evening's traffic on the stage. Even the action that emerges when one steps back far enough from the play is not without its peculiarities. The mutual attempts at conversion do not even proceed in a direct and straightforward, manner but are indirect and oblique. When Undershaft visits the Salvation Army shelter, Barbara does not spend any time trying to convert her father; she gives her entire attention to the conversion of Bill Walker. When Barbara comes to the munitions factory, her father spends only a few minutes talking to her; he devotes most of his time to converting Cusins, despite the remarkable, even obsessive, interest he had shown in Barbara during the two previous acts.

We have barely touched on the difficult *philosophical* issues of the play. It is not surprising that readers are confused by it, but at a good performance audiences are unaware of these difficulties. The play has a remarkable coherence in spite of all of these apparent irrelevancies and discontinuities. All of the complexities are resolved in the throughline of the play, which is ultimately simple, consistent, and unambiguous. A careful look at both the overall action and the details shows how they come together in an almost perfect whole.

An Illusory Conflict

The parable opposes two sets of seemingly irreconcilable principles, polar opposites that must be eternally at war: spirit against matter, religion against atheism, altruism versus egoism, heroic idealism opposed to cynical pragmatism. The triumph of Undershaft—or at least the triumph of Undershaft and Lazarus, Ltd., over the Salvation Army—can be interpreted as Chesterton saw it: "*Major Barbara* . . . contains a strong religious element; but when all is said, the whole point of the play is that the religious element is defeated" (190). A more popular view, at least among Shaw's fans, is that the play represents a Hegelian dialectic with the succession of Barbara and Cusins to the Undershaft throne as the final synthesis of spirit and power, idealism and pragmatism, growth and destruction (for example, Whitman 223–30). Although some, like Wisenthal, feel that Shaw successfully presents Cusins as an advance on Undershaft (and perhaps even Barbara), others are not convinced (*Marriage* 75–79). Turco, for example, believes that the play ultimately fails because Shaw does not succeed in presenting Cusins as a clear advance over his predecessor. Most critics now would reject Chesterton's view that religion, represented by Barbara, is defeated by materialism in the person of her father. Turco, in particular, has noted the many similarities between father and daughter. The difficulty is that critics are inclined to seek salvation in Cusins. Many find this view appealing, and there is evidence in the play to support it, but it is wrong. The play can be interpreted in a Hegelian manner, but Cusins does not represent the synthesis that emerges from the play as a whole. The real enemy is idealism, which is the refusal to look hard truths in the eye. Like *Candida*, but on a much deeper level, *Major Barbara* develops a conflict from an underlying unity, and the point is that the conflict is illusory or unnecessary. Many of the complexities and apparent contradictions are the result of the fact that the moral conflict, which first appears to Cusins so unavoidable, is artificial. The play does not deny the existence of evil, insisting emphatically that it cannot be avoided; it only denies the possibility of isolating and destroying it. Evil is not something that can be cut out like a cancer; it can only be transformed. It is part of us and we are part of it. We can try to repudiate it as alien to us, and we will find that we can do so only by choosing death over life, declaring a victory while accepting annihilation. But the play does represent the defeat of idealism, and if, like Chesterton, you are unable to see religion as other than a form of idealism, you must perforce agree with him about the moral of the play.

From such a point of view the play must be unbearably pessimistic. More important, much would appear irrelevant or incomprehensible, so complete understanding demands a realistic point of view. The play's purpose is to show us the path to heaven, a path forever invisible to idealist eyes. Only from the realist's point of view do all of the pieces of the dramatic picture—a map of the world and the spirit—fit meaningfully together.

Responsibilities and Choices

In *Major Barbara*, as in Shaw's other plays, the issues develop through the relationships of different sets of characters. One of Shaw's favorite devices is a triad of characters representing a range of approaches to a particular ethical or social problem. They might be presented in the abstract, like the Philistine, idealist, and realist of the *Quintessence*, or as three major characters in a play, such as Broadbent, Larry, and Keegan—in *John Bull's Other Island*. The use of three points of view permits greater complexity and avoids a simple dichotomy that would tempt us to see the issues as opposites of right and wrong. Here, the obvious trio is Undershaft, his daughter Barbara, and her fiancé Cusins, but nearly all of the characters are set off against each other in revealing ways. Sometimes the characters are paired and then bracketed with another person or set of characters. Lady Brit and Stephen are contrasted to Undershaft and Barbara. Mrs. Baines and Barbara represent different views of the mission of the Salvation Army. The four proletarians of the second act—Snobby, Rummy, Peter Shirley, and Bill Walker—serve as foils for and mirrors to each other.

Stephen and his mother, who open the play, are the representatives of the aristocracy, the traditional ruling classes. The scene between the two of them is not merely exposition; it begins, with a single note, the theme that will resonate in many complex chords later in the play. The issue is money, and the question is where to get it. Or so it seems, for we quickly learn, with Stephen, that the money must come from Undershaft's factory of death because there is no other possible source. Lady Brit's true objective in consulting with her son is not to ask for advice but to avoid responsibility for a moral decision that, although necessary, appears distasteful. She has made her decision and acted on it; she merely wants Stephen to take responsibility for it. In this scene, Lady Brit is the schoolmistress and Stephen her pupil. She instructs him, in word and deed, how the aristocracy approaches difficult moral questions. Stephen's horror of mentioning such "frightful" things as his father and his money produces this admonition from his mother: "It is only in the middle classes, Stephen, that people get into a state of dumb helpless horror when they find that there are wicked people in the world. In our class, we have to decide what is to be done with wicked people; and nothing should disturb our self-possession" (3:73). Thus we have the ruling-class solution: boldly face the facts, confidently take the money, and deftly shift the responsibility onto someone else.

This approach is not without its price. Lady Britomart steams into view as a classical dowager dreadnought, a moving mountain of indomitable will, but we later see that it is all bluff. She has no genuine power apart from her (very considerable) strength of character. When her husband, who has real power and knows it, opposes her, she is helpless. Even her son, who seemed so firmly under her thumb in the first scene, has only to declare his independence to achieve it. The strength that comes from position and the appearance of power is not inconsiderable, at least not until it is challenged by real power. In that way Stephen and his mother are alike. Had the business passed on to him, Stephen, like "all the other sons of the big business houses," would have had to hire a manager to run it. Even then the enterprise would run primarily on its own momentum, as Undershaft wisely notes (3:145). When that possibility is rejected by both Stephen and his father, the discussion moves to finding an alternative career. Stephen's aristocratic disdain for any ordinary profession eliminates all but one avenue: "He knows nothing and he thinks he knows everything. That points clearly to a political career," Undershaft sarcastically reminds them. Andrew may have had something of that sort in mind all along, as the other career choices were suggested merely as stepping-stones on the way to becoming prime minister. Even in the unlikely event that Stephen ever did make it to such a pinnacle of political eminence, his power would be circumscribed in much the same way that his mother's is, for in his next speech Undershaft declares, "I am the government of your country: I, and Lazarus." The moral choices of Andrew and his mother isolate

them from real power in ways that may not be readily obvious but are debili-
tating nonetheless. They are the "butts" of the piece, but Barbara and Cusins
are equally weakened by their attempt to take the moral high road. The differences between the aristocratic position of Stephen and Lady Britomart and
that taken by Cusins are obvious, but the similarities, which are crucial, are
overlooked. Stephen is sincere in his simplistic morality, but he is immature
and naïve. His mother's hypocrisy grows from an unwillingness to give up
either the moralism she shares with Stephen or the money and power she gets
from Undershaft. Cusins, as we shall see, suffers from a more subtle form of
the same disease.

The relationship of mother to son parallels in many ways that of Undershaft with Barbara and Cusins—both taken together and separately. Stephen
is his mother's protégé as Cusins and Barbara are Undershaft's. Stephen
has his position by virtue of birth and upbringing; Cusins and Barbara are
both, in a very real sense, adopted, for Undershaft has not previously known
his daughter. Seen from another viewpoint: Barbara and Cusins must both
qualify for their inheritance, while Stephen simply has the mantle laid across
his shoulders. More interesting, both heirs try to defy and even repudiate
the bequests, yet there is a real question how effective their claims to independence will be. Stephen declares his autonomy, but on the central questions of morality and power how different will he be—how different *can* he
be—from Lady Britomart? Even as he goes his own way, showing a healthy
ability to learn from his mistakes by apologizing to his father about his preju-
dices regarding Perivale St. Andrews, he reveals his naïveté afresh. Like the
educated gentleman he is, he caps his admiration for the wonderfully organized town with a quotation from Milton: "Peace hath her victories no less
renowned than War" (3:160). This is a stark contrast to Cusins, whose "it's
all horribly, frightfully, immorally, unanswerably perfect" shows him to be as
painfully sensitive to irony as Stephen is unconscious of it (3:158). Stephen's
hypocrisy is only slightly obscured by his confusion about the inconsistencies
in his position. These particular victories of peace are, of course, made possible
only by war. And why does he applaud the operation now that he has found
it to be clean and respectable? His objection was to the exploitation of war
and destruction; that has not changed. Did he imagine, like his sister, that just
because Perivale St. Andrews is engaged in the manufacture of weapons it
must have been "a sort of pit where lost creatures with blackened faces stirred
up smoky fires and were driven and tormented by [Undershaft]" (3:154)?
Yet he cannot escape his moralistic conviction that pain is good for the soul.
The pampered son of wealth and breeding worries that too much luxury will
destroy the workers' independence and sense of responsibility. Unlike Barbara, he has no comprehension that responsibility means having something

to do and knowing that if you do not do it it will not be done, not from having experienced egregious suffering. This superstition of the English upper classes allowed them to believe that having run a gauntlet of floggings at the hands of sadistic schoolmasters qualified them to govern an empire.

Parents and Children

If Stephen's independence of his mother is questionable, the same question can be raised about the succession of the Undershaft inheritance by Barbara and Adolphus. The closing line of the play—"Six o'clock tomorrow morning, Euripides"—underscores the unsettled nature of that question by reminding us that Cusins had not even agreed to the working hours Undershaft demanded.[3] How much will the next Andrew Undershaft be like or different from the present one? How much will the necessities imposed by the world and the realities of manufacturing and selling arms change the ideals of the saver of souls and the humanitarian professor of Greek? This is what the play is about: the spiritual and moral contest between father and daughter—solemnly agreed upon like a medieval joust.

The overturned expectations are nowhere more complex and enigmatic than in the relationship of the father, his daughter, and her suitor. All three are more than we might expect them to be, both in themselves and in their relations to the other two. Undershaft is the most obviously inscrutable. He is discussed as if he were a towering monster of evil; his first entrance reveals him as kindly, considerate, thoughtful, and somewhat embarrassed by being surrounded by a family he does not know. Money was the sole item on this meeting's agenda, but that is evaded—by the person who called the meeting—and the conversation is turned to religion—by Undershaft. He begins to question Barbara about the Salvation Army, and when his wife attempts to change this (to her) unpleasant subject by asking that Charles play something on his concertina "at once," he stops them by saying: "One moment, Mr Lomax. I am rather interested in the Salvation Army. Its motto might be my own: Blood and Fire" (3:88).

The reactions to this announcement are characteristic: Lomax is shocked, but Barbara, with perfect calm and unperturbed good nature, invites her father to come down to the shelter and "see what we're doing." She even has the audacity to ask the millionaire profiteer in mutilation and murder, the man who has all of Europe under his thumb, if he can play anything in their planned march. To Lomax's unspeakable amazement, he accepts as naturally and calmly as Barbara had asked. Father and daughter hit it off splendidly, and their common ground is religion. The opposition, for the moment, is represented by Lomax, who takes up the cause of moral purity championed earlier by Stephen and his mother. He succeeds in making the contradictions in that position even more obvious than had Lady Brit: "The cannon business may be necessary and all that: we cant get on without cannons; but it isnt right, you know." Lest anyone miss the point, Undershaft explains that he is not "one of those men who keep their morals and their business in watertight compartments." He is speaking for himself, as a munitions manufacturer, but his observation is valid for anyone who, like Lomax, regards the cannon business as necessary. This, as we shall see, includes just about everyone—and especially anyone who wishes to make the world a better place rather than just to deplore its wickedness.

Father is more firmly drawn to daughter in the exchange that follows his observation that there "is only one true morality for every man; but every man has not the same true morality." Stephen's contemptuous dismissal, that "some men are honest and some are scoundrels," is met by Barbara's "Bosh! There are no scoundrels." Immediately interested, Undershaft asks if there are any good men. When she assures him that there are neither good men nor scoundrels, he offers his challenge: "May I ask have you ever saved a maker of cannons?" Undershaft has clearly recognized something in his daughter that impels him to claim her, for if the audience suspects at this point that *he* is considering becoming one of *Barbara's* converts, they will be disabused in the next act.

The coda that resolves this scene is a counterpoint of religious attitudes. Barbara asks for "Onward, Christian Soldiers," Lomax volunteers "Thou'rt Passing Hence, My Brother," and Lady Britomart calls for prayers. The lines are drawn. Forced to choose, both Undershaft and Cusins declare their allegiance to Barbara's position rather than those of Lomax and Lady Brit, but there are differences. As usual, Undershaft is not explicit; he merely says that he has "conscientious scruples," but Cusins is diplomatically honest: he objects to the ritual confession of sin as unjust and untrue. He has worked for his moral rectitude, he has earned it and is proud of it, and he will not have it denied. His position is different from that of Lomax, Stephen, and Lady Britomart, or of Barbara and her father. He avoids the hypocrisy and confusion of the one by courage and honesty but lacks Barbara's cheerful rejection of moral stereotypes. Cusins does believe in scoundrels, or he would not work so hard to avoid becoming one.

Undershaft is, if anything, even more puzzling when we see him at the Salvation Army shelter. He is astonished that Barbara would suggest that he is a secularist, protesting that he is a "confirmed mystic," but pressed to identify his religion more specifically, he declares merely that he is a millionaire (3:110–11). When Cusins asks the same question, he explains that he believes that there are two things necessary to salvation: money and gunpowder. He does not explain the "mystical" nature of money, gunpowder, or his millions. Nor does he provide a metaphysical or spiritual basis for this "religion," other than to imply that it is the foundation on which ethical and spiritual values must necessarily rest (3:116). But his attraction to Barbara emerges more powerfully than ever. If there is doubt about the nature of his religion, there is none about his purpose here at the shelter: it is to win his daughter away from the Salvation Army to become apostle and missionary of the Undershaft religion. This is the exchange between Undershaft and Cusins:

UNDERSHAFT. . . . We have to win her; and we are neither of us Methodists.

CUSINS. That doesnt matter. The power Barbara wields here—the power that wields Barbara herself—is not Calvinism, not Presbyterianism, not Methodism—

UNDERSHAFT. Not Greek Paganism either, eh?

CUSINS. I admit that. Barbara is quite original in her religion.

UNDERSHAFT. Aha! Barbara Undershaft would be. Her inspiration comes from within herself.

CUSINS. How do you suppose it got there?

UNDERSHAFT [in towering excitement] It is the Undershaft inheritance. I shall hand on my torch to my daughter. She shall make my converts and preach my gospel—

CUSINS. What? Money and gunpowder!

UNDERSHAFT. Yes, money and gunpowder. Freedom and power. Command of life and command of death. (3:119–20)

This is a notable bit of dialogue. Undershaft sees more in Barbara than an intelligent and determined young woman deluded by religion. He is not like Peter Shirley, who thinks she would have been a "very taking lecturer on Secularism" if she had only learned to use her reason (3:111). Barbara's religion is her own; it is not something she has taken from the Salvation Army but something she has given it. Her father thinks it is his bequest. The unavoidable but amazing conclusion is that he sees his own religion in his daughter. He insists that the gospel she must preach is salvation by money and gunpowder.

The Undershaft Inheritance

What is the nature of Barbara's religion? Cusins sees that the power she uses is a power that uses her, just as later Undershaft speaks of being driven by a "will of which I am a part" (3:169). Is there a deeper reason for Undershaft to see himself in Barbara, or is he, as Cusins believes, simply mad? We see Barbara's religion at work in her treatment of Bill Walker. To understand

Barbara—and her relation to her father—we must look carefully at the way she handles Bill, but there is another clue to Barbara's spiritual power that is often overlooked.

In many ways Barbara's unique and individual religion is in harmony with that of the Salvation Army; this is why she could so easily find a home there. Cusins describes the Salvation Army as "the army of joy, of love, of courage," and we have many opportunities to see those qualities in Barbara personally (3:116). There is certainly no striking difference between Barbara and the Salvation Army with respect to what Shaw sees as the two opposing camps of Christianity: what he calls "Crosstianity" and (confusingly) Christianity. Crosstianity preaches salvation through the gibbet, while Christianity teaches the vanity of punishment and revenge. Logically, the two points of view are hopelessly irreconcilable, so that you would think that the division between them would form a major split dividing the followers of Jesus of Nazareth. Not so. It is a tribute to the powers of hypocrisy and muddled thinking that one can easily find members of the two camps sitting side by side in the same pew, listening to a sermon in which both of these contradictory notions are wholeheartedly endorsed. The reason the two are inconsistent is transparent. Salvation through the cross is the theory that two wrongs make a right carried to its most extravagant extreme. Evil must be balanced by evil, and the evil represented by the sins of humanity is so great that it can be wiped out only by the greatest imaginable wickedness: the torture and murder of God. The doctrine of atonement is thus deprived even of its only reasonable excuse: deterrence. God becomes humanity's whipping boy, but since the atonement was paid ere our own sins were possible, we need not even worry lest our sin bring pain to another; the sin has been paid for in advance and in full. It could be cynically argued that since God made man to sin, it is only right that God should be punished for it, but this is not what the Crosstians have in mind. The Christian doctrine of the Sermon on the Mount, in contrast, is (at least as Shaw understands it) a flat rejection of expiation as an attempt to cancel wickedness with more wickedness. The one belief is founded on the endorsement of atonement as solidly as the other is on its rejection. Barbara and the Salvation Army are in agreement here: they accept the injunction to judge not; they return good for evil, kindness for cruelty, and a helping hand for battering blows. They celebrate the life and teachings of Christ rather than His torment and execution.

There is a difference between Barbara and the others on this question, but it is subtle and largely latent—latent, that is, until Undershaft adds the catalyst that makes it manifest. On one level Undershaft's actions are plain: he wants to win Barbara over to Perivale St. Andrews, and the first step is to win her away from the Salvation Army. But how did he know his method would be effective? This question is not often asked. Most assume that he shows his daughter that the Salvation Army, because it is financially dependent on the likes of Bodger and Undershaft, is inescapably corrupt, but Shaw explicitly rejects this interpretation in his preface. Authors can be wrong about their own works, of course, but they at least deserve a hearing, and Shaw is emphatic on this point: he repudiates the notion that the Salvation Army "reduced itself to absurdity or hypocrisy" by accepting the donation of a distiller and a cannon founder. He condemns as idolatrous superstition the notion that certain coins are tainted by the hands through which they have passed. He notes with approval the assertion of an actual officer of the Salvation Army that "they would take money from the devil himself and be only too glad to get it out of his hands and into God's" (Pref. 3:35). An understanding of how Barbara's religion differs from that of the Salvation Army must begin at the most obvious and striking point of departure: the fact that Mrs. Baines accepts the money and Barbara does not. If the reason for Barbara's rejection is an unwillingness to accept tainted money, then Mrs. Baines is closer to Shaw's own position than is Barbara. That is unlikely. It would also mean that Mrs. Baines, in her open-eyed pragmatism, is closer to Undershaft than is his daughter. But if Barbara is *less* enlightened than the Salvation Army—from the *Undershaft* point of view—it is difficult to see why he should think her so special.

Religion and Responsibility

Barbara's disillusionment at the end of the second act illuminates the distinctive nature of her faith. It is special, for Barbara understands a fundamental truth missed by Mrs. Baines: the truth about the admonition to abstain from judgment. In the preface Shaw points out that "you can no more have forgiveness without vindictiveness than you can have a cure without a disease" (3:43). The essence of vindictiveness is the concept that a misdeed is something to be repaid. Forgiveness is the cancellation of a debt, and sin (to use Barbara's terminology) is not a debt. It cannot be erased; it can only be stopped. This, Shaw says, is a profound point of his disagreement with the Salvation Army, and Barbara is on his side, not the Army's. Barbara demonstrates the practical wisdom of the Sermon on the Mount in fighting brutality and cruelty. She treats Bill Walker as an equal, a fellow sinner and child of God. She talks about his assaults on Jenny and Rummy as casually as she might his clothing or his trade: she actually suggests it *is* his trade. She does not bully, threaten, or condemn him. In fact, she does nothing to save his soul, as that is generally understood. She merely encourages Bill's soul to save *him*. Rummy's violent vindictiveness justifies his brutality, and so, in a real sense, he is comfortable with her. Together they inhabit a world in which anger begets anger and violence excuses more violence. When Barbara tells Bill that he cannot buy his salvation, either in coin or in kind, what she really means is that she will not let him buy off his soul, she will not permit him to bribe his conscience. Moral responsibility, the theme raised and evaded in the first act, is the core of Barbara's morality and the expression of her religion. Her enemy is its evasion. In Barbara's religion, salvation is achieved not through works, not faith, and certainly not pain or atonement, but by responsibility to one's own soul. Anything that erects a wall between a man's conscience and his consciousness is her foe.

The wall closes like an iron gate when her father signs his check. Barbara treats her father and Bill Walker alike, as she sees it, they "are the same sort of sinner, and theres the same salvation ready for them" both (3: 89). Curiously, Undershaft invites the comparison. He first offers twopence to round out the meager collection from their meeting, then proposes to add ninety-nine pounds to the one Bill bids for the purchase of his soul. He appears to be testing his daughter, testing her devotion to the religion of responsibility. She does not waver: "You cant buy your salvation here for twopence: you must work it out" (3:123). Jenny Hill, an orthodox Salvationist, argues for taking the money. Barbara's refusal shows precisely where she differs from the Army. She understands, where Jenny does not, that the acceptance of conscience money, however desperately needed, defeats the work of saving souls—at least as Barbara conceives that work. Undershaft's action highlights the difference and reveals the strategic weakness in Barbara's position: she cannot do without conscience money because that is all the money available. Bill is not convinced that consciences cannot be bought here; he contends that he is not allowed to buy off his soul only because he cannot come up with the price.

All this leads to the scene of hushed awe in which Undershaft signs his check. The charged pause is broken by Bill's "Wot prawce selvytion nah?" Barbara's silence, maintained after her initial brief expression of dismay at the news of Bodger's offer, is over as well. Her father's check confirmed Bill's cynicism and justified his contempt. His conscience has been bribed by proxy. She must protest now, as keenly as she feels the Army's need for the money, because *her* vision of the Salvation Army is on the edge of annihilation. She cannot demand moral responsibility only from those who cannot afford the price of irresponsibility. Even if she could accept such inconsistency and discrimination, she knows that as long as the Bill Walkers of the world understand that consciences are for sale, her sword must turn to straw. After a valiant last stand, she accepts the inevitability of defeat. Like a soldier yielding his sword, she submits her badge of Salvation to her father. It is unconditional surrender.

Undershaft has helped to illuminate Barbara, but he himself remains a mystery. If anything, he has become more enigmatic: Why, short of maliciousness, has he done this? He robs her of her faith, but what does he offer in return but cynicism and pessimism? Undershaft challenges his daughter to seek a new and better faith when she sees that the old one has failed. Like Barbara, we would be glad for a better one, but can see only a worse. Does he want to break her spirit? To destroy the very qualities that had drawn him to her? Everything he has said suggests that he believes her particular religious inspiration allies her naturally with him, and not the Salvation Army; he wants Barbara *because* of her unique religion. The faiths of daughter and father become one in the final scene.

Father and Daughter

Barbara's attention is directed toward Bill Walker rather than her father in the second act, and Undershaft does battle with Cusins rather than his daughter in the third. This curious indirectness is the consequence of the point that Shaw makes: that there is no real conflict between father and daughter, that they are two sides of one coin, two manifestations of the same spirit. The apparent conflict between the two is a misunderstanding, the result of Barbara's youth and inexperience. In this parable, Barbara stands for religion, spirit, and morality; her father for matter, wealth, and destructive power. The third act brings them together by showing that the barrier between them is only a wall of lies erected to protect weak and sensitive consciences from reality. There is a genuine conflict in the play, however: a conflict between ideas. Barbara and Undershaft are on the same side. Theirs is the camp that views the world as one, not divided into good and evil. Their world has no scoundrels or good men, only children of the same Father: or in Shavian terms, different expressions of the Life Force. We see one side of that unity in the second act and another in the third. The reason that Shaw needs Bill Walker to provide a subject for Barbara's soul-saving skills is that, while they are effective and greatly needed in this soul-destroying world of ours, they would be useless against her father. They are not too weak; they are simply redundant. Retribution, atonement and repayment are the bricks and mortar with which Bill Walker, like most of us, builds walls of evasion around his soul; Barbara saves it by tearing down the walls. Bill is not allowed to escape from his conscience with money or pain. Andrew Undershaft does not attempt to avoid his soul; he takes pride in standing up and facing it. He refuses to spend money on "hospitals, cathedrals, and other receptacles for conscience money," and puts his spare cash instead into research on bombs and bullets (3:89). His motto is "Unashamed." Since he refuses to hide from his conscience, he can remain unashamed only by doing nothing shameful. His soul does not need salvation because it is already strong and free.

Undershaft's clear conscience is not enough to demonstrate an affinity between father and daughter if all it means is that her conscience is strong and healthy while his is dead or dying—if Barbara is a saint and Undershaft a scoundrel.[4] If that is so then Barbara's defeat does mean cynicism and despair. Dramatically, the question is whether Barbara can accept the cannon foundry and what it represents without compromising all that she represents. The answer to this question lies in Undershaft's "true faith of an Armorer" and the mottoes of the seven successive Undershafts. Barbara declares that there are no saints or scoundrels; she practices what Shaw calls moral equality, and she espouses, by her actions, the Christian precept to "judge not." The Armorer's faith is the logical extension of that rule. The second Undershaft was explicit on this point: "ALL HAVE THE RIGHT TO FIGHT. NONE HAVE THE RIGHT TO JUDGE" (3:168). The Armorer's faith still shocks and puzzles critics, although Shaw takes pains to explain it in his preface. It is not a glorification of machismo and combat for its own sake; it is the ultimate test of Barbara's principles of moral equality, an affirmation that you cannot divide the world into good people and bad. Undershaft, like his daughter, is an ethical anarchist. He is not necessarily a social anarchist, as we see both in his speech on social organization to Stephen and, more significantly, the experiments in social cooperation and community welfare he has created in Perivale St. Andrew. Undershaft understands the need for social organization, but he also understands that socialism must be founded on what Shaw called the "Anarchist Spirit" (*Impossibilities of Anarchism* 23). The organization of civilization must not outrage the consciences of its individual members. Whenever it does, it will justify the "morality of militarism" and individualist defiance that Undershaft represents. As Shaw observes, "the justification of militarism is that circumstances may at any time make it the true morality of the moment" (Preface 3:50). The one true morality for each man or woman, Undershaft maintains, is dependent on circumstances. His own circumstances include a financial dependence on the manufacture of arms, but all who find their consciences outraged by a social system that methodically degrades and brutalizes large numbers of its citizens will find that militarism must become their own true morality—if they have the courage to face reality. "The consent of the governed" has been the accepted foundation of our political theory for centuries, yet Undershaft's bald statement of its implications still shocks the very people who regard themselves as the champions of liberal democracy.

Foundations are not pretty, and Undershaft represents the foundation of the same principles of which Barbara embodies the superstructure. He makes this clear in the brief exchange he has with her in the final scene. He saved her soul from the crime of poverty and allowed her to become Major Barbara, to become a champion of spirit and saver of souls. Foundations, however hard to look at, are essential. You cannot free the soul without first freeing the body; you cannot serve others without first serving yourself; you cannot give to others if you have impoverished yourself. And you can only choose from the alternatives which are presented to you. Undershaft says:

> I had rather be a thief than a pauper. I had rather be a murderer than a slave. I dont want to be either; but if you force the alternative on me, then by Heaven, I'll chose the braver and more moral one. I hate poverty and slavery worse than any other crimes whatsoever. (3:174)

Make no mistake, when Undershaft says that poverty and slavery are crimes, he means that the pauper and slave are criminals. By accepting the degradation society has imposed on them they are guilty of unspeakable sins against the Life Force that can be redeemed only by the courage to rebel against it. Undershaft offers them the means. When bloodshed is the only alternative to degradation of oneself, "Thou shalt starve ere I starve" becomes the foundation of all ethics.[5] What is wanted is "courage enough to embrace this truth" (3:173).

That is why Andrew Undershaft needs Barbara. Undershaft points out that he "can make cannons: [he] cannot make courage and conviction" (3:169). That is what is wanted. He can provide the means for those who are willing to risk their lives in order to save their souls, but he cannot give them the will to do it. That is the truth about his own well-fed, comfortably housed, and self-satisfied workers. He has not only saved them, like his daughter, from the crime of poverty; he has saved them from the need to fight their way out of it. There is no reason to believe that they would have had the necessary courage and conviction if he had not. If the conviction needed is faith in their own equality, they would fail the test; Undershaft is the only one who thinks of the workers as equals: they want nothing to do with such radical notions. Andrew comments that the mosaic in the William Morris Labor Church, "No Man Is Good Enough to Be Another Man's Master," shocked his men. Obviously, the motto was his idea (this is explicit in the original manuscript) (3:162–63). There is plenty of hierarchy and inequality at Perivale St. Andrew, but none of it originates from Undershaft, save that which is a spontaneous reaction to his personality. It is created and enforced by the workers themselves, although the inequality in income that justifies the hierarchy and is justified by it merely augments the profits of the owner, as Undershaft wryly notes. Shaw is making the same point Gunnar Myrdal made the foundation of his 1944 study of American race relations:

> Our hypothesis is that in a society where there are broad social classes and, in addition, more minute distinctions and splits in the lower strata, *the lower class groups will, to a great extent, take care of keeping each other subdued*, thus relieving, to that extent, the higher classes of this otherwise painful task necessary to the monopolization of the power and the advantages. (68) (Emphasis in original)

Cusins, like most of the critics, sees nothing but cynicism in Undershaft's recognition of this truth, but Shaw's point is that this attitude among the exploited perpetuates their exploitation regardless of the wishes of the upper-classes. Most liberals and socialists come from the comfortable classes. The irony is not, as Cusins believes, that the workers are Undershaft's willing accomplices in his gulling of them; it is that no one can be forced to accept the responsibility of freedom who prefers the comfort and safety of slavery. If men are docile and acquiescent when forced into brutal and degrading circumstances, should we expect them to accept painful responsibility when they are well-fed and self-satisfied? Shaw believed that one of the worst effects of poverty was to maim souls beyond redemption, but nourished bodies do not necessarily produce flourishing souls. In the Derry manuscript, Undershaft tells Barbara that she is proof of the "principle that if you take care of people's bodies their souls will take care of themselves," but he also accepts Cusins's description of his workers as slaves: "To those who are worth their salt as slaves, I give the means of life. But to those who will not or cannot sell their manhood . . . I give the means of death" (200–06). In the revised version, he merely challenges Barbara to "Try your hand on my men: their souls are hungry because their bodies are full" (3:173). Some hearty souls, like Barbara's, will thrive untended if they have good soil, but most others require more careful attention. That is Barbara's job.

The unity that binds Undershaft and his daughter together is the unity in which they both believe. Neither is afraid of evil because neither believes in its existence as a separate entity, a formidable Other. Each has utter confidence in the basic goodness of other human beings: Barbara in Bill Walker, and Undershaft in the varieties of human beings to whom he sells his arms. Many otherwise perceptive critics go astray when confronted with Undershaft; they cannot comprehend how such a unity is possible because they imagine that Undershaft advocates indiscriminate murder, but that is not in the least what he is saying. Like his daughter, the sire of Major Barbara has faith in the consciences of his brothers and sisters—fellow children of God. Barbara trusts Bill's conscience to persuade him not to assault women, and Andrew appeals to the consciences of the poor to demand their freedom and dignity—and to be willing to kill if it is not granted. For Shaw, as for Undershaft, poverty and slavery are forms of living death, to accept them is to acquiesce in your own murder. If killing is the only alternative offered to you, to choose the sword is to choose life. The issue is whether to passively accept a large evil rather than actively choose a lesser one. Most tolerate the greater evil rather than allow themselves to feel contaminated by active participation in the lesser. Undershaft does not, and that is the source of his contempt for the lust after "personal righteousness."

Some critics imagine that Shaw is offering Undershaft as a kind of Savior of Mankind, an idea he vehemently repudiated (*Collected Letters* 3:629). The search for a savior is quixotic folly because saviors are an idealist delusion. If Shaw often depicted strong, positive and dynamic characters like Undershaft it was not because he was dotty about Great Men, as some imagine; it is because he believed in the future and wished to point us toward what we might become rather than rub our noses in our present follies. Caesar, Undershaft, Joan, and Lady Cicely are not supermen and superwomen, because the superman does not yet exist. They are only hints as to what he might become. Barbara and her father are both such beacons of the future because they have unified souls, they have faith in their own wills, and they have each dedicated themselves to a cause beyond themselves. They are both doing God's work because they have given themselves over to the Will of which they are a part, the piece of deity in each of them. They look at the world with open eyes and know the only way to combat the copious evil they see is to face and transform it. To flee only grants it possession of the field. They are realists. Barbara's vision was at first obscured by her youth and ignorance, but she has her father's eyes. The real conflict is not between father and daughter, but between realism and idealism. Idealism, not surprisingly, has many champions. Nearly everyone else in the play expresses some idealist notion, but the most important advocates of the idealist viewpoint are Stephen, his mother, and especially Cusins.

Cusins

Yes, Cusins is an idealist. He is the best example of that superior variety of the human species to be found in all of Shaw's plays. He is highly intelligent, strong in will, conscientious to the point of self-destruction, and remarkably perceptive. He illustrates in an extreme degree both the admirable and the pernicious traits Shaw saw as the marks of an idealist. The principle difference between his idealism and that of Lady Britomart or Stephen is that he is far more perceptive and clear-headed, so that idealism leads him to bitter irony and cynicism rather than hypocrisy and self-deception. Cusins is set apart ethically from Lady Brit and Stephen by the fact that they are moralists while he is conscientious. Undershaft makes the difference clear when he says to his wife: "My dear: you are the incarnation of morality. Your conscience is clear and your duty done when you have called everybody names." Morality tells us to condemn those whose behavior we find disagreeable; conscience tells us how we ourselves should or should not behave. Stephen's concern that too much pampering will be bad for the souls of workers is a more subtle form of morality because it is unconscious of any similar deleterious effect his own privileges might have on his character. Stephen regards a clear conscience as his birthright; Cusins knows he has to work for his. Stephen worries about maintaining the character of others (especially those in the lower orders), Cusins worries about his own. Undershaft, however, classes Cusins as a moralist along with his wife. Cusins's lust for a clear conscience he calls "patronizing people who are not so lucky as yourself" (3:177). This is an interesting statement of the principle of moral equality, implying that a person born with a flawed character is unlucky in the same way as one born with a club foot. Bill Walker is a ruffian largely as a result of his circumstances, according to Undershaft, for he ventures that he could save his soul more effectively than Barbara just by giving him a job and a decent income. Environment is not the only culprit: there are congenital character defects as well as physical ones, but a person born with a murderous temper is quite as unfortunate as one born with a withered arm. A moral disability is as worthy of compassion as a physical one. That is why Undershaft equates the lust for personal righteousness with "patronizing people not so lucky as yourself." It is Undershaft's equivalent of the Christian "There but for the grace of God, go I." The very fact that Cusins wants to avoid being a rascal means that he too divides the world into rascals and heroes. He would distribute the black and white hats differently from Stephen or Lady Britomart, but the principle is the same.

This is how Undershaft greets Cusins's claim to believe in love:

UNDERSHAFT. I know. You love the needy and the outcast: you love the oppressed races, the negro, the Indian ryot, the underdog everywhere. Do you love the Japanese? Do you love the French? Do you love the English?

CUSINS. No. Every true Englishman detests the English. We are the wickedest nation on earth; and our success is a moral horror.

UNDERSHAFT. That is what comes of your gospel of love, is it? (3:177)

This passage is an assault on liberal idealism that has puzzled even the best of Shaw's critics. When Shaw says that we are all expressions of the Life Force, imperfect manifestations of God's attempts to become perfect, Shavians nod in assent, but when he insists that is as true of the thief as the saint, or the capitalist as the worker, many cannot take him seriously. But the gospel of love falls apart when love is denied to those you have condemned as wicked: those less fortunate than yourself. So Cusins is a moralist as well, but rather than directing his moral scorn safely outward like Stephen and his mother, he directs it toward himself and those groups of which he is a member. If Barbara and her father are alike in possessing unified souls, Cusins's soul is marked by division and conflict. Shaw describes him as a man whose health is being destroyed by a perpetual struggle between his conscience and impulses of which he does not approve. To judge from the passages he quotes, his favorite Greek tragedy is *The Bacchae*, and like Pentheus, he is being torn apart. Pentheus is both drawn to and repelled by Dionysus; Cusins is drawn to both Barbara and Andrew Undershaft in spite of his conscience, and he casts both of them in the role of Dionysus.[6] Yet he calls Barbara his "guardian angel" and turns to her father to exclaim "Avaunt!" (3:156). He describes himself as a "poor professor of Greek, the most artificial and self-suppressed of human creatures" (3:117). His answer to bigotry, intolerance, and class snobbery is to reverse the roles of the condemned and the privileged. Instead of damning others, he damns himself. He identifies himself with the English when he calls England the wickedest nation on earth. After accepting the role of apprentice to Undershaft, he justifies himself by saying that he loves the common people and wants to arm them against the intellectuals, a group to which he himself conspicuously belongs. His love of the poor is only pity, which Undershaft contemptuously dismisses as the "scavenger of misery." His condemnation of the English and the intellectuals is self-hatred inspired by guilty consciousness of his own privileges and comforts. His attempt to achieve moral purity by avoiding contact with wickedness is doomed. It is not only ruining his health, but when the strain is brought to crisis at the conclusion of the second act, he suffers what amounts to a moral nervous collapse and wallows hysterically in what he is convinced is evil, even to the point of getting drunk with the man he calls the Prince of Darkness (who stays characteristically sober). Unlike Barbara and Undershaft, he views transgressions as debts to be repaid. He approves, to Barbara's dismay, of Bill's attempt to pay for his misdeed, and rejects forgiveness, not (like Shaw and Barbara) because the concept is fraudulent, but because "we must pay our debts" (3:114, 178). Many critics, themselves liberal intellectuals, believe that Cusins will be an improvement on the old Andrew Undershaft because of his commitment to arm the oppressed rather than the establishment. This is a desperate hope at best. The new Undershaft, like the old, will have to sell to whom he can in order to thrive, and can no more make courage and conviction than his predecessor. Barbara is the real hope, because the job at hand is to awaken dormant souls.

Revisions

There were two significant trends in the many changes Shaw made to the final scene of the play: one was to make Cusins a strong and more steadfast advocate of the idealist viewpoint. The other was to pull Barbara more into the background. The portrayal of Cusins in the Derry manuscript is dramatically unfocused; in the final version he is a stronger opponent to Undershaft. Speeches are added to set him apart from Undershaft and others deleted that had shown him coming over to the older man's position. The original ending was less ambiguous with respect to the struggle between Cusins and Undershaft. Barbara, on the other hand, has considerably less to say in the final version of the last scene. Some of her dialogue, like her reproach to her father about robbing from her a human soul, is moved to earlier in the play. Some minor lines are given to other characters, and others are cut. Curiously, the effect of this is to give her greater strength, as the men are engaged in a struggle for her—more specifically, for the spiritual power and moral authority she represents. The parable is also better served since some of her almost peevish objections to the munitions plant in the original undercut her final acceptance of it. The unity of father and daughter is made clearer while the ideological conflict of realism and idealism is made more vital through the strengthening of Cusins. There is no ambiguity about the philosophical meaning of the play: that is dear and consistent. The only question remaining at the end of the play is whether Cusins, the moralist, will change. Much depends on the answer. If he does not, if we go on dividing the human race into the righteous and the unrighteous, we will perpetuate evil rather than exterminate it. Barbara knows you cannot cure evil by either hiding or punishing. Only by facing it—with strength but without vindictiveness—can we begin to challenge the multitude of social evils our bungled and hysterical attempts at civilization have brought upon us. That is what *Major Barbara* is about.

Notes

1. A thorough and informative discussion of Shaw's numerous and substantial revisions of the play can be found in Bernard Dukore's Introduction to *Major Barbara: A Facsimile of the Holograph Manuscript*. Dukore's analysis details the many ways in which Shaw's changes improve the dramatic structure of the play.

2. Shaw implies at the end of the preface that the play should be considered as a parable when he "solemnly" denounces anyone foolhardy enough to claim it as a record of actual fact. Lest anyone miss the point, he made it utterly explicit for the British version of the film: "What you are about to see is not an idle tale of people who never existed and things that could never have happened. It is a PARABLE" (*Collected Screenplays* 485).

3. Shaw further emphasized the difference between Undershaft and his successor in his revision for the 1931 standard edition by changing "Six o'clock tomorrow morning, my young friend" to "Six o'clock tomorrow morning, Euripides." See Dukore, "Toward an Interpretation of *Major Barbara*."

4. In the Derry manuscript, Undershaft explicitly tells his daughter that the issue between them is whether or not he is, as Cusins had said, "a most infernal old scoundrel."

5. It is possible that Shaw got the expression from T. H. Huxley. In an essay called "The Struggle for Existence in Human Society," Huxley expresses very Undershaftian ideas. He discusses the difficulties in trying to achieve cooperation and peace among citizens with conflicting interests: "The moral nature in us asks for no more than is compatible with the general good; the non-moral nature proclaims and acts upon that fine old Scottish family motto, 'Thou shalt starve ere I want'" (93). The actual motto, that of the family of Cranstoun from the barony of Midlothian, was "Thou shalt want ere I want." Huxley stresses the egoism of the sentiment and Shaw the extremity of need.

6. In his hysteria at the end of the second act, Cusins says, "Dionysos Undershaft has descended. I am possessed," but he also says that the Salvation Army "reveals the true worship of Dionysos" to "the poor professor of Greek" and that he worshiped Barbara because he saw "Dionysos and all the others" in her.

LAGRETTA TALLENT LENKER

Make War on War: A Shavian Conundrum

On September 3, 1914, C. F. G. Masterman, England's propaganda chief, convened a meeting of well-known authors to appeal for their aid in building confidence for the British war cause. This meeting resulted in fifty-three of England's most eminent authors and dramatists signing a patriotic declaration supporting Britain's entry into World War I. George Bernard Shaw did not attend the meeting, nor did he sign the document, and the omission of his name from the list was a glaring one.[1]

Shaw, instead of attending the meeting, was busily completing one of his most infamous non-dramatic pieces, *Common Sense About the War*, which was distributed as an eighty-four page supplement to the Sunday, November 14, 1914, edition of the *New Statesman*. The article said, in effect, that no cause, not even patriotism, justified the terrible cost of war; however, popular sentiment erroneously interpreted *Common Sense* as a pro-German appeal. Consequently, Shaw was attacked on all sides as unpatriotic, and was especially vilified by his fellow writers who signed Masterman's document. As a result, several literary organizations, including the prestigious Society of Authors, expelled Shaw from their membership.[2] However, unbeknown to those public patriots, Shaw, despite his condemnation of the war, contributed twenty thousand pounds to the war campaign in 1915. Shaw reasoned that war is wrong but that once engaged in it, a country must responsibly provide

From *War and Words: Horror and Heroism in the Literature of Warfare*, edited by Sara Munson Deats, Lagretta Tallent Lenker, and Merry G. Perry, pp. 165–85. Copyright © 2004 by Lexington Books.

111

for those charged with waging it and not burden future generations with war debts.[3] As the dead and wounded began arriving home in England, popular sentiment began to embrace the philosophy espoused in *Common Sense*. Realizing this swing in public opinion, Shaw explained that his visionary thinking was both a blessing and a curse, "Shaw [speaking about himself] is often ten minutes ahead of the truth, which is almost as fatal as being behind time."[4]

Although Shaw was famous for his definite opinions on almost every topic, he continually presented multiple, often contradictory ideas about war. Perhaps this conflicting and conflicted viewpoint resulted from his visionary intellect or, perhaps, his Eros side was more dominant than his Thanatos side, or more than likely, he was dramatizing society's ambivalent attitudes toward war.[5] Alfred Turco distills the ideas found in Shaw's massive writings on war and peace:

> Although war is a human abomination that no amount of romanticizing or heroics can justify, nonetheless, Shaw believed, "when war overtakes you, you must fight.... One does not trouble about the danger of damp sheets when the house is on fire" (*WRW* [*What I Really Wrote About the War*], pp. 234, 232). The best outcome that can be hoped for from the "colossal stupidity of modern war" (*WRW*, p. 27) is a concluding peace conference capable of creating structures of international cooperation banning war as an instrument of future policy. Pacifism, while admirable in theory, is not practicable because "we must face the fact that pugnacity is still a part of human nature, and that civilization is still in its infancy" (*WRW*, p. 236) [6]

Even though Shaw's treatises, prefaces, and correspondence concerning war make fascinating study, this essay focuses on how Shaw's multivalent ideas on war influence his creation of five of his major plays: *Arms and the Man*, *Caesar and Cleopatra*, *Major Barbara*, *Heartbreak House*, and *Saint Joan*. Despite their various themes and settings, all five plays employ three discernable strategies to dramatize Shaw's love–hate fascination with war. I study these plays bearing in mind Turco's maxim that although patterns emerge in his work, Shaw never made the same point twice in exactly the same way.[7]

The first technique Shaw employs to interrogate his society's love/hate relationship with war is to create multifaceted, complex heroes. *Arms and the Man*, *Caesar and Cleopatra*, *Major Barbara*, *Heartbreak House*, and *Saint Joan* all feature military images usually associated with the hero; however, in a complicit yet subversive critique, the playwright also limns portraits that reveal the weaknesses and humanity of the very military figure or idea being valorized. Such treatments call into question the efficacy of war as well as the stature of the hero and illustrate the ambivalence of the culture that highly esteems bravery and military prowess while simultaneously deploring the violence, destruction, and horror that accompany any battle. As Richard Dietrich notes:

> Because of the considerable debunking of the hero that goes on in ... [a] Shaw play, Shaw was once thought one of the fathers of antiheroic literature, ... but to humanize the hero as Shaw has done is not to kill the hero. Shaw, in fact, was one of the last defenders of heroism in literature, seeking to rescue the hero by separating his essence from all the romantic claptrap that had grown up around him. "We want credible heroes," said Shaw.[8]

In keeping with Shaw's penchant for educating characters and by extension the public through his plays, each of the unconventional heroes considered here attempts to tutor another in his or her philosophy or practice of war. This professorial stance is one of Shaw's favorite means of supporting and sustaining his innovative drama of ideas.[9]

The second hallmark of these war plays concerns their settings—each takes place in a drawing room, court chamber, or royal encampment well away from the battlefield. These locales provide Shaw's characters with the ideal venue in which to hold their famous debates. Shaw, the ardent socialist and advocate of a "practical" league of nations, employed his dramas to explore and promote these ideas as they relate to war. These many discussions of preparations for war, philosophies of war (and peace), and causes of war constitute a kind of Shavian "war in the head," in which Shaw's war talk permeates the plays without a single blow being struck, without a shot being fired. One reason for the success of this cerebral strategy is that Shaw often presents his "enemy" as a social institution—such as capitalism, nationalism, or patriotism—instead of the conventional villain of melodrama and military romance.[10]

The third pattern characterizing these war plays is their ambivalent endings. These dramas end, not in battles won or lost, but in questions, hopes, and dreams. Perhaps Shaw's own ambivalence about war, as exemplified by his private, not public, support of England's war effort, informs the endings of these plays and makes closure difficult, if not impossible. Or maybe Shaw deliberately stages the open-ending approach to encourage audiences to consider these issues of war and peace long after leaving the theater.

Arms and the Man (1894), for example, features a handsome soldier with a realistic attitude toward war who deflates the romantic notions of the heroine concerning battle and the bravery of her betrothed. In this well-known farce, bits of chocolate substitute for bullets, and overcoats prove more useful than smart uniforms. Captain Bluntschli, the practical realist turned Shavian hero, debunks Raina's notions of the glamour of war with pronouncements such as: "All of them [soldiers are afraid to die] ... It is our duty to live as long as we can," and "nine soldiers out of ten are born fools."[11] Most deflating, however, is Bluntschli's description of the cavalry charge, led by Raina's betrothed Sergius, which has captured the romantic imagination of the Bulgarians. Raina asks the soldier who has intruded into her bedroom (Bluntschli, as it is later revealed) to describe the charge: "It's like slinging a handful of peas against a window pane: first one comes; then two or three close behind him; and then all the rest in a lump." When she presses for an account of Sergius' bravery, the mysterious stranger replies: "He did it like an operatic tenor.... We did laugh."[12] Here and elsewhere in the play, Shaw does not depict war, the ultimate in human aggression, as laughable; rather, it is the romantic glorification of war that Shaw finds silly.

As is usually the case, Shaw pairs a "conventional" soldier to serve as foil for the unconventional hero. In *Arms and the Man*, Sergius, the windmill-tilting fiancé of Raina, embodies the more traditional, romantic notions about war. Despite his fabled cavalry charge, Sergius soon learns that his victory was a hollow one, because the Serbs had the wrong ammunition, and that the astute soldier would have seen that the battle could have been won with little effort.[13] In a touch of Shavian irony, Bluntschli, the chocolate-cream soldier, must finish the business of war for the cavalry-charging hero and his soon-to-be father-in-law, Major Petkoff. The victors, Sergius and Petkoff, cannot manage the transfer of three cavalry regiments to another locale and ask for their former enemy Bluntschli's help. The professional, though unconventional, man of arms dispatches the troops after lunch while the Bulgarians sign forms and have tea. Is this an educational experience for Sergius and Petkoff? Perhaps not, but the episode wittily establishes Shaw's point about the identity of the true wartime hero. Grudgingly admired by the men, Bluntschli, the citizen soldier, the can-do pragmatist, the silent intruder who carries chocolate in his ammunition belt, becomes the first in a long line of Shavian non-traditional heroes, who grow ever more unconventional as Shaw's dramatic arsenal develops.

Shaw never dramatizes the actual military maneuvers that frame and incite the action of *Arms and the Man*; instead he presents descriptions of the battles in the boudoir, patio, and the much-touted library (complete with three bookshelves and an electric bell!) of the Petkoff home. Of course, dramatists, including the ancient Greeks and Shakespeare, have relied on messengers and other forms of report to relay the news of victories, defeats, and the horrors of warfare. Shaw, however, employs this technique not only for dramatic economy but also to provide a forum to discuss the social problems and issues that underlie even his romantic tales of chocolate soldiers. The result becomes a kind a "war in the head," in which the drama of ideas explodes to perform the real Shavian work. This discursive element in *Arms and the Man* portrays society's ambivalence about war as demonstrated by the description of the big cavalry charge, which is subsequently undercut; Sergius' report of being punished for winning an important battle in the wrong way; and Major Petkoff's asking his wife to give military orders and keep discipline. Moreover, for good measure, Shaw incorporates discussions on nationalism via the conflicts between the Serbians and Bulgarians, depictions of class warfare between the Petkoff's servants and their employers, and an exposé of the sham aristocracy. (Mrs. Petkoff announces: "Our position is almost historical: we can go back for twenty years.")[14] Certainly, in subsequent plays, the drama of ideas considers graver issues, but the foundation is laid here as one martial stereotype after another falls victim to Shaw's pen.

To conclude his "drama of real life," Shaw chooses not victory in battle, or bellicose speeches, but the age-old stage convention for comedic endings—marriage. However, this time, the unconventional hero not only gets his military rival's girl but also his admiration. As Bluntschli concludes his business of winning Raina's hand and dispatching the final bit of military deployment, Sergius—Bluntschli's rival in love and war—is heard to say "What a man! Is he a man!"[15] Thus, the victors do not receive the spoils: The military careers of the would-be serious soldiers Sergius and Petkoff are over, while Bluntschli, the practical man of the world, goes on to greater challenges. Thus the chocolate soldier, who prefers candy to bullets and efficient battle tactics to those that bring glory and fame, effectively subverts the big ending of the conventional warriors with their romantic pomp and visions of valor in battle. With this conclusion, Shaw debunks sentimental notions of war while showing an almost grudging admiration for the practical fellow who performs well in battle. Yet, as noted above, earlier in the play Bluntschli delivers brutally frank indictments of contemporary warfare. Having his unconventional hero profess the horrors of war yet execute exemplary feats in combat suggests Shaw's understanding of society's ambivalence toward war; having this hero assimilated into the family of his enemy through marriage demonstrates Shaw's notion that causes of battles are often shallow, unreasonable, and easily resolvable.

Interestingly, Shaw's audience for *Arms and the Man* consisted of a nation that had "seen only one serious war ... (the Crimean) in almost a hundred years," and they regarded it as shocking and almost traitorous that a dramatist should so demean the noble profession of arms.[16] Also, the critical debate over whether *Arms and the Man* is a charming little romance or stagecraft with political import took a real-world turn in 1903 when the Austrian government banned the play for fear of possible "political excitement about Macedonia and Bulgaria" and because of its dangerous revolutionary tendencies.[17] Shaw, stung by the British press' initial reception of his play, gloated: "I am charmed and flattered by the action of the Austrian government.... Here the critics persist in treating 'Arms and the Man' as comic opera or a burlesque. It has been left for the Austrian Government to see my original purpose and to discover that it is really a serious study of humanity with a revolutionary tendency."[18] Thus, although the play ends in the comedic tradition of marriage, the critical reviews and political implications are decidedly at odds.

Four years later, Shaw again considers the art of war and peace as he offers his portrayal of the legendary warrior and ruler, Julius Caesar.[19] Written in 1898, *Caesar and Cleopatra* offers the most nearly perfect, albeit unconventional, hero in the Shavian canon; in fact, Caesar often is called Shaw's Christ figure.[20] Shaw creates a striking contrast to Shakespeare's Caesar, who claims to be a god while overlooking his own human frailties. Both shattering and transcending stereotypes of aging and leadership, Shaw's Caesar is an unassuming, self-deprecating Titan who performs military and diplomatic feats worthy of a superman while laughing at his own humanity. Most particularly, Caesar continually points to his advancing age, which may deflate his heroic appearance but does not affect his heroic actions. His Egyptian friends counter his claims by calling Caesar not only a "conquering soldier, but also the creative poet-artist."[21] Caesar becomes another heroic character in the Shavian tradition who exhibits incongruity between an almost "bland, self-possessed manner of speech and startling, outrageous, or absurd matter."[22] Similarly these heroes are plain and direct in their speech yet larger than life in action.

Shaw deftly undermines the nineteenth-century tradition of the historical romance that the play's title evokes. Audiences of that time would expect to see a memorable romance blossom between the dashing older conqueror and the fair young queen, but instead Shaw delivers a play in which Caesar the warrior becomes the father figure, restructuring Egypt and guiding the sixteen-year-old Cleopatra toward adulthood and full royal power. Romantic love is out of the question but at the play's conclusion, Caesar promises to send Cleopatra a more traditional romantic warrior/hero (Mark Antony)—as if Caesar were a father choosing a husband for his daughter.

Many critics suggest that Shaw humanizes his protagonist by emphasizing qualities not typically associated with the hero, which, nevertheless, do not interfere with his abilities. Timothy G. Vesonder notes that Caesar's traits do not match the "age of the typical hero who is always in the prime of life, at the height of his physical prowess."[23] Instead of physical strength, Caesar embodies the heroic spirit, inverting the convention of youth overcoming age. Charles A. Berst argues that references to Caesar's age serve as anticlimactic devices. For example, at his first entrance, Caesar claims in soliloquy a lofty spiritual kinship with a sphinx, after which Cleopatra deflates him by addressing him as "Old Gentleman." Later, after Caesar has shown his capacity for action and donned his armor, he is mocked for being bald. At the play's end, the height of Caesar's glory, he jests that he is "old and ripe for the knife," a foreshadowing of his murder.[24] As Daniel Leary asserts, most late-nineteenth-century audiences knew Julius Caesar primarily from Shakespeare's tragedy, so an allusion to his murder would evoke the play's famous stabbing scene rather than a historical account of Caesar's death.[25]

Shaw creates a conspicuous contrast to Shakespeare's Caesar, at one juncture having his Caesar admit his own military mistakes, which have returned to haunt him, and affirm the lessons of clemency and peace that he now attempts to teach his officers. As Caesar the conqueror performs the unlikely act of freeing the Egyptians he has captured in the Alexandrian palace, the Egyptian leaders and generals of the Roman occupation army remind Caesar that they, acting in concert, beheaded the invading Pompey, Caesar's chief Roman rival. When Caesar expresses disgust at this fickle act, accusing the perpetrators of extracting unnecessary revenge and of backing the winning side, Lucius reminds Caesar of his own earlier actions involving a rival warrior: "You have seen severed heads before, Caesar, and severed right hands too, I think; some thousands of them, in Gaul, after you vanquished Vercingetorix. Did you spare him, with all your clemency? Was that vengeance?"[26] Thus, Caesar's attempt to lead others to peace by example fails in a very human fashion, but this lapse does not dissuade Caesar from his attempts to inculcate in another, younger warrior his principles of warfare. His trusted lieutenant Rufio does learn and practices "Caesar's boasted laws of life," killing his perceived enemy "Without punishment. . . . Without judgment."[27] For this and other acceptances of Caesar's theories of war and peace, Rufio, the son of a freedman, is made Governor of Egypt, while the queen of Egypt, another of Caesar's pupils but one who failed to embrace his philosophy, is almost forgotten as Caesar leaves Egypt for Rome.

Once again, the reports of battles and military intrigue are given primarily in palaces, throne rooms, and adjoining esplanades. Despite some minor saber rattling between Romans and Egyptians in acts one and two and a memorable scene at the lighthouse in the Alexandrian harbor, on-stage Shaw's Egyptian siege is "drawing room" war. Lucius describes Pompey's murder to the attendant crowd in Cleopatra's throne room; Cleopatra discusses the siege of Egypt in her boudoir; and Pothinus, the enemy of Cleopatra, warns Caesar of eminent mutiny and revolt on the splendidly decorated roof of Cleopatra's palace.[28] Although Caesar tells Cleopatra that to be a true queen she must "learn to look on battles," Shaw never requires this of his audience [29] Instead, we are treated to typical Shavian discourse on the pitfalls of nationalism as Caesar mocks the savage ways of his British secretary, who, in turn, derides Caesar for his frivolous Italian habits.[30] The more pertinent topics, however, deal with education, clemency, and leadership, all treated in the finest Shavian dialogue. Shaw's Caesar, the warrior antitype par excellence characterizes his preference for companions: "Oh, this military life! this tedious, brutal life of action. . . . we are mere doers and drudgers: a swarm of bees turned into men. Give me a good talker—one with wit and imagination enough to live without continually doing something!"[31]

Yet the ending of *Caesar and Cleopatra* perhaps most appropriately expresses Shaw's multivalent approach towards war. At the play's conclusion, Shaw's heroine has become a "New Woman" manqué, as she fails to grasp Caesar's doctrine of clemency and peace.[32] The glorious Egyptian victory is over, but Caesar's wars are not—he must engage in battle on his way back to Rome and realizes that he faces almost certain death. Most tellingly of all, however, Caesar forgets Cleopatra in his leave-taking. This slight is not mere absentmindedness but the result of Cleopatra's failure to learn; consequently, she has become irrelevant in his plans. When Cleopatra reminds him that he has not bade her farewell and tells him that he has treated her badly, he rewards her with the promise of a Roman toy (Mark Antony). As Caesar departs, Cleopatra displays a familiar ambivalence toward a Shavian warrior-hero: weary from attempting to attain Caesar's standards but still attracted by his strength and magnanimity, she begins to weep. When assured that he will return, Cleopatra replies, "I hope not. But I can't help crying, all the same," in a bittersweet bit of Shavian irony that foreshadows the stage departure of another legendary Shavian hero some thirty years later.[33]

The next play to be considered, *Major Barbara* (1905), is perhaps the most unlikely to be included in a study such as this. The drama features not practitioners of war, but the incongruous combination of munitions manufacturers and sincere salvationists—destroyers of bodies and savers of souls. In a complex scenario constructed around each person attempting to convert the other to his/her respective brand of "warfare," Barbara Undershaft, a major in the Salvation Army; Andrew Undershaft, wealthy arms magnate and Barbara's estranged father; and Adolphus Cusins, professor of Greek and Barbara's fiancé, compete for each other's souls and ultimately create a kind of holy trinity to, as Andrew Undershaft states "make war on war."[34] Thus, instead of the singular hero, Shaw produces a synthesizing triumvirate, a strategy that according to Dietrich confuses literary critics searching for traditional heroes:

In his middle period we mostly find that certain characters possess only pieces of that synthesis and must work with others to achieve an effective whole. And the idea of synthesis seems to be replaced by that of maintaining a fruitful tension between opposites. No wonder critics have been bewildered by *Major Barbara* (1905), for they have tried to locate in a single character what Shaw intended for the ensemble. Here Barbara ... finds that salvation is a complicated matter requiring more than simple faith. To be effective that faith must engage in dialectical play, ... which in practical terms, in this play, means marrying a professor of Greek and making a pact with her "devil" of a father.[35]

Subsequently, Barbara and her father join in a wager to attempt to convert each other to their respective religions, and Barbara, while losing the bet, gains her soul—rather the Shavian version of it—free from the hypocrisy of organized religion and the crime of poverty. Her father offers his crusading daughter the opportunity for effecting genuine salvation through "money and gunpowder": "It is cheap work converting starving men with a Bible in one hand and a slice of bread in the other. . . . Try your hand on my men: their souls are hungry because their bodies are full." As Barbara experiences the enlightenment that Undershaft desires, he turns to Cusins: "Plato says . . . that society cannot be saved until either the Professors of Greek take to making gunpowder, or else the makers of gunpowder become Professors of Greek."[36] When Cusins agrees that Undershaft's gunpowder is the more universal power, Shaw forges an unholy alliance, all three united under the Salvation Army's unlikely banner of "Fire and Blood."

Consequently, the clash between the militant salvationists and the unashamed armorer propels the play into a fierce discussion of the morality of war, religion, and capitalism. This play's most aptly labeled "war in the head" takes place not on a battlefield or military garrison but in a fashionable London home, a Salvation Army Shelter, and a manufacturing plant—without a real soldier in sight, Yet Shaw peppers the ensuing discussion with bellicose phrases such as "make war on war," "Blood and Fire" (the Salvation Army's motto that Undershaft says could be his own), and "money and gunpowder," to highlight the actual topic of the play.[37] In addition to the enticing epigrams, the dialogue of the play explores the seemingly irreconcilable conundrum of humanity's fascination with war and how force may be employed for the advancement of society. Four examples will serve. First, early in the play as the estranged Undershaft family attempts to renew their acquaintance with the father, Charles Lomax, suitor to the younger Undershaft daughter, asks her father if he believes war will be abolished once it becomes too destructive. Undershaft retorts: "Not at all. The more destructive war becomes the more fascinating we find it." As the debate over the forces of salvation and destruction escalates, Undershaft and Cusins consider Barbara's possible role in Undershaft's world. Undershaft proclaims that his daughter will carry his torch and message. When Barbara and her father engage in heated controversy, he states fervently that he would like to kill poverty, and she in turn taunts that killing is his answer to everything. Undershaft replies: "It is . . . the only lever strong enough to overturn a social system, the only way of saying Must."[38]

In another Shavian twist, the social system Undershaft refers to is his own—capitalism, the villain that sustains poverty and social slavery. Shaw identifies this "villain" early on, through one of the Salvation Army's clients, Snobby Price, who avers that he is not the Salvation Army's usual clientele: his intelligence places him above the social niche into which the "capitalists" have placed him.[39] A few scenes later, the shelter comes under the influence of that arch-capitalist, Andrew Undershaft. Dietrich labels him "the millionaire owner of a 'devilish' munitions factory that supplies weapons to whoever has money to buy, in the best capitalist tradition. Capitalism in this repressive society being one of the few accepted vents for self-assertion, strong spirits such as Undershaft tend to overindulge."[40] In Shaw's philosophy, the leaven to capitalism must be the trinity that synthesizes intellect, love, and power.[41]

However, for all the "glory hallelujahs" and fire and brimstone rhetoric on both sides of the debate, Shaw, once again, crafts an ambivalent ending. At the climactic point of the formation of this unconventional trinity, Barbara turns from her partners in the forging of a new society to her mother to discuss a most conventional topic—housekeeping. Shaw thus subverts his big scene, hinting that the redemption into the Trinity is not absolute, characterized not by the Salvation Army's anthem "Onward Christian Soldiers" but by the Shavian conundrum "make war on war." With this battle cry, Undershaft, Barbara, and Cusins unite to live both in the world and of the world. Redemption or Damnation? Shaw's play answers with the conjecture that the manufacture of these instruments of war offers a more effective means of feeding humanity's bodies and souls than does the charity of the Salvation Army. This unsettling hypothesis demonstrates how deeply the dual aspects of war pervade modern society.

Images of war even penetrate Shaw's fantasies. *Heartbreak House* (1917) symbolizes "cultured, leisured Europe before the war" and, as such, suffers from a malignant ennui, what Shaw terms "indifference and neglect."[42] In his preface to the play, Shaw concedes that nineteenth-century England had been spared the horrors of war on her own soil, but that security was destroyed by the events of World War I. In Shaw's mind, the "Plague of London" could have been avoided if the privileged classes had acted responsibly.[43] Those who could have prevented the plague of war inhabit *Heartbreak House*, a play more concerned with war "than might be inferred from its oblique treatments."[44] *Heartbreak House* features the fantastic Captain Shotover, a bellicose octogenarian who conducts experiments with dynamite. Although Shotover attempts in vain to abdicate his role as father, head of the household, and, by extension, patriarchal ruler of his clan, the closely related roles of leader, savior, and even unconventional hero will not release him from their literal and metaphorical hold. In *Literature of Crisis 1910–22*, Anne Wright presents a cogent analysis of Shotover, the play's unlikely and reluctant hero:

> His claim to the title is implicitly considered in what he says and does.... Shotover's denunciation of capitalism and materialism is in the vein of Carlyle and Ruskin. With them he shares a faith in strong leadership, which connects with his career as a sea captain. The ship is the dominant dynamic (and male) symbol for *Heartbreak House*, which overlays . . . the static (and female) symbol of the house, centre of personal relationships. The ship of state—for this is indeed a metaphor for the organization of society—needs direction and responsible leadership: navigation.[45]

Wright continues by discussing how Shotover possesses a mystical element, which combines with his "Christian moralistic fervour," to produce a "prophet-preacher" who announces the arrival of judgment, calls himself the hand of God, and "speaks for 'God's way'; but with a hint as well of magical, even diabolical power." Furthermore, Wright sees Shotover as a forerunner of the wisdom and power of the Ancient in Shaw's next play, *Back to Methuselah*.[46]

Yet for all of his heroic qualities (if tinged with the mystical and diabolical), Shotover supports the inhabitants of Heartbreak House by passionately exploring the forces of darkness and death. His goal, as he explains to his son-in-law Hector, is to "discover a ray mightier than any X-ray: a mind ray that will explode the ammunition in the belt of my adversary before he can point his gun at me." Nevertheless, his daughter Hesione reminds him that there is more money to be made in weapons of mass destruction: "Can't you think of something that will murder half Europe with one bang?" As he returns to his experiments, Shotover, in a statement that perhaps contradicts another Shavian unlikely hero, Andrew Undershaft, intones, "Give me deeper darkness. Money is not made in the light."[47] Thus, Shotover's moral philosophy involves his "steering of the ship" of his family, and, by extension, the ship of state; however, his business is the invention of the trappings of war.[48]

Heartbreak House presents another Shavian triangle of an older man and two younger individuals who fall under his influence and/or debate his wisdom. Ellie Dunn, the ingénue disappointed in love and life, turns to the ancient captain for wisdom, while his son-in-law Hector Hushabye serves as his debating partner in the consideration of the morality of war and peace. Hector, described by Wright as a Byronic "Hero manqué," is tied to home and hearth by his wife, one of the fascinating Shotover sisters who enchant men for sport. His escape becomes a rich fantasy life wherein he adopts the pose of Marcus Darnley, revolutionary soldier. Wright labels Hector's theories of evolution as "natural selection imbued with a moral imperative"; however, "Unlike Hector, Shotover would kill, not spare, the enemy. The 'political philosophy' of *Heartbreak House* is expressed largely as a debate between these two characters: Hector with his swordstick, Shotover with his twentieth-century dynamite."[49] Nevertheless, Hector expresses sincere concern for the survival of society. When he implores Shotover to tell him how to affect this salvation, the Captain advises that he "learn your business as an Englishman," which Shotover regards as "navigation," the responsible steering of the ship of state upon which England's future depends.[50] Thus, Ellie and Hector each fall under Shotover's tutelage in much the same fashion as Rufio and Cleopatra in *Caesar and Cleopatra*. Yet, in *Heartbreak House*, Shaw reverses the outcome. Hector/Marcus, deluded by fantasy, remains the spoiled, pessimistic romantic who questions all, waits for war's death, and is disappointed when it does not come.[51] After Shotover saves her from a mercenary marriage to the capitalist Boss Mangan and shares with her his thoughts on attaining the seventh degree of concentration, Ellie gives her "broken heart and . . . strong sound soul to its natural captain, my spiritual husband and second father."[52] Consequently, Ellie and the Captain find "life with a blessing" and carry the Shavian message of calling for the bombs of war to clear away the dead in society to make room for a new world order—from war to peace.[53]

Heartbreak House only considers war, presumably, far away from the battlefields of World War I at a country estate garden party on a lovely afternoon and evening, until the war comes to Heartbreak House and its inhabitants in a spectacular, almost surreal, manner. Preliminary discussions of war are even more oblique than those between Hector and Shotover at the end of act one (noted above). In act three, as the setting moves to the terrace, almost every character has a comment on how to solve society's problems: how to rescue "This soul's prison we call England."[54] Boss Mangan reveals that his capitalist talents are a sham and that he cannot offer suggestions on how to better the country; Addie nominates her colonial-governor husband as England's leader; Hector admits his natural abilities are bound up in his enthrallment to women; and Hesione advocates the appreciation of beauty as an antidote to discontent.[55] Louis Crompton analyzes the action: "What is remarkable about this scene is that for all its intellectual intentions . . . the dialectical structure remains largely implicit. The characters . . . assert their own convictions and express their feelings very much as if the others were not present."[56] However, even in this idyllic, if ethereal scene, war mania looms. Hesione avers that they are all madder than usual, or, as Wright says, "madness, heartbreak and violence are endemic."[57] For just as Hesione and Mazzini Dunn rise in defense of beauty and bohemianism (Dunn gushes that the peace found in the bohemian nature of Heartbreak House is more meaningful than in all his previously supported social causes), the first bombs fall onto the English countryside.[58]

Shaw introduces the bombs into the madness, tedium, and bohemianism not merely as a spectacular ending to fantasy but in large measure as an antidote for a social system that he had fought against all of his adult life. In *Heartbreak House*, capitalism has a name and a human form: Boss Mangan. As Wright proposes, "*Heartbreak House* is intensely committed to defining, or redefining, the Enemy, as well as to finding the Savior. The play identifies the Enemy within as the international adversary, capitalism, in the representative figure of Boss Mangan the financier."[59] Boss is lumped with the Burglar Billy Dunn and killed in the Captain's dynamite pit in what has been termed the symbolic end of capitalism. However, Shaw's old adversary does not surrender easily, even in his own plays. As we shall see, those afflicted with the ennui born of the capitalist system wherein the privileged few, even for all of their advantages, find no peace and contentment and miss the meaning of the drama's big event.

At the end of the play, an air of expectation pervades the moonless evening. Ellie announces that she is always anticipating something but does not know what. Hector avers that not all of their talking can last. Shotover expects Providence to intervene although he realizes that "the Church is on the rocks." Moreover, just as the idealistic Mazzini assures the group that nothing will happen, a far-away rumbling begins.[60] As the crescendo builds and the danger comes closer to Heartbreak House, the doldrums give way to terror and then, most tellingly, to an electric excitement. Although two lesser beings are killed and the German Zeppelin pilots run a terrible risk, Ellie and Hesione, perhaps having the courage to express what the rest of those caught in the group madness feel, compare the concatenation of bombs to Beethoven and trill at the exhilaration of danger:

Hesione: But what a glorious experience! I hope they'll come again tomorrow night.

Ellie: (radiant at the prospect) Oh, I hope so.[61]

Are these the expressions of silly, unthinking women, or an uncensored portrayal of "civilized" society's true feelings about war? The delight of Shotover's family and guests in the pyrotechnics of the German air raid underscores the ennui of early twentieth-century England and clearly portrays humanity's fascination with the paradoxical beauty and horrors of war. Lady Augusta Gregory reported that Shaw had difficulty ending the play because it was "so wild."[62] Perhaps the difficulty came not only from the fantastic nature of the drama and its characters but also from Shaw's own ambivalence towards war. Although *Heartbreak House* was published in 1919, Shaw withheld production of the play until 1921.[63] Even then, the play was misunderstood by the English, who remembered Shaw's *Common Sense About the War* and who were perhaps still not ready to acknowledge their own Janus-faced attitudes about war.

Christianity's ambivalent association with military might denaturalizes Shaw's chronicle play, *Saint Joan* (1923) in which the "angel dressed as a soldier" persuades the authorities that she is on a heavenly mission to teach the French to fight so that "the will of God may be done in France." The legendary Joan had been one of the most famous and popular female figures in fin de siècle England, and Shaw's treatment of Joan followed those by Tom Taylor and others.[64] Yet Shaw's transition from the fantastic, bohemian, and almost ephemeral figures of twentieth-century *Heartbreak House* to the bold, confident girl of the Middle Ages is not as severe as one might think. Shaw's treatment of the Maid also features unconventionality and ambivalence about war. Joan's being a mere girl of seventeen who presumptuously challenges secular and religious authorities renders her Shaw's most unconventional and subversive military hero. She boldly bests men of the Church and government and is ultimately burned at the stake for embarrassing them by being right when they were wrong.[65] Although Joan confidently commands the French army, wins near-miraculous battles, and glories in her self-proclaiming fulfillment of God's will on earth, she cannot ignore the realities of war. In scene one, Robert de Baudricourt, one of Joan's first supporters in the military, warns her about the brutality of the English soldiers. Joan responds that good people always turn evil when they invade another country and that she would become wicked, too, if she attempted to conquer England without God's blessing. Later in their conversation, Joan offers Robert a practical assessment of the French soldiers' motivation for fighting: She avers that in battle men fight for self-preservation and the only way to insure that one will survive the battle is to turn and run. Joan promises to teach the French to fight for a higher purpose and to drive the inevitably wicked from French soil.[66]

After Joan has succeeded in having the Dauphin (Charles VII) crowned at Rheims Cathedral, she becomes uncharacteristically melancholy, longing for the exhilaration of battle and victory at Orleans. Then she confesses to harboring all too familiar emotions so prevalent in the Shavian canon: "I am frightened beyond words before a battle; but it is so dull afterwards when there is no danger: oh, so dull! dull! dull!" La Hire, another French soldier, chimes in as Joan prepares to leave court: "You will miss the fighting. It's a bad habit, but a grand one, and the hardest of all to break yourself of." And so, even the Saint who fights for the Glory of God is not immune to the seductive thrill of war, as she and her French comrades readily admit.[67]

Thus, more capable than Church and State, Joan becomes a liability. After being captured by the Burgundians and sold to the English, she endures a lengthy trial by those whom she embarrasses, complicated by their inability to decide whether she is a witch or a heretic. Finally branded a heretic, Joan is burned at the stake and dies in scene six, at least for the moment. However, before this ignominious end, Joan attempts to teach her betters the art of war for the glory of her heavenly father. As self-appointed tutor to the Dauphin, Joan attempts to teach the uncrowned king how to pray, how to be a father to his own son, and how to be God's soldier.[68] In this Shavian inversion of the traditional education model where the venerable teach the lowly, the Maid from Lorraine instructs the King of France, albeit with mixed results. Charles accepts Joan's tutelage but still relies on her strength and martial accomplishments to fight his battles and to help him accede to the throne.

Saint Joan, along with *Caesar and Cleopatra*, becomes one of Shaw's most militaristic plays, featuring battle encampments, soldiers in war garb, and prison towers, yet the actual war is once again "in the head," as Shaw crafts one of his most famous dramas of ideas. In *Saint Joan*, too, battles are vividly described and reported, most notably the siege at Orleans led by "the invincible" Dunois and the battle at Compiègne that resulted in Joan's capture by the Burgundians.[69] Nevertheless, even if no blows are struck on stage, the verbal pyrotechnics are vintage Shaw. Although the exchange of ideas occurs throughout the play, as soldiers debate war strategy, noblemen discuss affairs of state, and churchmen argue theology, the dominant theme throughout features the rise of the twin tides of Nationalism and Protestantism, both shown from multiple perspectives.[70]

The major debate takes place in scene four, often termed the Drama of Ideas section, among those officials on both the French and English sides of the war who plot Joan's capture. Shaw foreshadows the importance of the play's predominant discussion scene when his powerful Archbishop, in response to a question about miracles, observes that an old era is dying and a new epoch is waiting to begin.[71] The angst caused by this "new spirit" may be observed intermingled with the plotting of Joan's possible capture and trial. First the English Earl of Warwick and Chaplain de Stogumber review the many defeats of the

English forces at the hand of the Maid but soon digress into talk of "labels" for groups of men from various regions. The Chaplain identifies himself as an "Englishman," and the Earl, representing feudalism (a form of social organization that knew no national borders), teasingly questions his embracing of this modern concept. The Chaplain demurs, but admits that he does have a patriotic "feeling" for English soil. Next, the Chaplain calls their enemy Dunois a "Frenchman," and this time the Earl responds with more passion: "If this cant of serving their country once takes hold of them, goodbye to the authority of their feudal lords, and goodbye to the authority of the Church. . . . goodbye to you and me."[72] After the French conspirator, the Bishop of Beauvais, arrives, the talk soon turns to Joan's supposed heresy, her direct appeal to God without intercession through the Church. The collusion between these two warring factions is affirmed, as they, in turn, explicate each other's interests. The English Earl identifies Joan's religious heresy as Protestantism, while the French bishop, returning the favor, connotes Joan's presumptive crimes in the secular arena as Nationalism. Thus, momentarily laying aside their differences that have caused such bloody wars, representatives of the Church and State embark on another war—against a seventeen-year-old "angel dressed as a soldier." The English Earl concludes the parlay that seals Joan's earthly fate with a catchy phrase that perhaps applies to wider ideals than the maid: "if you will burn the Protestant, I will burn the Nationalist."[73]

Dietrich suggests, "However much we have outgrown both Nationalism and Protestantism, Shaw showed how in Joan's fifteenth century they were necessary to historical dynamics."[74] Perhaps, however Shaw uses the shift from feudalism to Nationalism and from Catholicism to Protestantism as an analogy for what he saw as the next step in modern human progress—the advent of a multinational world where global interests supersede those of individual countries and a more tolerant and open religious community where respect, love, and peace are key—a practical league of nations.[75]

Shaw's most subversive feature of his tale of the Maid remains the Epilogue, which takes place twenty-five years after Joan's burning and allows her to confront those individuals from Church and State who convicted her of heresy and inflicted their most cruel punishment upon her. After constructing the proper tragedy of her life and death, Shaw creates a comic dream sequence in which King Charles, Brother Martin, the Bishop, her favorite soldier Dunois, the English Chaplain and Earl, and the Executioner each appear before Joan in the King's bed chamber (it is, after all, his dream) and good naturedly express regret at their respective parts in her bad end.

Charles issues what may be a general confession/apology for the entire group: "It is always you good men that do the big mischiefs," seemingly excluding himself.[76] Yet when Joan asks if she should come back to earth as a living woman, each man, friend and foe alike, recoils in horror at the idea of another encounter with the Maid and quickly disappears from the reverie. Interestingly, the last man remaining with Joan is not a king or bishop but a simple soldier who, in many respects, is the most sympathetic character in the Epilogue. At Joan's burning, the Soldier, a mere person in the crowd watching the execution, heard Joan's plea for a cross, tied two wooden sticks together, and gave the make-shift cross to her as she stood in the flames. For this one good deed, the Soldier, now dead, receives one day a year out of hell as his reward. Through an anonymous soldier, a man of war, who shows such kindness to Joan when all others had forsaken her, Shaw undercuts the bellicose images of the king and princes of Church and State and adds an element of ambivalence to the play's ending in which a burned soldier-saint will not stay dead. Thus, Shaw writes beyond the traditional ending of the legend to have the Maid of Orleans return about the time of her rehabilitation and then canonization. Again, the images are martial as Saint Joan relives her now famous military accomplishments. Thus, the complicit critique probes the tension between the glories of war and those of salvation.

The age-old ambivalence of humanity towards war is difficult to comprehend and still more difficult to express. Perhaps as Captain Shotover intuits, human beings. must "feel the fear of death sharply in order to feel the life in themselves more intensely."[77] More than any other playwright of the nineteenth and twentieth centuries, Shaw's work provides an emblem of this perplexing paradox and shows us ourselves confronting the issue of war, which is both the anathema and the apotheosis of man- and womankind.

Notes

1. Stanley Weintraub, *Journey to Heartbreak: The Crucible Years of Bernard Shaw 1914–1918* (New York: Weybright and Talley, 1971), 37–39. For their work on Shaw and war, I am indebted to Professor Weintraub as well as Anne Wright, Alfred Turco, and Gordon Bergquist.

2. Weintraub, *Journey*, 118–20.

3. Weintraub, *Journey*, 108.

4. Shaw qtd. in Weintraub, *Journey*, 69.

5. See Chris Hedges, *War Is a Force that Gives Us Meaning* (New York: Public Affairs, 2002), 157–85. Hedges gives a cogent discussion of the concepts of Eros and Thanatos.

6. Alfred Turco, "On War and Peace," *SHAW* 16 (1996): 165. Turco also gives a useful summary of Shaw's writings on war and peace. Turco's list of pertinent works includes *Arms and the Man* and the follow-up essay "A Dramatic Realist to His Critics"; *Heartbreak House* and its preface; letters Shaw wrote during World War I, many of which are available in *Collected Letters, 1911–1925*, ed. Dan H. Laurence; *What I Really Wrote About the War; The Intelligent Woman's Guide to Socialism and Capitalism*; and *Everybody's Political What's What?* (188–90).

7. Turco, "War and Peace," 165.

8. Richard F. Dietrich, *British Drama 1890–1950: A Critical History* (Boston: Twayne Publishers, 1989), 99.

9. Lagretta Tallent Lenker, *Fathers and Daughters in Shakespeare and Shaw* (Westport, Conn.: Greenwood Press, 2001). This work contains several discussions of Shaw's penchant for having characters, especially fathers and daughters, educate one another.

10. Gordon N. Bergquist, *The Pen and the Sword: War and Peace in the Prose and Plays of Bernard Shaw* (Salzburg, Austria: Institute für Englische Sprache und Literatur, 1977). See p. 68 passim for a discussion of Shaw's views on capitalism, nationalism, imperialism, and war.

11. George Bernard Shaw, *Arms and the Man*, in *The Bodley Head Bernard Shaw: Collected Plays with their Prefaces*, ed. Dan H. Laurence, 7 vols. (London: Max Reinhardt, 1970–1974), I:396, 398. All quotations of Shaw's work are from the seven-volume *Bodley Head* collection.

12. Shaw, *Arms and the Man*, I:403, 404.

13. Shaw, *Arms and the Man*, I:404.

14. Shaw, *Arms and the Man*, I:420, 443, 470.

15. Shaw, *Arms and the Man*, I:472.

16. Bergquist, *Pen and the Sword*, 44.

17. Shaw qtd. in Samuel A. Weiss, "Shaw, *Arms and the Man*, and the Bulgarians." *SHAW* 10 (1990): 27–28.

18. Shaw qtd. in Weiss, "Arms," 28.

19. Lagretta Tallent Lenker and Valerie Barnes Lipscomb, "Reflections of the Aging Caesar: Drama as Cultural Perspective," in *Journal of Aging and Identity* 7, no. 4 (December 2002): 275–86. Portions of my discussion of Shaw's Caesar as unconventional hero are drawn from this article.

20. Dietrich, *British Drama*, 100.

21. George Bernard Shaw, *Caesar and Cleopatra*, in *The Bodley Head Bernard Shaw: Collected Plays with their Prefaces*, ed. Dan H. Laurence, 7 vols. (London: Max Reinhardt, 1970–1974), II:270.

22. David J. Gordon, "Shavian Comedy and the Shadow of Wilde," in *The Cambridge Companion to George Bernard Shaw*, ed. Christopher Innes (Cambridge: Cambridge University Press, 1998), 131.

23. Timothy G. Vesonder. "Shaw's Caesar and the Mythic Hero." *Shaw Review* 21 (1978): 74.

24. Charles A. Berst, "The Anatomy of Greatness in *Caesar and Cleopatra*," *Journal of English and Germanic Philology* 68 (1969): 74–91.

25. Daniel Leary, "Shaw and Shakespeare: Why Not!" *Independent Shavian* 23 (1985): 6–8.

26. Shaw, *Caesar and Cleopatra*, II:208.

27. Shaw, *Caesar and Cleopatra*, II:289.

28. Shaw, *Caesar and Cleopatra*, II:207, 255, 263.

29. Shaw, *Caesar and Cleopatra*, II:223.

30. Shaw, *Caesar and Cleopatra*, II:241 and 287, 243.

31. Shaw, *Caesar and Cleopatra*, II:261.

32. Shaw, *Caesar and Cleopatra*, II:255, 282.

33. Shaw, *Caesar and Cleopatra*, II:292.

34. George Bernard Shaw, *Major Barbara*, in *The Bodley Head Bernard Shaw: Collected Plays with their Prefaces*, ed. Dan H. Laurence, 7 vols. (London: Max Reinhardt, 1970–1974), III:178.

35. Dietrich, *British Drama*, 117.

36. Shaw, *Major Barbara*, III:173, 178.

37. Shaw, *Major Barbara*, III:178, 88, 120.

38. Shaw, *Major Barbara*, III:89, 174.

39. Shaw, *Major Barbara*, III:96.

40. Dietrich, *British Drama*, 118.

41. Dietrich, *British Drama*, 121.

42. George Bernard Shaw, *Heartbreak House*, in *The Bodley Head Bernard Shaw: Collected Plays with their Prefaces*, ed. Dan H. Laurence, 7 vols. (London: Max Reinhardt, 1970–1974), V:12, 18.

43. Shaw, *Heartbreak House*, V:18.

44. Anne Wright, *Literature of Crisis, 1910–22* (New York: St. Martin's Press, 1984), 7.

45. Wright, *Literature of Crisis*, 84.

46. Wright, *Literature of Crisis*, 85.

47. George Bernard Shaw, *Heartbreak House*, V:102, 103, 105; Wright, *Literature of Crisis*, 80.

48. Weintraub, *Journey*, 166.

49. Wright, *Literature of Crisis*, 82–83.

50. Shaw, *Heartbreak House*, V:177.

51. Shaw, *Heartbreak House*, V:181.

52. Shaw, *Heartbreak House*, V:168.

53. Dietrich, *British Drama*, 130.

54. Shaw, *Heartbreak House*, V:177.

55. Louis Crompton, "*Heartbreak House*," in *Bernard Shaw's Plays*, ed. Warren Sylvester Smith (New York: W.W. Norton, 1970), 428.

56. Crompton, "*Heartbreak*," 428.

57. Shaw, *Heartbreak House*, V:103; Wright, *Literature of Crisis*, 3.

58. Crompton, "*Heartbreak*," 428–29.

59. Wright, *Literature of Crisis*, 70.

60. Shaw, *Heartbreak House*, V:177.

61. Shaw, *Heartbreak House*, V:181.

62. Lady Augusta Gregory qtd. in Weintraub, *Journey*, 183.

63. Weintraub, *Journey*, 330.

64. George Bernard Shaw, *Saint Joan*, in *The Bodley Head Bernard Shaw: Collected Plays with their Prefaces*, ed. Dan H. Laurence, 7 vols. (London: Max Reinhardt, 1970–1974), VI:95; Elaine Showalter, *Sexual Anarchy: Gender and Culture at the Fin de Siècle* (New York: Viking Penguin, 1990), 29.

65. Shaw, *Saint Joan*, Preface VI:15–16.

66. Shaw, *Saint Joan*, VI:94–95.

67. Shaw, *Saint Joan*, VI:141, 144–45.

68. Shaw, *Saint Joan*, VI:112–13.

69. Shaw, *Saint Joan*, VI:104 and 129, 158 and 172–73.

70. Shaw, *Saint Joan*, VI:38–39; 124–40.

71. Shaw, *Saint Joan*, VI:107.

72. Shaw, *Saint Joan*, VI:126.

73. Shaw, *Saint Joan*, VI:99, 140.

74. Dietrich, *British Drama*, 135.

75. See Bergquist, *Pen and the Sword*, 159, for a discussion of Shaw's views on a practical League of Nations.

76. Shaw, *Saint Joan*, VI:197.

77. Ronald Bryden, "The Roads to *Heartbreak House*," in *The Cambridge Companion to George Bernard Shaw*, ed. Christopher Innes (Cambridge: Cambridge University Press, 1998), 188.

JAN MCDONALD

Shaw among the Artists

For art's sake alone I would not face the toil of writing a single sentence.

Shaw (1976: 35)

I have, I think, always been a Puritan in my attitude towards Art.

Shaw (1946c: xii)

George Bernard Shaw (1856–1950) was a committed socialist, a successful, if controversial, dramatist, an inspired theatre director of his own work and an influential commentator on contemporary music, drama and fine art. In all his endeavours he demonstrated an indefatigable zeal to reform existing social conditions, sterile theatrical conventions and outworn artistic orthodoxies.

In this chapter I shall focus on Shaw's views on art and artists, examining some of his many critical and theoretical writings, but concentrating on how his opinions were expressed in dramatic form in plays which particularly engage with such issues, namely, *Candida* (1895), *Caesar and Cleopatra* (1899), *Mrs Warren's Profession* (1902), *Man and Superman* (1905), *The Doctors Dilemma* (1906), *Pygmalion* (Berlin: 1913; London: 1914) and *Back to Methuselah* (New York: 1922; London: 1923).

Towards a Shavian Aesthetic?

Shaw's opinions on art and artists are scattered throughout his work, in his critical and journalistic writing, in letters and notebooks, as well as in his

From *A Companion to Modern British and Irish Drama: 1880–2005*, edited by Mary Luckhurst, pp. 63–74. Copyright © 2006 by Blackwell Publishing.

plays and the prefaces to them. These observations, spanning many years, are not consistent and can seem almost wilfully contradictory. His comment that 'Wagner can be quoted against himself almost without limit' (Shaw 1930: 265) is at least as applicable to Shaw. As Sidney P. Albert among others has pointed out Shaw was much influenced by his reading of Hegelian dialectics, a methodology well suited to his inclination to play with conflicting ideologies, particularly in his dramas (Albert 1956: 423–4). In addition, his taste for polemics, his mischievous flying of multi-coloured kites and his sense of irony—which he engaged on occasion to subvert ideas that he had previously endorsed—all militate against the expression of a structured aesthetic philosophy.

Finally, and most importantly, for much of his life Shaw was politically engaged, both theoretically and practically, as a socialist, and his writings demonstrate his attempt to balance a utilitarian ethic of improving social conditions with a deep attachment to the creative and performing arts. 'I am an artist, and, it is inevitable, a public moralist', he announced in a letter to Robert W. Welch in September 1905 (Laurence 1972: 560).

Judith B. Spink believes that Shaw failed to achieve the desired equilibrium and that his aesthetics were seriously compromised by his politics: 'Shaw's complete commitment to the socialist cause led him eventually to such contorted views on art as are perhaps more familiar from more uncompromisingly Marxist critics and artists' (Spink 1963: 83). It is certainly true that Shaw passionately eschewed the notion of 'Art for Art's sake', as the first epigraph above makes clear, and he repeatedly asserted that his prime motive for engaging in aesthetic pursuits was to promote political ideas. The preface to his first play, *Widowers' Houses* (1892), is unequivocal: 'It is not my fault, reader, that my art is the expression of my sense of moral and individual perversity rather than my sense of beauty' (West 1950: 115). In a letter to Henry Arthur Jones (8 January 1899), he went further, asserting not only that a work of art should have a social function, but that a sense of purpose and social responsibility was essential, a *sine qua non* of excellence: 'The best established truth in the world is that no man produces a work of art of the very first order except under the pressure of strong conviction and definite meaning as to the constitution of the world' (Laurence 1972: 71). In this, as in many other respects, Shaw was a true Platonist. Plato, as Albert has noted, 'praised art only when it is allied with philosophy in the pursuit of the Form of Beauty which is also intellectually viewed, Truth, and morally considered, the Good' (Albert 1956: 430). The artist-philosopher was the only artist Shaw took seriously. On occasion he implied that art was *only* of value as a means of making radical ideas pleasing. He wrote in the preface to *Mrs Warren's Profession*: 'I am convinced that fine art is the subtlest, the most seductive, the most effective instrument of moral propaganda in the world' (Shaw 1946b: 7).

In practice, in Shaw's best work, the 'art' is not merely the handmaiden of his favoured philosophy, whether he is promoting Fabian socialism, the Schopenhaurian Life Force, the Nietzschean Superman or the theories of Lamarck, Bergson et al. on Creative Evolution. Nevertheless, it is, paradoxically, in two passages in which the art of the dramatist is least effective that Shaw expounds his aesthetic theory at some length, the 'Don Juan in Hell' episode in *Man and Superman* and Part V of *Back to Methuselah*, 'As far as thought can reach'. A brief comparison of these non-dramatic sections—'non-dramatic' because the two-dimensional characters are merely mouthpieces for opposing ideologies—is useful, bearing in mind the twenty years between the two plays, years which encompassed World War I. The latter is rarely performed in whole or in part, and Shaw himself gave permission to the directors of *Man and Superman* to omit the 'hell' scene.

Both passages have as their subject Creative Evolution; in the first the instrument of humankind's ascent is the Nietzschean 'Superman': in the second, it is time and abstract thought. Shaw believed that in *Man and Superman* as a whole the 'message' had been obscured in order to fit the drama to the tastes of his contemporary audience; that is, one might say, to engage with the 'art' of playwriting. The later development of the 'religion' of Creative Evolution makes no such concessions.

In 'Don Juan in Hell' the artist-philosopher, Don Juan/John Tanner, rails against the aesthetic hedonism of the Devil, comparing his religion of love and beauty to 'sitting for all eternity at the first act of a fashionable play' (Shaw 1976: 139). 'Hell is the home of the unreal and the seekers of the happiness'; the 'masters of reality' inhabit Heaven (139)—artists such as Rembrandt, 'a fellow who would paint a hag of seventy with as much enjoyment as a Venus of twenty' (171) and Mozart, and by implication from the preface, Bunyan, Hogarth, Ibsen and Tolstoy among others, artists who committed to a struggle for reform, artist-philosophers like Shaw himself.

In Part V of *Back to Methuselah* the 'artist-philosopher' becomes the 'artist-prophet' while retaining much of his earlier Platonism. Believing that great art of the past was 'great' because of the religious conviction that inspired its creation, Shaw seeks to be 'an iconographer of the religion of my time [i.e. Creative Evolution] and thus fulfil my natural function as an artist' (Shaw 1945: lxxxv).

In a futuristic pastoral nightmare, beautiful children play at love and art; they abandon both pursuits by the age of four. At the 'Festival of the Arts' the sculptor Arjillax shocks his spectators by producing busts of the Ancients; that is, he seeks to represent the reality of the world around him rather than an idealized prettiness. Martellus goes further for, in collaboration with the scientist Pygmalion, he creates two 'living' creatures. 'Anything alive is better than anything pretending to be alive', he asserts (ibid.: 240). But they have made mere automata, and Pygmalion dies at the bite of his female 'monster'. The She-Ancient, a true Platonist, rebukes the artists and aesthetes: 'Art is the magic mirror you make to reflect your invisible dreams in visible pictures' (ibid.: 268). 'You can create nothing but yourself' (ibid.: 267). As art and artists dissolve into an abstract world of thought, however, the future seems bleak and cold, a '*reductio ad absurdum*' of [Shaw's] puritanic distrust of the senses' (Woodbridge 1963: 111).

If 'As far as thought can reach' is the piece by Shaw that is most 'anti-art', his great defence of art and artists is his response to Max Nordau's celebrated treatise on *Degeneracy* (1895). This first appeared as 'A Degenerate's view of Nordau—an Open Letter to Bernard Tucker in NY Weekly, LIBERTY, 27 July 1895', and was reprinted in 1908 as *The Sanity of Art*. The kernel of Nordau's thesis was thus summarized by Shaw: 'Nordau's message to the world is that all our characteristically modern works of art are symptoms of disease in the artists, and that these diseased artists are themselves symptoms of the nervous exhaustion of the race by overwork' (Shaw 1930: 328). Many of the works which Nordau characterized as 'degenerate' were by artists whom Shaw regarded as outstanding contributors to contemporary culture: Ibsen, Wagner and Tolstoy, for example. The fact that Nordau identified such geniuses with 'the refuse of our prisons and lunatic asylums' (ibid.: 339) only confirmed to Shaw that Nordau was 'the dupe' of a fashionable theory, namely psychiatry. He dismissed the theories of the German writer as 'nothing but the familiar delusion of the used-up man that the world is going to the dogs' (ibid.: 326–7). While admitting that when a new movement in art, literature or music is initiated a great deal of imitative rubbish can be accepted temporarily by critics seeking to embrace new forms, Shaw remains adamant (and eloquent) about the intrinsic possibilities of the creative and performing arts improving the human condition. His spirited defence was much appreciated in the United States, where his response was first published. The *Kansas City Journal* was only one paper to review it enthusiastically: 'Probably never before has there appeared such a wonderful defence of modern art and music as Mr Shaw has given us in his criticism' (see Edwards). But—and there is always a but with Shaw—in his Lecture on Art at Bedford (10 December 1885) he wrote: 'The arts contain methods of seeking happiness: and they are mischievous or beneficial, moral or immoral, just as other methods of seeking happiness are' (Weintraub 1989: 59). There is no special pleading for art as a 'palliative for social gangrene', and all artists are not equally worthy either in their pursuit of their vocation or as members of the community. In seeking to examine further Shaw's complementary or contradictory views, I shall turn to his dramas for illumination.

Shaw's Portraits of the Artists

Spink commented that Shaw attributed to his fictional artists 'less of heroic stature and more of biting satire that one has any reason to expect in so inveterate an artist' (Spink 1963: 82). There are clear parodic elements in his approach at times, but rather than describe the overall approach as 'satiric', I would suggest that he is attempting a comprehensive and objective appraisal of representative samples of a genus of which he is a member.

The artists (and the art lovers) will be investigated, first through their physical appearance, secondly by testing the quality of their creative production, and thirdly by assessing the manner in which they relate to the other characters, in order to extrapolate, if possible, their place in society.

With the important exception of Eugene Marchbanks in *Candida*, the artists in Shaw's plays are explicitly endowed with a handsome appearance, tastefully dressed, perfectly groomed, amiable, engaging and socially at ease. There is more than a hint in the descriptions that the characters have self-consciously created themselves according to some preconceived image of the artist or aesthete. In *Man and Superman* even Octavius's mourning dress is a carefully contrived costume to enable him better to undertake the role of the bereaved, one in which he takes some pleasure. The artists present themselves with a studied attention to their appearance, more commonly associated with women than with men. In this gallery of charming matinée idols, Eugene Marchbanks is an alien creature, '*so uncommon as to be almost unearthly*', described variously as '*a strange shy youth of eighteen*'—he is younger than the others—'*slight effeminate with a delicate childish voice and a hundred tormented expressions*'. His clothes are '*anarchic*' and '*there is no evidence of his ever having brushed them*' (Shaw 1946a: 120). He is nervous and socially inept. His youth, unkempt appearance and vulnerability naturally appeal to Candida's indefatigable maternalism. The description of Eugene as '*effeminate*'—Dubedat is specifically labelled '*not effeminate*'—requires some investigation. A review in the *Manchester Guardian* (15 March 1898) described him as a 'childlike creature . . . a boy of eighteen got up to look like Shelley, not a man, femininely hectic and timid and fierce' (see Evans 1976: 71). The association of Eugene with effeminacy has led critics such as Sally Peters in *The Ascent of the Superman* first to associate the Shavian artist with homosexuality, and secondly, by viewing the character of Eugene as a self-portrait of the young Shaw, to deduce that he himself had veiled homosexual sympathies. Her carefully documented argument concludes: 'Shaw created a vaguely allusive atmosphere that bathed Marchbanks in a coded homosexuality—a character with autobiographical parallels to the playwright' (Peters 1996: 165). 'Coded' messages are always seductive, but the final deduction is not proven. Nevertheless, leaving aside Shaw's personal gender preferences, which are irrelevant here, it is useful in the context of examining his representation of the artist to probe further. Praed, 'hardly past middle-age' (Shaw 1946b: 211), is unmarried, and is the only one of the older generation in *Mrs Warren's Profession* who has not taken advantage of the services she offers. In *Man and Superman*, Ann Whitefield observes, 'Tavy will never marry'; 'The poetic temperament's a very nice temperament, very amiable, very harmless and poetic, I daresay; but it's an old maid's temperament' (Shaw 1976: 204). Shaw may have been influenced in the representations of some of his fictional artists by the *fin de siècle* fascination with homosexuality—popularly but by no means solely associated with Oscar Wilde—and the sexologists' investigations into the 'Uranian' or 'Urning', the intermediate sex, that was, as some would have it, superior to the male and the female. Edward Carpenter, for example, himself a homosexual, associated this gender type specifically with the artist's nature and the artist's sensibility and perception (Carpenter 1908). Was Shaw rendering some of his artists and aesthetes 'barren' because he was influenced by Carpenter and others, or because he was intent on effecting a meaningful opposition between the artist and the procreative dynamic of the Life Force? Or, in Eugene's case, was he simply showing the first immature heterosexual impulses of an adolescent boy?

How Talented are Shaw's Artists?

In the plays under examination, Shaw portrays two poets, an easel painter, an artist-craftsman, an architect and two sculptors. One might add the two 'Pygmalions', creators of living things, Henry Higgins in *Pygmalion* and the Martellus/Pygmalion partnership in Part V of *Back to Methuselah*. There is no musician and no actor, surprising perhaps if one considers that Shaw focused on the portrayal of such artists in his novels. And there are no women artists. In the Epistle Dedicatory to *Man and Superman*, Shaw wrote: 'I am sorry to say that it is a common practice with romancers to announce their hero as a man of extraordinary genius, and then leave his works entirely to the reader's imagination' (Shaw 1976: 26). Hence the inclusion of 'The Revolutionist's Handbook' in the appendix to the printed play text. This prompts the question: what is the perceived quality of the work of the artists represented in Shaw's drama, and how does he convey that quality to an audience?

The quality of Octavius's literary endeavours (perhaps they do not exist) remains unknown. A review in the *Times Literary Supplement* referred to him as an 'alleged' poet: 'So far as the play is concerned the "poet" might just as well have been a dry-salter' (Crompton 1971: 113). A. M. Gibbs astutely remarked that 'In the larger allegory of the play, Octavius is associated with sentimentality, debased romanticism and the poetic idealization of women ... the qualities he is associated with . . . are seen forming part of the condition of hell' (Gibbs 1983: 124). The quality of the work of Eugene, Louis Dubedat, Apollodorus, and the Martellus and Pygmalion partnership is more germane to the theme of the play in which each appears. Charles Berst asserts that, in Eugene's case, 'his spirit is more poetic than his talents' (Berst 1973: 57). Eugene's passages of poetic prose, notably the speech about his dream of taking Candida away to 'where the marble floors are washed by the rain and dried by the sun; where the south wind dusts the beautiful green and purple carpets' (Shaw 1946a: 142), are meretricious, no doubt deliberately so. This example, together with the description of Candida as the Madonna (ibid.: 161), might be designed as parody, assigning Eugene to the category of poets described by Shaw in *The Sanity of Art*, 'who have nothing to versify but the commonplaces of amorous infatuation' (Weintraub 1989: 383). The truth of Eugene's poetic genius remains suspect, and Shaw does not provide the audience with any of his original work—probably because the dramatist himself was no poet.

One is left in no doubt as to the genius of Louis Dubedat in *The Doctors Dilemma*. It is an integral feature of his character and of the 'dilemma' explored in the play. The doctors are agreed about his brilliance as a painter, but this is difficult for the audience or the reader to judge. Shaw, however, evolved a clever device for actualizing Dubedat's talent. The painting on which he is working in Act III is of his wife, and Jennifer is seen modelling for it on the throne, beautiful, caring and draped in brocade. We can have a clear impression of what the picture will be—Louis, having 'Pygmalion-like' transformed a naïve young Cornishwoman into the splendid creature she now is, will continue posthumously to create beautiful Jennifers according to his preordained instructions. But Louis's art is not only two-dimensional. Today, he would be credited with a talent for 'installations' or 'live art', as witnessed by his staging of his own death-scene before an invited audience. In his invalid's chair, flanked by Jennifer and Sir Ralph, he occupies the position in which his easel was previously placed, the embodied 'picture' replacing the painted one. Louis is '*making the most of his condition, finding voluptuousness in languor and drama in his death*' (Shaw 1987: 169). Urging his wife to remarry and always to remain beautiful, and assuring her that he will live on in her, he utters his artist's creed: 'I believe in Michael Angelo, Velasquez, and Rembrandt; in the might of design, the mystery of colour, the redemption of all things by Beauty everlasting, and the message of Art that made these hands blessed. Amen. Amen' (ibid.: 174). His final posthumous work of art is the appearance of Jennifer created according to his directions, '*wonderfully and beautifully dressed and radiant, carrying a great piece of purple silk, handsomely embroidered, over her arm*' (ibid.: 179). With this cloth she covers his dead body: another triumph for the artist.

Dubedat's paintings are on exhibition in the gallery which is the setting for Act V, but are hardly sufficiently visible for an audience to make any serious judgement. On the occasion of the first production at the Royal Court, however, Shaw borrowed paintings from the Carfax Gallery to dress the stage. As Weintraub describes, these were the works of 'Beardsley, Rothenstein, Augustus John, Charles Ricketts and Charles Shannon' (Weintraub 1989: 28). This evinced a scathing notice from Max Beerbohm in the *Saturday Review* (24 November 1906): 'Dubedat seems to have caught, in his brief lifetime, the various styles of all the young lions of the Carfax Gallery ... Masterpieces of painting must be kept to an audience's imagination. [...] only by suggestion can these masterpieces be made real to us.' The solecism was, however, committed by Shaw the director, not Shaw the dramatist. In *Caesar and Cleopatra* Apollodorus's exquisite taste in craftsmanship, very much in the style of William Morris, Shaw's mentor and friend who promoted the art of the beautifully useful, is evident in his sword: 'designed as carefully as a medieval cross [which] has a blued blade shewing through an openwork of purple leather and filigree' (Shaw 1946c: 184). This, 'the only weapon ft for an artist' (ibid.: 189), is put to use by its owner, who is an accomplished duellist, Cleopatra's 'perfect knight' (ibid.: 188), and a not inconsiderable soldier besides.

The work of those who 'create' or 'transform' human creatures is also available for judgement as to its quality. In *Pygmalion* Henry Higgins does 'make' a beautiful duchess from the apparently unpromising material of Eliza Doolittle (with help from Pickering and his mother), but his creation takes control of herself, and surpasses the imagination of her creator. Martellus and Pygmalion in *Back to Methuselah* (Part V) are less fortunate in their collaborative project and produce only primitive monsters, who are finally exterminated. Except in the last two examples, it is difficult to convey on stage the genius of the artist. It is much easier, as in the case of Octavius (*Man and Superman*) and Eugene (*Candida*), to indicate the absence of it, but using the devices with which he engages in *The Doctors Dilemma*, Shaw makes a most convincing attempt.

The Artist in Society or Who Changes the World?

In all of Shaw's dramas which feature an artist or an aesthete, that character is brought into direct confrontation with one who holds a contrasting view of life—variously, soldiers, scientists, rationalists and social reformers. This section will examine how, or if, the conflicts are resolved.

Three of the plays, *Candida, Man and Superman* and *The Doctors Dilemma*, have a triangular pattern of characterization, with a woman at the apex, and the artist and the other with whom he is in opposition or competition at the base. The woman is given an additional symbolic dimension: Candida 'is' the

Virgin Mother, Ann 'is' Everywoman, and Jennifer 'is' the Muse. In compet-
ing for her, the men are, therefore, not merely sexual rivals but philosophical adversaries. Eugene is matched with James Morell, a Christian socialist;
Octavius with Jack Tanner, a revolutionary and philosopher; Louis Dubedat
with Ridgeon, a physician/scientist. Shaw thus 'tests' his artists in the boxing
ring of contemporary social preoccupations.

In *Candida*, Morell, the charismatic preacher, and Eugene, the embryonic
poet, are both equally engaged with words. Neither, however, has any sympathy with the manner in which the other chooses to deploy them. Candida is
impressed by neither; she trivializes the effects of Morell's oratory, attributing
his rhetorical effectiveness to his sex appeal, and Eugene's verses bore her. She
would rather he reverted to his usual conversational 'moonshine'. The men's
accomplishments are directly juxtaposed in Act III. The exhilaration of the
returning Lexy and Prossy, in Dionysian high spirits, intoxicated not only by
Burgess's champagne but by the excitement of Morell's revolutionary socialism, is set in sharp contrast to Candida's strictures on temperance and her
failure to engage with Eugene's poetic endeavours. The 'artist' emerges as the
'stronger' man in terms of his self-sufficiency and capacity for coping with an
independent existence, but Morell's successful commitment to social reform,
in which Eugene has absolutely no interest, renders him the more effectual
member of society.

Octavius Robinson in *Man and Superman*, would-be poet and playwright, is a highly conventional young man, firmly embedded in the manners
and mores of English upper-middle-class society. His role as a poet is largely
constructed by Jack Tanner. As Berst has pointed out: 'To prop his metaphysics [Tanner] gives Octavius a role which is entirely disproportionate to the
ineffectual, untalented, romantic stripling' (Berst 1973: 114). Tanner has to
create his generic adversary for the hand of Ann; Shaw does not provide one.
Tanner's 'true artist' who 'will let his wife starve, his children go barefoot,
his mother drudge for his living at seventy, sooner than work at anything
but his art' (Shaw 1976: 61) is a to miles from Octavius Robinson. Just as
Candida decides that Morell will better serve her maternal purposes, Ann
selects and pursues Tanner because she needs a father for the Superman, and
the barrenness of the so-called 'poetic temperament' is of no use to her. Jack
Tanner's revolutionary fervour, his endless quest to improve society, as well as
his sexual energy, select him as the chosen partner of 'Everywoman'. In each
play, the 'poet' is defeated by the social reformer.

The Doctor's Dilemma, while broadly adhering to a similar triangular structure and maintaining the confrontational trope of the other plays,
engages with these dramaturgical strategies to develop a somewhat different
issue. True, in this last instance, the artist wins the woman who does not even

notice the existence of his rival, but Shaw's purpose is to show the similarities between the artist and the man of science rather than their differences. The 'dilemma', as Sir Patrick expresses it, is 'a plain choice between a man and a lot of pictures', but 'the most tragic thing in the world', ironically articulated by Ridgeon, is 'a man of genius who is not a man of honour' (Shaw 1987: 176). Neither Dubedat or Ridgeon is an honourable man, although each is a highly gifted one. Ultimately the artist is the victor, for he achieves immortality for Jennifer, his Muse, and for his art. Ridgeon saves lives for this world alone.

The 'dilemma', or to be more explicit, the contest between the artist's output and his contribution to society, is further explored in two other plays by Shaw that do not adhere to the 'triangle' formula described above. In *Mrs Warren's Profession*, described by Berst as 'A moral allegory—the Battle for the Soul of Vivie Warren' (Berst 1973: 29), Praed is the most attractive tempter whom she encounters. Crofts, Frank and even her mother (finally) are more easily dismissed. But Praed is not tainted like the rest. He represents a cultured and civilized world, demonstrating to Vivie, and to the audience, that the capitals of Europe may be the sites of a chain of capitalist whorehouses but they are also centres of great art. Vivie's crude dismissal of the Gospel of Art which Praed preaches diminishes her and renders her final appearance alone in the putative seat of 'honour', the actuary's office, a bleak picture.

In *Caesar and Cleopatra*, Apollodorus, the Sicilian patrician, whose universal password 'Art for Art's sake' should render him among the damned, is not so much in an adversarial position in relation to Caesar as a complementary one. Caesar is represented as a great soldier and a wise and judicious ruler. He is a successful 'man of the world' in the best sense of the phrase. Although he jestingly dismisses Apollodorus as a 'popinjay' (Shaw 1946c: 216), he immediately acknowledges the wit and imagination of his conversation. On Caesar's departure from Egypt, he leaves Apollodorus in charge of the art of the 'colony' with the words (surely ironic and referring to the British as well as the Roman Empire):

CAESAR: Remember: Rome loves art and will encourage it ungrudgingly.

APOLLODORUS: I understand, Caesar. Rome will produce no art itself; but it will buy up and take away whatever the other nations produce.

CAESAR: What! Rome produce no art! Is peace not an art? Is war not an art? Is government not an art? Is civilization not an art? All these we give you in exchange for a few ornaments.

(Shaw 1946c:239)

Caesar and Cleopatra reaches a nice balance in endorsing aesthetic sensibility as having a rightful place in the ideal state and in extending the concept and function of creativity to permeate all aspects of government. Thus, in the plays, as in his theoretical writings, Shaw questions the nature of art, the function of art, the engagement of art with political and social concerns—with the same ambiguities and the same dialectic.

Pictures in the Plays and on Stage

The printed texts of Shaw's dramas abound in references, explicit and implicit, to works of art, and his directorial notes to actors and scenic artists frequently offer advice on costume and setting. A key visual property in *Candida*, described as a 'modern Pre-Raphaelite play' (Shaw 1946a: vi), is the '*large autotype of the chief figure in Titian's Assumption of the Virgin*' (ibid.: 104) which hangs above the mantelpiece in Morell's study. One learns much about the characters and the meaning of the play from this picture (Adams 1966). Shaw notes in the stage directions that: '*A wise-hearted observer . . . would not suspect either [Candida's] husband or herself of . . . any concern with the art of Titian*' (ibid.: 104). Candida and Morell belong to the practical everyday world, of domestic chores in her case, and of social work in his. Shaw later was to comment that the picture has been 'boiled down to a cockney Candida' (Weintraub 1989: 20). It was a gift from Eugene, chosen because of the resemblance he perceived between Candida and the depiction of the Madonna. Eugene is the aesthete, the Pre-Raphaelite whose adoration of Candida is, as Margery Morgan aptly observes, 'a blend of erotic with religious emotion' (Morgan 1972: 76), expressed in his idealized description of her: 'Her shawl, her wings, the wreath of stars on her head, the lilies in her hand, the crescent moon beneath her feet' (Shaw 1946a: 161). The choice of Titian's painting over Shaw's earlier selection of Raphael's 'Sistine Madonna' was made because the former did not include the Christ child. There are no distracting children in *Candida* either. Conveniently the 'real' ones are still recuperating in the country where their mother has left them, and she makes virtually no reference to them throughout the play. It is first Eugene, and then Morell, who sits in the child's chair. Of the two adults whom Candida reduces to childhood, paradoxically but not surprisingly, it is the artist who leaves, taking with him the much-debated 'secret' in his heart. The man, poet or not, who saw the Madonna (Raphael's or Titian's) in a commonplace and predatory suburban housewife—'a sentimental prostitute', according to Beatrice Webb (Morgan 1972: 72)—having the scales lifted from his eyes, must effect his escape. As for the mysterious 'secret', there is no reason to doubt Shaw's own explanation:

> The poet then rises up and says 'Out, then into the night with me'—Tristan's holy night. If this greasy fool's paradise is happiness,

then I give it to you with both hands: 'life is nobler than that'. That is 'the poet's secret'. (Letter to James Huneker, 6 April 1904; Laurence 1972: 415)

Weintraub also draws attention to pictorial references in stage settings which give the spectator or reader important insights into character, for example the interior decoration of Roebuck Ramsden's study in Act I of *Man and Superman* and Mrs Higgins's drawing room in *Pygmalion*. The former contains '*autotypes of allegories by GF Watts*' (Shaw 1976: 25), a fashionable Victorian painter, first husband of the actress Ellen Terry. (Is this a Shavian quip, one wonders, considering his amorous correspondence with the lady?) Watts's allegories fit well with Ramsden's inherent conservatism and conventional moral attitudes. The collection of busts of John Bright and Herbert Spencer again attests to Ramsden's erstwhile radicalism, and the impression of the whole room gives physical corroboration to the description of him in the stage directions, namely that he '*believes in the fine arts with all the earnestness of a man who doe not understand them*' (ibid.: 42). Similarly, in *Pygmalion* the decor of Professor Higgins's laboratory, with its arid engravings of architectural perspective drawings, is sharply contrasted with the elegance of his mother's Chelsea drawing room, with its Morris wallpaper and soft furnishings, and a selection of paintings in the Burne-Jones manner.

It is difficult to determine the extent to which an audience, certainly a twenty-first-century audience, would be qualified to read such visual references. But it is likely that at a time when women's fashions and home decoration were dictated by 'society drama' on the West End Stage, Shaw's contemporaries would be visually sophisticated. Even if specific references proved elusive, the overall effect of Shaw's artistic choices in terms of setting could not fail to illuminate an understanding of character and theme.

Conclusion: Platonist, Philosopher, Puritan and Playwright

It is easy to become enmeshed in the complex web of Shaw's opinions on art and artists. A few constants do, however, emerge: a work of art must be grounded in the society from which it grows and must contribute to the progress of that society, spiritually, morally or practically. Romance, prettiness and superficial sentiment will not serve. Great artists, be they poets, painters, craftsmen or dramatists, must be philosophers, moralists or prophets of their own 'religion', from which their art will draw its power. Shaw's own work is testimony to his aesthetics.

Primary Reading

Shaw, George Bernard (1930). *Major Critical Essays*. London: Constable.

Shaw, George Bernard (1931). *Our Theatre in the Nineties*. 3 vols. London: Constable.

Shaw, George Bernard (1945). *Back to Methuselah*. Oxford: Oxford University Press.

Shaw, George Bernard (1946a). *Plays Pleasant*. London: Penguin. (Includes *Candida*.)

Shaw, George Bernard (1946b). *Plays Unpleasant*. London: Penguin. (Includes *Mrs Warren's Profession*.)

Shaw, George Bernard (1946c). *Three Plays for Puritans*. London: Penguin. (Includes *Caesar and Cleopatra*.)

Shaw, George Bernard (1976). *Man and Superman*. London: Penguin.

Shaw, George Bernard (1987). *The Doctor' Dilemma*. London: Penguin.

FURTHER READING

Adams, Elsie B. (1966). 'Bernard Shaw's Pre-Raphaelite Drama', *PMLA* 81:5, 428–38.

Albert, Sidney P. (1956). 'Bernard Shaw: The Artist as Philosopher', *Journal of Aesthetics and Art Criticism* XIV:4, 419–38.

Berst, Charles A. (1973). *Bernard Shaw and the Art of Drama*. Urbana, IL, and London: University of Illinois Press.

Carpenter, Edward (1908). *The Intermediate Sex: A Study of Some Transitional Men and Women*. London: Allen and Unwin.

Crompton, Louis (1971). *Shaw the Dramatist*. London: Allen and Unwin.

Doan, William J. (2001). '*The Doctor's Dilemma*: Adulterating a Muse', *Annual Conference of Bernard Shaw Studies* 21, 151–61.

Edwards, Sashona 'The Worthy Adversaries: Benjamin R. Tucker and G. Bernard Shaw'. www.uncletaz.com/liberty/shaw.html.

Evans, T. F. (ed.) (1976). *Shaw: The Critical Heritage*. London: Routledge and Kegan Paul.

Gibbs, A. M. (1983). *The Art and Mind of Shaw*. London: Macmillan.

Laurence, Dan H. (ed.) (1972). *Bernard Shaw: Collected Letters: 1898–1919*. London, Sydney and Toronto: Max Reinhardt.

Meisel, Martin (1984). *Shaw and the Nineteenth-Century Theatre*. New York: Limelight Editions.

Morgan, Margery M. (1972). *The Shavian Playground*. London: Methuen.

Peters, Sally (1996). *The Ascent of the Superman*. New Haven, CT, and London: Yale University Press.

Spink, Judith B. (1963). 'The Image of the Artist in the Plays of Bernard Shaw', *Shaw Review* 6, 82–8.

Weintraub, Stanley (1989). *Bernard Shaw on the London Art Scene*. University Park and London: Pennsylvania University Press.

West, Alick (1950). *A Good Man Fallen Among Fabians*. London: Laurence and Wishart.

Woodbridge, Homer (1963). *Bernard Shaw: Creative Artist*. Carbondale, IL: South Illinois University Press.

MICHAEL GOLDMAN

Shavian Poetics: Shaw on Form and Content

Shaw's plays bristle with ideas, and the more one looks at his works for the stage, the more complicated becomes the relation between these ideas and the style in which they are expressed. The apparently clear-cut social positions become elusive, perplexingly bound up with the energy and impulse, the music and texture of theatrical performance. It would seem important, then, to try to get a grip on the relation between style and idea in Shaw's art. Historically, this effort has proved harder than one might expect, in part because of a peculiar critical distortion of Shaw's work that has persisted almost from the beginning of his dramatic career.

Even a famous author can be a victim of his or her reputation. For some writers, time eases the burden relatively quickly. T. S. Eliot was soon understood to be a passionate and personal poet, rather than a coldly cerebral one. By now Jane Austen is safe from the reputation of maiden delicacy. But will Shaw (1856–1950) ever recover from being thought entertaining? In his case, of course, the reputation is deserved—as far as it goes. He is entertaining, like his beloved Mozart, who, Shaw said, had taught him "how to write seriously without being dull." Shaw faces greater problems than Mozart, however, because even his reputation for seriousness has hurt him. So, even as he is considered too much of an entertainer, too given to gags and paradoxes to

From *Princeton University Library Chronicle*, vol. LXVIII, pp. 71–81. Copyright © 2006 by Princeton University Library.

be taken seriously, at the same time reviewers and critics continue to insist that his plays are not really art but a kind of platform oratory.

The enduring popular picture of Shaw seems to be of a kind of combination of merry prankster and socialist demagogue, a writer who will do anything for a laugh yet is at bottom drily didactic. Certainly no play of his can be performed in New York without the *Times* reviewer using the word "soapbox" somewhere in his article, as if it explained everything, or anything. Behind this paradoxical and patronizing attitude lies the assumption that the relation between style and content in Shaw's work is of the crudest kind; the practiced orator finds snappy diversions to punctuate his harangue.

Surprisingly, among the many ways to deal with this misapprehension, one that is seldom tried is to treat Shaw seriously as an analyst of his own art, particularly of the way in which what we usually call "ideas" operate in his work. In the discussion that follows, I look at a few of his statements about art, aesthetics, and meaning that I think help one to grasp the complexity of his understanding of these issues. Focusing on some passages from his prefaces, especially the preface to *Man and Superman* (1901), I want to attempt some close reading of a type that is usually not directed at Shaw's prose, presumably because it is considered unnecessary.

Shaw is at ease in his prefaces. He is writing free of the tight demands of dramatic time and structure, and so there are garrulous, overly relaxed moments but also flashes of free-form brilliance on all subjects—and sometimes the flashes are impressively sustained and the brilliance deeply penetrating. I intend to look at a couple of places where Shaw emerges as an extremely interesting literary theorist, with results that are revealing for his own plays and indeed for literature in general. They treat the subject of content in the arts in unexpected fashion; that they have been generally ignored would be remarkable, except that the reasons are all too obvious. First, no one wishes to credit Shaw with this kind of seriousness. And second, they are so much fun to read, so brimming with Shaw's Mozartian vitality that it is easy to enjoy them without thinking too hard—or rather, to assume that they are saying simply what one has always expected Shaw to say.

* * *

Some of Shaw's comments on style may leave us wondering if we can be right to approach him in terms of art at all. Coming to maturity in the era of art for art's sake, Shaw typically takes a very strong line against purely stylistic considerations and tends to dismiss formal or aesthetic analysis, of his work, preferring to emphasize its content instead. When he was shown an analysis of his prose style, he commented, "It was very much as if I had told him his house was on fire, and he had said, 'How admirably monosyllabic.'" In *Man and Superman*, Hell seems to be the appropriate destination for devotees of aesthetic pleasure, with the Devil voicing a particularly powerful version of what elsewhere Shaw calls the Gospel of Art. Yet Shaw was himself a superb technical analyst of drama, particularly of acting, and a notable appreciator of art and music. And even in *Man and Superman*, we note that Mozart, for Shaw the greatest of composers, quickly finds Hell boring and chooses to reside in Heaven instead.

We sense this complication as early as *Caesar and Cleopatra* (1898), where we encounter the engaging dandy Apollodorus, who smuggles Cleopatra to Caesar concealed in an expensive Persian rug. Apollodorus proudly insists on his status as an artist, and Shaw pokes a certain amount of fun at his aesthetic pretensions. But Apollodorus is a man of parts, a brave and skilled swordsman, and Caesar admires him as much for his artistic and intellectual flair as for his daring. In *Caesar and Cleopatra*'s hierarchy of best-and-brightest (a hierarchy that is a feature of most of Shaw's plays), Apollodorus ranks high, perhaps next to Caesar. And even the critique to which his aestheticism is exposed is subtler than expected. Finding his way barred by a Roman sentry, Apollodorus declares, "My motto is art for art's sake." Unimpressed, the sentry replies that this is not the password of the day. We are nudged toward historical awareness here. A scant three years after Oscar Wilde's trial, "Art for art's sake" was certainly not the password in 1898. More important is a more general point, the same one that Bertolt Brecht was to make when he said that you can sail with the wind or, against the wind, but you cannot sail with yesterday's wind or tomorrow's. The power of art cannot be separated or insulated from the demands of the historical moment, the ever-changing passwords of the day. Apollodorus has to shift his tactics, but he finally prevails, and this conscious artist (who sings, turns phrases, arranges exquisite banquets, and manages to sell a few rugs on the side) turns out to be the character who best understands Caesar's mind.

In fact, Shaw's attack is never on art itself or its aesthetic qualities, but on a certain kind of aestheticism, the worship of art as one might worship sensual pleasure, as the following passage from the preface to *Three Plays for Puritans* (1900) suggests: "I am as fond of fine music and handsome building as Milton was, or Cromwell, or Bunyan; but if I found that they were becoming the instruments of a systematic idolatry of sensuousness I would hold it good statesmanship to blow every cathedral in the world to pieces with dynamite, organ and all, without the least heed to the screams of the art critics and cultured voluptuaries."[1] This statement seems designed to provoke *our* screams as art lovers, but the mention of Milton, a supremely sensuous writer, reinforces the distinction Shaw is pursuing. He writes as someone at home with the sumptuosities of great art. Nor does he ever, in any sense, prefer the ideas or themes of art over its formal beauties. Indeed, if we read his most searching comments on art carefully, we see that for Shaw this distinction is meaningless and misleading.

I turn now to my main exhibit, a passage from the preface to *Man and Superman*. Because it is by Shaw, who is not supposed to be theoretically complex, especially on aesthetics, scholars have tended to look right past such statements. (How differently they would be treated if they were by T. S. Eliot or Jacques Derrida!) Shaw's analysis is in fact as subtle and original a discussion of form and content as any I know, and it deserves to be quoted—and examined—at length:

> My contempt for *belles lettres*, and for amateurs who become the heroes of the fanciers of literary virtuosity, is not founded on any illusion of mine as to the permanence of those forms of thought (call them opinions) by which I strive to communicate my bent to my fellows. To younger men they are already outmoded; for though they have no more lost their logic than an eighteenth century pastel has lost its drawing or its color, yet, like the pastel, they grow indefinably shabby, will grow shabbier until they cease to count at all, when my books will either perish, or, if the world is still poor enough to want them, will have to stand, with Bunyan's, by quite amorphous qualities of temper and energy. . . ."[f]or art's sake" alone I would not face the toil of writing a single sentence. . . . Effectiveness of assertion is the Alpha and Omega of style. He who has nothing to assert has no style and can have none; he who has something to assert will go as far in power of style as its momentousness and his conviction will carry him. Disprove his assertion after it is made, yet its style remains. Darwin has no more destroyed the style of Job nor of Handel than Martin Luther destroyed the style of Giotto. All the assertions get disproved sooner or later; and so we find the world full of a magnificent debris of artistic fossils, with the matter-of-fact credibility gone clean out of them, but the form still splendid.[2]

The best way to navigate this remarkable passage is to follow the apparently simple distinction with which Shaw begins: the distinction between form and content, the oldest and usually most cliché-ridden of critical binaries. The idea is normally expressed in language that suggests the clearest and simplest of oppositions. On the one side we are accustomed to find style, form, texture, expression, beauty; on the other, content, ideas, meaning, truth.

At first Shaw seems to insist on the contrast in the boldest, even the crudest terms. In the opening words of the passage, an interest in style is associated with the mincing "fanciers of literary virtuosity," a phrase of the same ilk as "the screams of art critics and cultured voluptuaries," and it mimes Shaw's "contempt" for an aestheticism that is again none too delicately linked to effeminacy. "Belles lettres" and "amateurs" reinforce the effect.

But watch how quickly the style/content distinction gets obscured, how Shaw keeps inserting new terms for the two sides of the binary. Each substitution is made as if the simplest contrast were being pursued, but in fact each introduces a nuanced, complicating spin. Halfway through the first sentence, the phrase "forms of thought" is substituted for "content" and in turn immediately replaced by "opinions." And these more evanescent formulations are seen as merely the vehicles not of some truth, idea, or even a point of view, but of what Shaw calls his "bent."

"Bent" is the crucial word in the passage. It diminishes the ideational status of content, yet replaces it with something more personal that opens up an entirely more nuanced vision of the artistic process. "Bent" is a wonderfully simple, casual, very English word. It is diffident, apparently dismissive—Shaw refers not to his ideas, discoveries, beliefs, or even opinions, but to a tendency, an attitude, a leaning. And yet a bent is directed, human, individual, dynamic. It involves the whole personality; it connects an impulse to a person and through that person connects the impulse to action.

By the second sentence, then, we are looking at a new binary—not style/content, but forms of thought/bent. These forms of thought, Shaw now reminds us, are subject to rapid historical decay; already, younger men find them "outmoded." What remains of them is their "logic." This word returns us to the more enduring, presumably more substantial side of the binary, the "content" side. But again, the ground is shifting. Logic suggests rigor and strictness of thought, but of thought's formal process rather than its subject matter. And suddenly—we are still in the second sentence—logic is equated with the "drawing" and "color" of an eighteenth-century pastel, with the formal qualities, that is, of a nondiscursive art. The content side has again dissolved into form; but at the same time we are being invited to think of formal qualities in a new way.

A little further in the same sentence, the startling introduction of Bunyan shows us how far we have come. Having first equated what is permanent in his writing with the line and color of an elegant pastel, Shaw now equates both with the enduring value of a great Christian writer. Content, ideas, beliefs would seem absolutely central to the author of *Pilgrim's Progress*, yet Shaw reminds us that most readers of Bunyan today are not drawn to him because they credit his religious opinions. Rather, they appreciate the "qualities of temper and energy" they find in his work. Temper and energy—do these qualities refer to style or content? They are deeper and more lasting than ideas, but harder to assign to one pole of the binary. Like the idea of a bent, they direct us toward a personal quality that is deeper than any formulation, a marshaling of the impulse toward life.

For Shaw, personal qualities of this sort are of the greatest ethical and historical importance. He usually uses a word like "energy" with a sense of its scientific definitions, in this case the capacity to do work in the world. Indeed, many of the most appealing effects in Shaw's plays derive their force from dramatizing a superior use of energy. In *Caesar and Cleopatra*, for instance, Shaw introduces a steam engine eighteen centuries ahead of its time. The anachronism has been seen as cheekily perverse—Shaw making fun of the whole enterprise of historical drama—but the point is that a steam engine seems amazing, supernatural in a culture that makes much less efficient use of energy, just as the Roman legions and Caesar's rational generalship seem miraculous to the Egyptians over whom he triumphs. Much theatrical fun is had with the steam engine—it is the device that hoists Cleopatra and her rug up to Caesar on the Pharos—and we see it in elaborate operation. Not surprisingly, it fascinates Caesar, even in the midst of a military crisis. As with the play's enormously entertaining presentation of Caesar himself, the theatrical fun associated with the steam engine celebrates the ability to do the world's work, to put energy to use in a superior way. The brio of its theatrical deployment is a metaphor for Caesar's own "temper and energy." In *Man and Superman*, a "practicable" motorcar is used to very similar effect. There, too, it's impossible to separate the energy, the color, the bold wit of the theatrical presentation from ideas about power, history, and human excellence.

But now in the paragraph we are reading, Shaw—after having apparently replaced the sharply defined notion of a readily formulable content with more fluid terms like "bent," "temper," and "energy"—seems to change direction and swing back to the emphatic favoring of content over style, a trumpetlike affirmation of the priority of what one has to say over how one says it. "Effectiveness of assertion is the Alpha and Omega of style." Power of style, he declares, depends on having "something to assert." We quickly discover, however, that what is important about the assertion is not finally its message, its content as a fixed and formulable idea. Style, rather, is the enduring element. "Disprove his assertion after it is made, yet its style remains." The link between assertion and style is the "momentousness and conviction" of what is asserted. Effectiveness of assertion is not so much a matter of putting one's point across as of communicating one's bent.

Shaw drives his argument home by invoking the stylistic power of three religious artists: the author of the book of Job, George Frideric Handel, and

Giotto. The last two introduce a typical Shavian twist or enrichment. Their appeal is in the first instance sensual, and Shaw knows full well that we do not think of them as didactic: they continue to speak profoundly to people who share not a single one of Handel's or Giotto's convictions. All convictions—everything we normally think of as "content"—are doomed to pass. All assertions will be disproved—Shaw's as much as Darwin's or Luther's. What remains, the enduring quality behind any assertion, is something we can feel with special force in the greatest of books or paintings or works of music. With a full sense of the reversal of the by now thoroughly dismantled binary, Shaw calls this quality "form." "And so we find the world full of a magnificent debris of artistic fossils, with the matter-of-fact credibility gone clean out of them, but the form still splendid." He can still poke fun at the pretensions of aestheticism by calling the great works of the past "fossils," while nevertheless making the grandest claims of value for the aesthetic dimension.

We have come a long way in a short paragraph. Appropriately enough for Shaw's subject, it is hard to sum up in a simple formula the rich conception that has emerged. Yes, to make great art one has to have a point, a belief, an attitude to life. But one's point is not the point. And the idea of form has been transvalued too. By now we think of form, of its "splendor," as inextricably linked to the power of conviction, that is, to the power of communicating a bent, a vital thrust of mind and spirit. Shaw has quite literally, in the purely Derridean sense, deconstructed the form/content binary. Importantly for Shaw, however, the aim of deconstruction in his hands is not a *mise en abyme*, which is finally no more than a sophisticated way of throwing up one's hands at the presumed insufficiency of language. Rather, Shaw uses this kind of analysis as an instrument of education, a way of breaking down outmoded forms of thought to achieve a more enlightened understanding. It conserves and renews what it has disassembled. It is a Fabian performance, not destructive but reconstitutive.

*   *   *

If art is about communicating a bent, how is a bent communicated? What is the content of a bent? A complete answer would require a study of Shaw's poetics, a book that remains unwritten. But one answer may be found in another idea that is broached a little later in the preface to *Man and Superman*—the idea of resistance:

> If you study the electric light ... you will find that your house contains a great quantity of highly susceptible copper wire which gorges itself with electricity and gives you no light whatever. But

here and there occurs a scrap of intensely insusceptible, intensely resistant material; and that stubborn scrap grapples with the current and will not let it through until it has made itself useful to you as those two vital qualities of literature, light and heat. Now if I am to be no mere copper wire amateur but a luminous author, I must also be a most intensely refractory person, liable to go out and to go wrong at inconvenient moments, and with incendiary possibilities.[3]

It's no accident, of course, that Shaw chooses an image drawn from electricity, for—as with Caesar and the steam engine—the question of putting power to use is central to his politics and to his view of history as well as to his idea of art. The passage reminds us that, in reading Shaw, we should look not only for the opinions the characters utter but also for the clash of those opinions with our own, their resistance to our ideas and to currents of belief, action, and expectation generated by the play that sets them in motion. It is this resistance-to-the-current that creates the dramatic experience.

In *Major Barbara* (1905), for example, Andrew Undershaft, the Nietzschean arms manufacturer, argues persuasively, movingly, delightfully that developing weapons of mass destruction and selling them to whoever can pay top dollar is the most moral undertaking possible, specifically more virtuous than sheltering the homeless, feeding the poor, and following the Ten Commandments. In a drama that everywhere resonates with Shaw's impassioned socialist critique of society, this brilliant capitalist carries the day and converts the play's most charming and morally intelligent characters to his point of view. We spend the play resisting his arguments, while, thrillingly, their impulse carries the play along.

Not surprisingly, *Man and Superman* provides a particularly neat illustration of the process. The whole play is about a man resisting a current, the current of the Life Force embodied by the woman who is determined to make him her husband. By marrying Ann Whitefield, Jack Tanner gives in to the Life Force, as no doubt he should, but by *resisting* it for four acts, he makes the drama. He allows us to see and enjoy what it is all about. And in making Jack Tanner both an articulate socialist of the most advanced intellectual positions and a poor jerk who cannot see what's obvious to everyone else and who has no chance of escaping Ann, Shaw is really expressing the same point he makes in the preface when he talks about form and content. Jack's intellectual opinions, valid as they may be, are at best of transitory value and are relatively trivial compared with the Life Force, which uses them up, is illuminated by them—and then moves on.

Compared with some of Shaw's heroes and heroines, with Undershaft and Caesar and Major Barbara, Tanner is relatively limited in his gifts. It is probably a mistake to play him as he is often played, made up to look like Bernard Shaw. But he is like Shaw in at least one respect: he makes a contribution that Shaw feels characteristic of art. When the play ends, Ann speaks to him tenderly but condescendingly, "Never mind . . . dear. Go on talking." Tanner's—and the play's—last word is an exasperated "Talking!" which Shaw follows with the stage direction, "*Universal laughter.*" His friends are laughing at Jack's expense, of course, but Shaw's direction—with typical tongue-in-cheek arrogance—also refers to the laughter he is confident will issue from the delighted theater audience, from all audiences of *Man and Superman* everywhere. But "universal" aims even wider than that; it points to the general pleasure of the universe, of the Life Force itself, which may be amused at the pretensions of individual men to truth and understanding, but which thrives on their efforts toward greater knowledge and enlightenment. Jack Tanner has made his contribution. He has added to the growing, blooming, value-creating energy of the living world. Though they may not quite understand him, he has communicated his bent to his fellows. And if we wish to understand what a Shaw play communicates, we must look first and finally to its complex liveliness as a work of art, to the life-tendencies it imparts to us, to the splendor of its form.

Notes

1. *Three Plays for Puritans* (New York: Brentano's, 1906), xx.
2. "Epistle Dedicatory," in *Man and Superman, and Three Other Plays* (New York: Barnes and Noble, 2004), 329–30.
3. "Epistle Dedicatory," 331.

EMIL ROY

G. B. Shaw's Heartbreak House *and Harold Pinter's* The Homecoming: *Comedies of Implosion*

G. B. Shaw's *Heartbreak House* (1919) and Harold Pinter's *The Home-coming* (1965) are two of twentieth-century British drama's premier plays. Shaw's debt to Chekhov's *Cherry Orchard* is too well known for rehearsal here, while the Pinter play mines preoccupations displayed as early as *The Room*, reflecting his indebtedness to Samuel Beckett's fiction among others. Though nearly half a century separates these two works and though Shaw had no discernable influence on Pinter, a side-by-side comparison illuminates not only their differences but underlying preoccupations they share, emanating from formal and social values.

Both playwrights are outsiders, Shaw famously considering himself a "downstart" Irish protestant, and Pinter a secular Jew. Born in 1930, twenty years before Shaw's death, Pinter, like Shaw, works within the conventions of fourth-wall realism. As Christopher Innés says of Pinter, both plays are "models of power structures," though unlike Shaw, Pinter depicts "political themes in purely personal terms."[1] Shaw views his play as a scrim through which to visualize a corrupt, demoralized European society, emphasizing his point through his lengthy commentary and ship interior set standing in for imperial England. Pinter's down-at-the-heels setting obliquely acknowledges a larger urban context, but reduces "politics to a worm's eye view."[2]

From *Comparative Drama* 41, no. 3 (Fall 2007): 335–48. Copyright © 2007 by *Comparative Drama*.

155

If we consider how interchangeable the two plays' titles are, their under-lying similarities reverberate even more meaningfully. Both plays exploit an enduring archetype deeply rooted in the dramatic form: the impact of one or more outsiders on a closed, emotionally conflicted family group, eliciting long-buried antagonisms and flimsy lies, the unforeseen death of a minor character and, in both plays, futile attempts, after the departure or expulsion of an outsider, at reforming the shattered social group. Quite ironically, both playwrights work twists on this time-honored plot device: Shaw's "outsider" Ellie becomes through "heartbreak" an "insider," in effect the third of Sho-tover's daughters, defeating her rival, Hesione Hushabye, and discarding her putative lover, Mangan. In *The Homecoming*, Ruth rejects her husband, Teddy, who may have offered marriage as a form of redemption. She then seamlessly re-enters her former profession on her own terms.

Neither Shaw nor Pinter has available the highly artificial Elizabethan convention of the soliloquy, which allowed characters to reveal their inner thoughts to the audience. However, characters in both their plays feel driven to embarrassing, self-abnegating confessions that serve much the same pur-pose. Their enigmatic characters let slip buried snippets of memory, giving the audience few guideposts to distinguish truth from fiction—if Pinter even considers the distinction meaningful. Shaw's characters are knowable, if com-plex and neurotic, occasionally breaking into recitations of agonized, but rec-ognizably truthful insights into their pasts. Pinter's characters, like Shaw's, are often self-deluded but even more distanced from reality, both theirs and ours: they are all unreliable narrators at times. Where Shaw overexplains, Pinter's dialogue is spare, even cryptic. What Shaw achieves in scope and breadth, Pinter gains in depth and ambiguity. Their plays can be called "comedies of implosion" as, despite the final offstage explosions in Shaw, the characters in self-destructing reveal the emptiness they had struggled to conceal from both themselves and us. Rolf Fjelde approvingly quotes R. D. Laing's definition of "implosion" as "the final precipitation of a state of dread which experiences the full terror of the world as liable at any moment to crash and obliterate all identity,"[3] language that aptly describes the moods of both the Shaw and Pinter plays.

In dismissing Pinter's Jessie as "*no more* than an offstage, inarticulate figure" (italics mine), Mireia Aragay slights the grip offstage, unseen char-acters exert on the behavior of both playwrights' onstage figures.[4] Shaw's Hastings Utterword and Shotover's unnamed "Negress" (Shaw's word) wife occupy archetypal positions roughly analogous to Pinter's MacGregor and Jessie. These characters all appear sharply bifurcated, joining power and pas-sivity, eliciting both idealization and fearful contempt from onstage figures. Though Hastings exemplifies great political authority as "governor of all the crown colonies in succession,"[5] his wife has not only completely domesticated him, but she has also deserted him—as she once left home—in her quest for "heartbreak," an all-consuming submersion in passion. For his part, Shotover recommends a West Indian as an "excellent wi[fe]" (76). Shotover never explains why they separated after only two years of marriage.

Pinter's wraithlike dead characters also reveal mismatched contraries: father/betrayer (MacGregor) and mother/whore (Jessie). Though Max lauds MacGregor as a quick study in the butcher trade, Sam blasts him as a "lousy stinking loudmouth."[6] Just as Hastings first tamed Ariadne before he alienated her, MacGregor could have conceivably displaced Max by fathering one or more of his sons, as Sam hints before his collapse. The actor Paul Rogers suggests,"MacGregor is . . . almost the ruling idea in that household."[7] Macgregor's parentage perhaps accounts for differences in the sons' personalities and temperaments, though all of them are spiritually empty and, possibly, physically impotent, except for Teddy. Similarly, Max both idealizes Jessie as "the backbone to this family . . . a will of iron, a heart of gold and a mind"(62), while maligning her "rotten face"(25). In both plays, then, dichotomized parent/spousal figures project infantile confusion toward parent figures, between nurturing, protective images, on the one hand, and threatening, intimidating symbols, on the other. These characters, especially the men, exert their power subtly and pervasively not by the direct application of brute force—"any fool can govern with a stick in his hand"(145), Shotover announces dismissively. They do so through political or sexual charisma, their effects magnified rather than diminished by physical absence.

Both playwrights express a deep uneasiness with all of society's ways of controlling and channeling the sex drive: marriage, prostitution, platonic attachments, and celibacy, among others. Their men and women fight out the "war of the sexes" on traditional grounds, using sex, love, and money as pawns in their quest for unhampered power. Instead of romanticizing the conventional "gay couple," Margaret Croyden has observed, Shaw, like Pinter, presents the calculating "shrewd couple."[8] The stakes are high in Shaw and— until the last few minutes—almost laughably trivial in Pinter. Both men and women view romantic infatuation as entrancing madness (in Shaw) or obsessive possessiveness (in Pinter). In neither play do men or women understand the other sex nor have they reconciled the yawning splits within their own psyches. Romance or infatuation (for Shaw) and sexual encounters (for Pinter) pass too quickly, and marriage for both lasts too long.

Both plays are preoccupied with women's nature: her status, rights, and prerogatives. In particular, women insist on choosing their own mates or partners. This demand violates social dictates that only men exercise this right, a longstanding preoccupation of English literature at least since

Chaucer. Helplessly enthralled and often resentful, even misogynistic, men seem driven to extreme lengths to captivate women with plumage, money, or words. They both crave and resent the power of sirens who tantalize them with a magnetic, uncontrollable allure. Mazzini Dunn claims mildly that Ellie is "such a lovely girl" because he had "been in love once" (104). Shotover grumbles that "fellows like Mangan" "bring forth demons to delude us, disguised as pretty daughters ... for whose sake we spare them" (87). He goes on to ask, "Is there any slavery on earth viler than this slavery of men to women?" (137). Randall—termed "the Rotter" by Ariadne—bitterly grouses that he has "loved this demon [Ariadne] all [his] life" but "have paid for it" (136). Mangan chimes in: "When you [Hesione] gave me the glad eye ... ,you were making a fool of me" (111–112). Hector and his sister-in-law, Ariadne, succumb to the sudden, irrational attraction others have experienced, recognizing the social hypocrisy masking adultery: "If you do and say the correct thing, you can do just what you like" (83). Betrayed by his loss of control, Hector angrily assails a "damnable quality" of fascination in Shotover's daughters that "destroys men's moral sense, and carries them beyond honor and dishonor" (82).

In *The Homecoming* Pinter's equivalent of the Hector–Ariadne encounter involves Teddy's wife, Ruth, and his brother, Joey, which proceeds nearly wordlessly. After Lenny puts on music, dances with and kisses Ruth, Joey embraces then lies heavily on her; they roll onto the floor. Like Hector, however, Joey recognizes bitterly that Ruth like Ariadne is available to others, that powerful emotion is no guarantee of possession: "I don't want to share her with a lot of yobs!" (89). In *The Collection* Bill explains preconceptions implied in *The Homecoming*: "Every woman is bound to have an outburst of ... wild sensuality at one time or another. . . . It's part of their nature. Even though it may be the kind of sensuality of which you yourself have never been the fortunate recipient."[9] Underlying the struggles for dominance among men and women in both plays is, on a deeper, more internal level, a contest between independence and interconnectedness.

If both playwrights' men are torn by wishes for sexually beguiling temptresses, they also yearn paradoxically for homebodies devoted to household upkeep and children. A few exceptional men, like the never-seen "numskull" Hastings, seem to thrive on marriage: "So long as Ariadne takes care he is fed regularly, he is only too thankful to anyone who will keep her in good humor" (132). For his part, Randall Utterword accepts the disadvantages of a "platonic" relationship to Ariadne with none of the advantages of marriage. Yet if men successfully confine women to traditional homebody roles, the men quickly feel bored and imprisoned. The self-loathing Hector complains, "I might as well be your lapdog. . . . What a damned creature a husband is anyhow!" (89). The Captain tells Ellie, "It's a dangerous thing to be married right up to hilt, like my daughter's husband." He adds, in the same vein, that a husband resembles a broken-in horse.

While Pinter's men, like Shaw's, recognize a woman's sexual allure—"[Ruth's] a lovely girl. A beautiful woman" (75)—they too seek control, to diminish her freedom to choose. Even after Ruth has sealed her agreement with Lenny to return to prostitution, the family seeks to domesticate her, fearing "She won't . . . be adaptable" (97):

Max: And you'd have the whole of your daytime free, of course. You could do a bit of cooking here if you wanted to.

Lenny: Make the beds.

Max: Scrub the place out a bit.

Teddy: Keep everyone company. (93–94)

Ruth evidently turns a deaf ear. She may have no intention of mothering the brood, father and sons. Pinter's conclusion may require his audience to believe two contradictory things: Ruth gains both the freedom of the whore (without a housewife's status) and freedom from entrapment in Teddy's bourgeois marriage (without the freedom to choose sexual partners).

Shaw's women, like his men, acknowledge the power their sexual allure gives them over men's imaginations. Ariadne is married to a powerful, successful man and possesses a "strange fascination" that keeps men "hanging about her" (133). Finding herself lovesick, Ariadne had returned to her father's house in a desperate quest for psychic health. Yet her perverse search for romantic enchantment confirms its mythic power: she had "never been in love in her life, though she has always been trying to fall in head over ears" (84), Hesione muses. They also decry its transitory impact, leaving their men mere husks of the heroes they once captivated. For both Ellie and Hesione, their infatuation with Hector made a stunning impact followed by ennui and regret. "We were frightfully in love with one another . . . an enchanting dream" (84), Hesione recalls, anticipating Ellie's agonized sorrow at her dashed fascination with Hector's imposture: "In the world for me is Marcus and lot of other men of whom one is just the same as another" (108). The women's mingled fascination by and fear of passion—and its concomitant loss of control—emerges in Hesione's brief flirtation with Mazzini Dunn: "Women have flirted with me because I'm safe," he sighs, "but have tired of me for the same reason" (104). Shaw's women are as confused and distraught as his men: "What do men want?" Hesione agonizes: "They have their food, their firesides, their clothes mended, and our love at the end of the day. Why are they not satisfied?" (90). Dazzled by fantasies of unattainable romantic liaisons, yet deeply frustrated by their intangibility, Shaw's women seek—like Strindberg's Miss Julie—to impose codes of conduct on others they themselves blatantly evade.

If Shaw's women cannot sustain their own and their lovers' burning passion, they desperately try other stratagems: throwing beautiful women in their husbands' paths, somehow burnishing their partners' heroic qualities, engaging in unconsummated fantasy romances. Hesione had "invited pretty women to the house" to give Hector "another turn, but it has never come off?" (84) she regrets. For her part, Ellie stubbornly persists in believing she could reinvent a dwindling husband as dashing hero: "I would have made a man of Marcus, not a household pet" (109), she taunts Hesione. Like Ruth, Ellie is "both a threat and an object of desire," in Varun Begley's terms.[10] Ellie's final liaison with Shotover results as much from despair and resignation as it does from love. In the process of disillusionment, termed "heartbreak," she gives up Hector, rejects Mangan, and attaches herself, finally, to the oblivious Shotover, her "spiritual husband and second father" (149). *Heartbreak House* thus continues Shaw's imaginings of young women mentored if not entranced by older men in such plays as *Major Barbara*, *Pygmalion*, and *Saint Joan* (if we may, for the moment, think of God in the latter play as an "older man").

Just as Shaw's Ariadne posits a fanciful societal polarity between *Heartbreak House* and Horseback Hall, Pinter's Ruth contrasts a dystopian view of Arizona with that of her husband's more benign Utopian vision. "It is so clean there, you can bathe until October," Teddy protests, and adds (in his mind) a laughable clincher: "You can help me with my lectures" (71). Ruth responds with parched, sterile, and biting imagery: "It's all rock. And sand. It stretches … so far … everywhere you look. And there's lots of insects there" (69), repeating the last phrase for emphasis. Like Ariadne's failed homecoming and Mangan's promises of a house in the country, neither Teddy's trip to Venice nor his hopes of entangling Ruth in his teaching duties save their marriages. Male characters in both plays seek refuge from sexual frustration at times in passivity and escape. Despite his short-lived, model marriage, Shotover voices the play's insistent misogyny: "Go, Boss Mangan, and when you have found the land where there is happiness and where there are no women, send me its latitude and longitude, and I will join you there" (114). Pinter's Joey, the failed boxer, boasts of picking up girls, running off their "escorts," and forcing sex upon them. Yet his dalliance with Ruth consists entirely of impotent foreplay. Of his inability to reach orgasm with Ruth, he says lamely, "Now and again … you can be happy … without going any hog" (84).

Past and present violence defines both playwrights' patriarchs, though instigated by female greed and perfidy. Shaw's Shotover is a merchant of death, supporting his household by inventing weapons of mass destruction: "Living at the rate we do," Hesione prods him, "You cannot afford life-saving inventions. Cant you think of something that will murder half Europe at one bang?" (89). On a much smaller scale, Pinter's Max is a one-time butcher, hinting at flesh-peddling involving his wife Jessie. His apparently unmotivated violent outburst—hitting first Joey in the stomach and then Max across the head—closely follows his angry abuse of Ruth: Teddy, he claims, "brings a filthy scrubber off the street. . . . Have you ever had a whore here?" (58). His outrage rings ironically hollow, considering his late wife's profession.

Sometimes, in both plays, violence stems directly from sexual frustration. Alternately tempted and enraged by the wiles of Ariadne, his wife's sister, Hector complains bitterly, "You got your claws deeper into me than I intended" (83). After Ariadne humiliates Randall, Hector seizes Ariadne by the throat and throws her forcefully into a chair. Shaw suggests wryly she is *"not in the least put out, and rather pleased by his violence"* (136). The incident, of course, reflects a misogynist fantasy that women not only court but enjoy violence. In a later scene, Shaw hints that Shotover's dynamite, buried in a cave outside, serves much the same purpose as Chekhov's first-act gun. Infuriated by Randall's acquiescence to Ariadne's bullying, Hector shouts. "Oh women! women! women! (*He lifts his fists in invocation to heaven*) Fall. Fall and crush" (138). When bombs fall in the third act, they respond as much to Hector's misogynist curse as to all the characters' wish for anarchy. Pinter's Lenny recounts physical abuse toward women, one of them a supposedly diseased prostitute, the other a woman who had asked him to help move a heavy laundry appliance. Given the triviality of the women's misdemeanors, Lenny's brutality seems entirely motivated by misogyny.

In both plays women seal their advantage over male antagonists in bargaining scenes formalized in Restoration drama, a staple since Elizabethan times. Ellie and Ruth discard lovers and husbands, if a bit reluctantly at first, at least in Ellie's case. Ellie accuses Hesione, "You were born to lead men by the nose" (107). Heartbroken by her loss of the solidly married Hector, she coolly blackmails Boss Mangan into promising her both the luxuries she craves and an open marriage before rejecting him. She later recalls hypnotizing her father, a feat she repeats onstage with Mangan. Finally, Ellie bullies Mangan into marriage by threatening to place Hesione beyond his reach. Quite ironically, as Irving Wardle suggests, in Ellie's bargaining scene with Mangan, as in Ruth's with Lenny, she translates sexual power into real estate.[11] Ellie wonders before she rejects Mangan, "whether there are any nice houses to let down here" (93) near Hesione, that is.

In *The Homecoming* Ruth rejects her husband heartlessly in the process of driving a hard bargain with the pimp Lenny. She overcomes Teddy's feeble resistance to their separation, then the family's attempts at subjugation, with a combination of guile and ruthlessness. Her deal administers a shock to the system for both Max and Sam, (possibly) killing one of them and deeply humiliating the other. As Francis Gillen's cogent analysis of Pinter's drafts makes clear, the author "develop[s] Ruth as a woman of strength able to convey and accomplish her own agenda."[12] In a reversal of dramatic tradition, both Shaw and Pinter treat marriage comically while courtship is tinged, if not with tragedy, at least with the darkest irony.

Shaw and Pinter instill in their plays the logic of the unconscious: love must be paid for, sometimes in coin of the realm for both Ellie and Ruth, sometimes at an even more terrible cost. Mangan is stripped of both pretensions and illusions by the relentless assaults of the other characters. He is driven finally to admit that his power and arrogance have no basis in reality, that his managerial prowess is fake. In the logic of the unconscious, again, characters in both plays believe, "If I hurt myself, you'll love me." Mangan's rush into the cave where Shotover has stored his dynamite mingles a search for refuge from approaching bombers with a disguised suicide attempt, as though any reason for living has disappeared.

In Pinter, recognizing that Jessie's death like her profession have made her forever unavailable to him, Sam shouts, "MacGregor had Jessie in the back of my cab as I drove them along" (94), then collapses. Sam's confession mocks the *liebestod* of classic romantic literature, closely linking Jessie's and Ruth's professions, their replacement of husbands with nameless strangers, and their three sons. Sam may faintingly join Jessie in fantasy, or his collapse may re-enact his despairing shock at seeing her enjoy sex with MacGregor. Again, in the logic of the unconscious, Sam's death (if that's what it is) and Max's final, groveling plea for Ruth's favors are unanswered calls for unconditional love.

Both Shaw and Pinter link the scarcity of food and drink to lovelessness, a loss of psychological underpinnings and social instability. Giving or withholding food involves the exercise of power, ways of taking advantage, or showing approval or disdain while a plenitude of food and drink—though much rarer—suggests love, security, acceptance, and order. "There is no love," says Shaw's Jack Tanner, "sincerer than the love of food." Disorder, uneasiness, and distaste often emerge in food imagery, as food providers give or withhold food in lieu of love. In *Heartbreak House* Ariadne Utterword equates mealtime irregularity with rational and emotional anarchy. She had entered a loveless marriage to compensate, in part, for the House's failure to nurture her: "no regular meals, nobody ever hungry because they are always gnawing bread and butter or munching apples, and, what is worse, the same disorder in ideas, in talk, in feeling" (55). After pouring out stale tea, Shotover favors the still-innocent Ellie with his special brew. Nurse Guinness comments, "O, miss, he didn't forget you after all! You have made an impression" (57). The lovelorn overeat or engage in fruitless complaint. While the Captain favors Ellie's self-aware if humble father, with a macaroni meal, Mangan's digestion has been ruined, suggesting his inner turmoil and insecurity: "Too rich: I cant eat such things" (92). For the unlovable "captain of industry" has overindulged disastrously: "he has ruined his liver eating and drinking the wrong things; and now he can hardly eat at all" (102).

In *The Homecoming* Ruth associates a nostalgic memory of her premarital work as a "photographer's model" with a rare abundance of drink and food: "when we changed in the house we had a drink. There was a cold buffet" (73). Ruth's wistful recollection passes nearly unnoticed. Seemingly trivial struggles over food and drink mask disdain, barely concealed battles for dominance, even vengeance. As Michael Billington comments about a film (*The Quiller Memorandum*), "Pinter uses the consumption of food as a constant metaphor for a kind of moral blankness."[13] By suggesting Max is "cooking for a lot of dogs," Lenny slyly reveals the family members' animality. Ruth later contests Lenny over an otherwise inconsequential glass of water, a struggle Ruth sexualizes and turns to her advantage:

Lenny: Just give me the glass.
Ruth: No
    Pause
Lenny: I'll take it then,
Ruth: If you take the glass . . . I'll take you.

Lenny recognizes their byplay as a sexual contretemps: "What are you doing, making me some kind of proposal?" (30) Later, Teddy steals Lenny's cheese roll, another seemingly trivial contest masking a complex power struggle. When confronted, Teddy admits, "I took it deliberately" (80). His petty, evidently unmotivated theft deflects his resentful loss of Ruth's love upon his brother; it also pays Lenny back for asking embarrassing philosophical questions; furthermore, it anticipates Lenny's deal returning Ruth to prostitution.

Both playwrights use clothing symbolically, not only to shield nakedness but as a stand-in for society's weakening repressions. Clothing is a proxy for lying, gratuitous display, subjugation, spurious self respect, and social hypocrisy. In *Heartbreak House* Hector's costumes paradoxically symbolize female desire to his wife, entrapped male will to Hector. They signify his wife Hesione's much-regretted grip on his imagination, the powerful role of romantic fantasy in their marriage. Yet the same costumes ensnare Hector, who calls them the "chains" of "the escaping slave" (114). Nakedness, on the other hand, connotes self-awareness and truth-telling, experiences often striking characters with the force of an epiphany. Mangan, having seen the façade of his power and prestige ripped to shreds, threatens hysterically to tear off his clothes, "blowing his cover," so to speak. "Weve stripped ourselves morally naked: well, let us strip ourselves physically naked as well" (146–47). Later, as the group gathers outdoors, Mazzini Dunn appears completely at ease in his pajamas. Hesione favorably contrasts his behavior with that of the shallow Mangan, who "as a practical business man, has tried to undress himself and has failed ignominiously; whilst you, as an idealist, have succeeded brilliantly" (150). As Hesione notes, Mazzini's near-nakedness reflects his poise, his secure sense of belonging.

Pinter too views clothing as both camouflage and enticement, meant to blind observers and accentuate female sexuality. Lenny's uncanny echo of *Heartbreak House*, "Isn't it funny? I've got my pyjamas on and you're fully dressed" (45), calls attention to Ruth's charisma. Ruth's complaint about her inability to find satisfactory shoes in America glances obliquely at both her once-forsaken role as streetwalker and her ill-fitting role as a professor's wife. Oddly, the play's only two lyrical passages invoke gifts of clothing to symbolize rare moments of affection. In one of them, Max congratulates himself on his "generosity" to Jessie, invoking clothing to idealize his otherwise ambivalent relationship to his dead wife. He recalls promising Jessie "a dress in pale corded blue silk, heavily encrusted in pearls, and for casual wear, a pair of pantaloons in lilac flowered taffeta" (62), a fantasy masking a profession usually conducted in the nude. In an unusually tender reminiscence, Lenny recalls poetically, "I bought a girl a hat once. . . . It had a bunch of daffodils on it, tied with a black satin bow, and then it was covered with a cloche of black veiling" (73). Like Max's over-refined dress imagery, Lenny's hat gift invokes a male fantasy of female submission and obedience.

Ruth later exploits the clothing-nakedness paradox with her verbal striptease, a simultaneous act of revealing through concealing. Ruth tantalizes the family while remaining fully clothed. She suggests they visualize her body clad only in underclothes, that they consider her body language, the movements of her lips, quite apart from any words she may speak: "Look at me. I . . . move my leg. That's all it is. But I wear . . . underwear . . . which moves with me . . . it . . . captures your attention" (68–69). In effect, Ruth verbally and gesturally pre-enacts Sam's report of the sex act Jessie had performed blatantly in the back of his taxi as he watched, helplessly enthralled. After Teddy confesses his theft of Lenny's cheese roll, Lenny pointedly ties up food, dishonesty, and social hypocrisy with a clothing metaphor: "this is something approaching the *naked* truth, isn't it?" (80; italics mine). Pinter has tellingly acknowledged that "speech is a constant stratagem to cover nakedness."[14] In both plays references to clothing heighten the imagined sex appeal of naked bodies while pointing up their authors' preoccupations with love's scarcity and loss. They also suggest social inhibitions the characters all yearn to sustain and evade, illustrating the psychological maxim, "What we desire we also fear." Both plays, then, probe the deeper implications of an essential item of stagecraft—clothing, with its power to manifest, hide, and titillate, all at the same time.

In *Heartbreak House* and Pinter's work, both playwrights have not so much abandoned the hackneyed conventions of the well-made, three-act play as they have hollowed it out, slowed its pace and sought poetic, highly evocative language and action. They build their mastery of stagecraft on the ruins of earlier dramatic contrivances designed either to hide their often flimsy plotting (think letters, pistols hanging on walls, revelations of concealed parentage, birthmarks, and the like) or to be parodied, most brilliantly in much of Shaw and Oscar Wilde (consider naming confusions, memoir-writing ingénues, and concluding mass marriages in *The Importance of Being Earnest*, for example). Bert States's shrewd insight applies to both authors: "Fidelity to experience, moral qualm, truth, these are indeed perpetuated, but in terms of the medium."[15] Shaw still clings to the pretense that his characters are artfully constructed amalgams of opposites, complicated but knowable. For his part Pinter affirms a deeply rooted uncertainty principle regarding the knowability of his characters indebted as much to his social ambience as to Beckett. Shaw maintains the useful pretense that a rigid class structure dominates and represses the English body politic, calling as much in despair as in hope for its literal destruction. Austin Quigley's suggestive comment applies to both: "The recognition of irrevocable loss is matched by recognition of an inescapable future."[16] Shaw's outdated social distinctions have not so much disappeared in *The Homecoming* as they have been posited, then undermined and negated. They leave in their stead a rootless, alienated society driven primarily by naked, self-lacerating struggles for love, money, power, and status.

NOTES

1. Christopher Innés, *Modern British Drama: The Twentieth Century* (Cambridge: Cambridge University Press, 2002), 332.

2. Ibid.

3. Rolf Fjelde, "Plotting Pinter's Progress," in *A Casebook on Harold Pinter's "The Homecoming,"* ed. John Lahr (New York: Grove Press, 1971), 98.

4. Mireia Aragay, "Pinter, Politics and Postmodernism," in *The Cambridge Companion to Harold Pinter*, ed. Peter Raby (Cambridge: Cambridge University Press. 2001), 250.

5. George Bernard Shaw, *Heartbreak House* (1919; reprint, Baltimore: Penguin, 1964), 55. (Subsequent citations of Shaw's play refer to this edition.)

6. Harold Pinter, *The Homecoming, in Complete Works: Three* (New York: Grove, 1978), 34. (Subsequent citations of this play refer to this edition.)

7. "An Actor's Approach: An Interview with Paul Rogers," in *A Casebook on Harold Pinter's "The Homecoming"* 169.

8. Margaret Croyden, "Pinter's Hideous Comedy," in *A Casebook on Harold Pinter's "The Homecoming"* 50.

9. Harold Pinter, *The Collection, in Complete Works: Two* (New York: Grove, 1977), 151.

10. Varun Begley, *Harold Pinter and the Twilight of Modernism* (Toronto: University of Toronto Press, 2005), 68.

11. Irving Wardle, "The Territorial Struggle," in *A Casebook on Harold Pinter's "The Homecoming"* 44.

12. Francis Gillen, "Pinter At Work: An Introduction to the First Draft of *The Homecoming* and its Relationship to the Completed Drama," in *The Pinter Review: Collected Essays 1997 and 1998*, ed. Frances Gillen and Stephen Gale (Tampa: The University of Tampa Press, 1999), 42.

13. Michael Billington, *The Life and Work of Harold Pinter* (London: Faber & Faber, 1996), 183.

14. Ronald Hayman, *Harold Pinter* (London: Heinemann, 1968), 79.

15. Bert O. States, "Pinter's *Homecoming*: The Shock of Recognition," in *Harold Pinter*, ed. Harold Bloom (New York: Chelsea House, 1987), 17.

16. Austin E. Quigley, *The Pinter Problem* (Princeton: Princeton University Press, 1975), 227.

Chronology

1856	Born on July 26 in Dublin, Ireland, the son of George Carr Shaw and Lucinda Elizabeth Shaw.
1871–1876	Works for land agent in Dublin.
ca. 1876–1885	Joins mother in London. Works as writer and commercial laborer. In 1884, cofounder of the Fabian Society.
ca. 1885	Starts as book reviewer, also as art critic and music critic.
1889	Editor of *Fabian Essays in Socialism*.
1891	Publishes *The Quintessence of Ibsenism*.
1892	*Widowers' Houses*, his first play, produced.
1894	*Arms and the Man* produced.
1896	*The Devil's Disciple* produced.
1898	Marries Charlotte Payne-Townshend. *Plays Pleasant and Unpleasant* published.
1904–1906	Several plays produced, including *Man and Superman*, *John Bull's Other Island*, *Major Barbara*, and *The Doctor's Dilemma*.
1908	*Getting Married* produced.
1909	*The Shewing-up of Blanco Posnet* produced.
1910	*Misalliance* produced.

1911   *Fanny's First Play* produced.

1913   *Pygmalion* produced.

1914   *Common Sense About the War* published.

1920   *Heartbreak House* produced.

1922   *Back to Methuselah* produced.

1923   *Saint Joan* produced.

1925   Awarded Nobel Prize for literature.

1929   *The Apple Cart* produced.

1931   Travels to Moscow.

1932   Publishes *The Adventures of the Black Girl in Her Search for God*.

1933   The Shaws travel to numerous countries, including the United States.

1934   Publishes *Prefaces*.

1938   Academy Award for screenplay of *Pygmalion*. *Geneva* produced.

1939   *In Good King Charles's Golden Days* produced.

1943   Wife dies.

1944   Publishes *Everybody's Political What's What*.

1950   Dies in November.

Contributors

HAROLD BLOOM is Sterling Professor of the Humanities at Yale University. Educated at Cornell and Yale universities, he is the author of more than 30 books, including *Shelley's Mythmaking* (1959), *The Visionary Company* (1961), *Blake's Apocalypse* (1963), *Yeats* (1970), *The Anxiety of Influence* (1973), *A Map of Misreading* (1975), *Kabbalah and Criticism* (1975), *Agon: Toward a Theory of Revisionism* (1982), *The American Religion* (1992), *The Western Canon* (1994), *Omens of Millennium: The Gnosis of Angels, Dreams, and Resurrection* (1996), *Shakespeare: The Invention of the Human* (1998), *How to Read and Why* (2000), *Genius: A Mosaic of One Hundred Exemplary Creative Minds* (2002), *Hamlet: Poem Unlimited* (2003), *Where Shall Wisdom Be Found?* (2004), and *Jesus and Yahweh: The Names Divine* (2005). In addition, he is the author of hundreds of articles, reviews, and editorial introductions. In 1999, Professor Bloom received the American Academy of Arts and Letters' Gold Medal for Criticism. He has also received the International Prize of Catalonia, the Alfonso Reyes Prize of Mexico, and the Hans Christian Andersen Bicentennial Prize of Denmark.

JOHN A. BERTOLINI is a professor at Middlebury College. Much of his work is on Shaw, including the introduction and notes to two editions of Shaw's works. Professor Bertolini is also a founding member of the International Shaw Society and serves on its advisory council. Additionally, he is on the editorial board of *Shaw: The Annual of Bernard Shaw Studies*.

JEAN REYNOLDS is a professor at Polk State College in Winter Haven, Florida. She is the author of several textbooks and has published in *Shaw: The Annual of Bernard Shaw Studies* and other journals.

169

CELIA MARSHIK is an associate professor at Stony Brook University. She is the author of *British Modernism and Censorship*.

STUART E. BAKER has been a professor of theater at Florida State University. He is the author of *Georges Feydeau and the Aesthetics of Farce* and many essays devoted to a multidisciplinary approach to theater studies.

LAGRETTA TALLENT LENKER has been director of the Office of Graduate Certificates and codirector of the Center of Applied Humanities and the Florida Center for Writers at the University of South Florida. She authored *Fathers and Daughters in Shakespeare and Shaw* and coedited *Shaw and War*.

JAN MCDONALD is emerita professor of drama at the University of Glasgow and vice president of the Royal Society of Edinburgh and of the Citizens' Theatre, Glasgow. She has published *The New Drama, 1900–1914* and *Drama and the Actor*.

MICHAEL GOLDMAN is emeritus professor at Princeton University. He is author of a number of books, including *Shakespeare and the Energies of Drama, Ibsen: The Dramaturgy of Fear*, and *The Actor's Freedom: Toward a Theory of Drama*.

EMIL ROY is an emeritus professor at the University of South Carolina at Aiken. He published *British Drama Since Shaw* and coauthored *Studies in Drama* and *Studies in Fiction*.

Bibliography

Astell, Ann W. *"Joan of Arc and Sacrificial Authorship."* Notre Dame, Ind.: Notre Dame University Press, 2003.

Bennett, Benjamin. *All Theater Is Revolutionary Theater.* Ithaca, N.Y.; London: Cornell University Press, 2005.

Bentley, Eric. *Bentley on Brecht.* Evanston, Ill.: Northwestern University Press, 2008.

———. *Bernard Shaw.* New York: Applause, Theatre & Cinema Books; Milwaukee, Wis.: Sales & distribution [in] North America, Hal Leonard Corp.; Paddock Wood, Tonbridge, Kent: [in the] UK, Combined Book Services Ltd., 2002.

Bermel, Albert. "A Shavian Whodunit: The Mysterious Mr. Warren." *Independent Shavian* 38, nos. 1–2 (2000): 6–15.

Berst, Charles A. "As Kingfishers Catch Fire: The Saints and Poetics of Shaw and T. S. Eliot." *Shaw: The Annual of Bernard Shaw Studies* 14 (1994): 105–25.

Bertolini, John A., ed. *Shaw and Other Playwrights.* University Park: Pennsylvania State University Press, 1993.

Black, Martha Fodaski. *Shaw and Joyce: The Last Word in Stolentelling.* Gainesville: University Press of Florida, 1995.

Carpenter, Charles A. *Bernard Shaw as Artist-Fabia.* Gainesville: University Press of Florida, 2009.

Coelsch-Foisner, Sabine. "Spinsters Versus Sinners: A Late-Nineteenth-Century Paradigm in G. B. Shaw's Plays." *Imaginaires* 2 (1997): 91–111.

Crawford, Fred D., ed. *Shaw Offstage: The Nondramatic Writings.* University Park: Pennsylvania State University Press, 1989.

Davis, Tracy C. *George Bernard Shaw and the Socialist Theatre.* Westport, Conn.: Greenwood Press, 1994.

171

Dukore, Bernard F. "Shaw and American Drama." *Shaw: The Annual of Bernard Shaw Studies* 14 (1994): 127–43.

———. *Shaw's Theater.* Gainesville: University Press of Florida, 2000.

Dukore, Bernard F., ed. *Bernard Shaw on Cinema.* Carbondale: Southern Illinois University Press, 1997.

Evans, Judith. *The Politics and Plays of Bernard Shaw.* Jefferson, N.C.; London: McFarland, 2003.

Falocco, Joe. "Mother Ireland: An Oedipal Reading of *John Bull's Other Island.*" *New England Theatre Journal* 15 (2004): 49–62.

Gahan, Peter. *Shaw Shadows: Rereading the Texts of Bernard Shaw.* Gainesville: University Press of Florida, 2004.

Gainor, J. Ellen. *Shaw's Daughters: Dramatic and Narrative Constructions of Gender.* Ann Arbor: University of Michigan Press, 1991.

Guy, Stéphane. "'A Hollow Sham': The Representation of War in Bernard Shaw's Victorian Plays." *Cahiers Victoriens et Édouardiens* 66 (2007): 497–517.

Haddad, Rosalie Rahal. *Bernard Shaw's Novels: His Drama of Ideas in Embryo.* Trier: WVT, 2004.

Handley, Miriam. "Chekhov Translated: Shaw's Use of Sound Effects in *Heartbreak House.*" *Modern Drama* 42, no. 4 (Winter 1999): 565–78.

Holroyd, Michael. "Bernard Shaw the Immature Novelist." *Irish University Review: A Journal of Irish Studies* 30, no. 2 (Autumn–Winter 2000): 209–19.

———. *"Bernard Shaw: vol. 4, 1950–1991: The Last Laugh."* London: Chatto & Windus, 1991.

———. *"Bernard Shaw: vol. 3, 1918–1950: The Lure of Fantasy."* London: Chatto & Windus, 1991.

Hugo, Leon. *Bernard Shaw's* The Black Girl in Search of God: *The Story behind the Story.* Gainesville: University Press of Florida, 2003.

———. "Britons, Boers, and Blacks: Bernard Shaw on South Africa." *Shaw: The Annual of Bernard Shaw Studies* 11 (1991): 79–95.

Innes, Christopher. "The Shaw Factor: Retrospective Modernism and British Theater." *Shaw: The Annual of Bernard Shaw Studies* 14 (1994): 95–103.

Kauffmann, Stanley. "Ibsen and Shaw: Back to the Future." *Salmagundi* 128–129 (Fall 2000–Winter 2001): 275–80.

———. "The Late Beginner: Bernard Shaw Becoming a Dramatist." *South Atlantic Quarterly* 91, no. 2 (Spring 1992): 289–301.

Leary, Daniel. "*Heartbreak House*: A Dramatic Epic." *Independent Shavian* 37, nos. 1–2 (1999): 3–13.

McDiarmid, Lucy. *The Irish Art of Controversy.* Ithaca, N.Y.; London: Cornell University Press, 2005.

Morrison, Harry. *The Socialism of Bernard Shaw*. Jefferson, N.C.: McFarland & Co., 1989.

Muggleston, Lynda. "Shaw, Subjective Inequality, and the Social Meanings of Language in *Pygmalion*." *Review of English Studies: A Quarterly Journal of English Literature and the English Language* 44, no. 175 (August 1993): 373–85.

Pagliaro, Harold. *Relations between the Sexes in the Plays of George Bernard Shaw*. Lewiston, N.Y.: Edwin Mellen Press, 2004.

Peters, Sally. *Bernard Shaw: The Ascent of the Superman*. New Haven: Yale University Press, 1996.

———. "From Private Drama to Political Drama: Shaw and Transcendence through Socialism." *Independent Shavian* 30, no. 1/2 (1992): 16–25.

Rusinko, Susan, ed. *Shaw and Other Matters: A Festschrift for Stanley Weintraub on the Occasion of His Forty-second Anniversary at the Pennsylvania State University*. Selinsgrove [Pa.]: Susquehanna University Press; London: Associated University Presses, 1998.

Saddlemyer, Ann. "*John Bull's Other Island*: 'Seething in the Brain.'" *Canadian Journal of Irish Studies* 25, nos. 1–2 (1999): 219–40.

Sri, P. S. "Shaw's *St. Joan* (1923): A Platonian Tragedy?" *Text & Presentation: The Comparative Drama Conference Series* (Supplement 4)(2007): 185–95.

Stafford, Tony. "'The End of the Hearth and the Home': The Deconstructing Fireplace in Shaw's Early Plays." *Independent Shavian* 44, no. 1/2 (2006): 17–30.

Sterner, Mark H. "Shaw's *Devil's Disciple*: The Subversion of Melodrama/the Melodrama of Subversion." *Modern Drama* 42, no. 3 (1999): 338–45.

Von Albrecht, Michael. "Bernard Shaw and the Classics." *Classical and Modern Literature: A Quarterly* 8, no. 2 (Winter 1988): 105–14.

Weintraub, Stanley. Bernard *Shaw: A Guide to Research*. University Park, Pa.: Pennsylvania State University Press, 1992.

———. "'The Hibernian School': Oscar Wilde and Bernard Shaw." *Shaw: The Annual of Bernard Shaw Studies* 13 (1993) 25–49.

———. "Who's Afraid of Virginia Woolf? Virginia and G. B. S." *Shaw: The Annual of Bernard Shaw Studies* 21 (2001): 41–62.

Wisenthal, J. L. "Shaw's Utopias." *Shaw: The Annual of Bernard Shaw Studies* 17 (1997): 53–64.

"Wilde, Shaw, and the Play of Conversation." *Modern Drama* 37, no. 1 (Spring 1994): 206–219.

Wolf, Milton T., ed. *Shaw and Science Fiction*. University Park: Pennsylvania State University Press, 1997.

Acknowledgments

John A. Bertolini, "*Saint Joan*: The Self as Imagination." From *The Playwrighting Self of Bernard Shaw*. Published by Southern Illinois University Press. Copyright © 1991 by the Board of Trustees, Southern Illinois University.

Jean Reynolds, "The Shavian Inclusiveness." From *Pygmalion's Wordplay: The Postmodern Shaw*. Copyright © 1999 by the Board of Regents of the State of Florida. Reprinted courtesy of the University Press of Florida.

Celia Marshik, "Parodying the £5 Virgin: Bernard Shaw and the Playing of *Pygmalion*." From *The Yale Journal of Criticism* 13, no. 2 (2000): 321–41. Copyright © 2000 by Yale University and the Johns Hopkins University Press.

Stuart E. Baker, "*Major Barbara*." From *Bernard Shaw's Remarkable Religion: A Faith That Fits the Facts*. Copyright © 2000 by Stuart E. Baker. Reprinted courtesy of the University Press of Florida.

Lagretta Tallent Lenker, "Make War on War: A Shavian Conundrum." From *War and Words: Horror and Heroism in the Literature of Warfare*, edited by Sara Munson Deats, Lagretta Tallent Lenker, and Merry G. Perry. Copyright © 2004 by Lexington Books.

Jan McDonald, "Shaw among the Artists." From *A Companion to Modern British and Irish Drama, 1880–2005*, edited by Mary Luckhurst. Copyright © 2006 by Blackwell Publishing, editorial material and organization, © 2006 by Mary Luckhurst.

175

Michael Goldman, "Shavian Poetics: Shaw on Form and Content." From *Princeton University Chronicle* 68 (2006–2007): 71–81. Copyright © 2006 by Princeton University Library.

Emil Roy, "G. B. Shaw's *Heartbreak House* and Harold Pinter's *The Homecoming*: Comedies of Implosion." From *Comparative Drama* 41, no. 3 (Fall 2007): 335–48. Copyright © 2007 by *Comparative Drama*.

Every effort has been made to contact the owners of copyrighted material and secure copyright permission. Articles appearing in this volume generally appear much as they did in their original publication with few or no editorial changes. In some cases, foreign language text has been removed from the original essay. Those interested in locating the original source will find the information cited above.

Index

Characters in literary works are indexed by first name (if any), followed by the name of the work in parentheses

177

JUN 2011

George Bernard Shaw